T0275121

CROSSING
THE PARK

The Men Who Dared to Play for Both
Liverpool & Everton

Peter Kenny Jones
Foreword by Rafa Benitez

First published by Pitch Publishing, 2023

Pitch Publishing
9 Donnington Park,
85 Birdham Road,
Chichester,
West Sussex,
PO20 7AJ
www.pitchpublishing.co.uk
info@pitchpublishing.co.uk

© 2023, Peter Kenny Jones

ISBN 978 1 80150 384 6

Typesetting and origination by Pitch Publishing
Printed and bound in Great Britain by TJ Books, Padstow

Contents

Dedicated to Karen Elizabeth Jones – Mum
Everything I do, everything I am and everything I want to be is because of you. The bravest person I'll ever know, missed every single day. When it comes to mums, you're the best there was, the best there is and the best there ever will be.

'*If ever there is a tomorrow when we're not together,
there is something you must always remember,
You are braver than you believe, stronger than you seem and smarter than you think,
But the most important thing is, even if we are apart, I'll always be with you.*'

Winnie the Pooh,
A.A. Milne

Foreword by Rafa Benítez

THE PEOPLE of Merseyside love football, I think it's in their blood, part of their life, part of the day to day of many people. The fans identify with their team in such a way that it's one of the most important things in their life.

To be one of two men to have managed both teams is nothing special. The decision to sign for Liverpool was easy, because of its history and past, the present and the prospects for the future. Signing for Everton was more a professional and family-oriented decision, considering the possibilities of what they'd told me would be a project, and my friends and family, to be able to stay in a city where we had a good relationship with the people.

There are so few men to have played for both teams because of what I said at the start about having a passion for your team, because of what it means to people even in the day to day.

The rivalry is unusual, but there are other cities with teams where something similar happens – Madrid with Real Madrid and Atlético de Madrid would be similar, for example. Sevilla with Sevilla and Betis is especially similar. Then in Italy, Inter and Milan is more like Madrid and Atlético.

When I first arrived at Anfield I was surprised by the people, they were very friendly, they tried to help with adapting to the new place from day one. Then at Everton, there were a lot of friendly people, but the difference was that some looked at you differently, they couldn't forget the past with Liverpool.

I feel at home in Merseyside, my family is completely at home here and that is important. The Liverpool fans are still kind and close today, many of the Everton fans know what actually happened and are, let's say, friendly.

My best moment with Liverpool was the Champions League in 2005, along with many other good memories; the worst moment was the feeling towards the end that something was changing for the worse and that I had to leave. With Everton, the best moment was the 2-1 win in December against Arsenal. I'd rather not talk about the bad moments.

I don't think that managing Everton tarnished my reputation at Anfield; the Liverpool fans understood that my family and my home are here and that I hadn't been managing for a while, so many accepted this. At the start many of the Everton fans saw it as an opportunity to take advantage of my experience to reach another level, but others still didn't see it clearly. I think this has settled a bit now.

I can't say I'm more Liverpool or Everton today. Logically, in six years there were a lot of highs at Liverpool, but I still have good friends amongst the Everton fans. I couldn't pick an all-time Merseyside XI either because this is a complicated one, I don't like to leave anyone out and I think I could make several teams, they're all excellent players. But my favourite Merseyside derby memory is Luis García's goal at Anfield in 2006 when we were down to ten men.

Acknowledgements

THERE ARE always too many people to mention, and I can only start with an apology for the people I'll forget.

This book is dedicated to my mum; I wish she could have the chance to read this and be part of the future of everything I do but, unfortunately, life doesn't work out like that. It's been a really tough year without you but you taught me everything I need to know, in order to cope with not having you here with us all. I miss you.

Dad, the reason I'm football mad, and the co-author (with no royalties or naming rights) to everything I do. Nothing is ever too much to ask and you'll always do anything for me. It's been harder for you in the past year than I can ever imagine but you've just shown us how lucky Mum was to be with you.

Annie, because of you I'm writing this book. I never thought anyone could make me change my outlook on my love and hate in football. I always want my team to win but you've shown me that rivalries get in the way of the love for your own club. I love mine and, because I love you, I don't want you to be upset. I don't show that I know, but I'm so lucky to have you and I can't wait for what our future holds together. My timetable writer, spreadsheet compiler and sometimes late-night garage-working companion – thank you. Also, I haven't even asked you yet at the time of writing but thanks for saying yes and I can't wait to marry you!

Thomas and Rebecca – thank you both for always being there for me and for being my back-up parents. We've all had a tough time of it but we'll always share something special and I appreciate everything you've both done for me.

Gray, I can't wait to test you on my books once you're going to the match and loving it like we all do. You can have a few more years of dinosaurs, Minecraft and SpongeBob in the meantime though. Laura, I'll try to make the next one a kids' book so you can have some mild use out of anything I write.

The lads and all of my mates, thank you for always taking an interest in my hobbies and boring stories. I didn't want to leave anyone out (sorry if I have), so I can't say too much, but thank you and love you all; thanks for all being there for me in the past year too. Let's hope none of you split up or this will be awkward: Tom Helowicz, Ailish Taulty, Jonny Allen, Lauren Davies, Jay Sharples, Freya Wright, Jack Baguley, Hope Bradbury, Dan Mythen, Meg Evans, Ryan Irvine, Lucy Flynn, James Lee-Hindle, Sam Walker, Chris Nugent, Warren McCann, Dan Smith, Niamh Whitehouse, Mike Campbell, Lev Bratt, Jake Atkin, Peter Robinson, Dr Johnson, everyone else and, of course, the mighty Seed City.

Netty, Steve and Joe, thank you for welcoming me into your family and helping us both whenever called upon. The Dunning library has been very useful once again. Looking forward to the next cruise!

To everyone who took part in the questionnaire I used to help with some stats and facts later in the book. Everyone who took the time is much appreciated and those who wanted their name to be printed in the book were: Tommy Jones, Steve Dunning, Paul Dunning, Tony Gore, Phil Bickerstaff, Allan Woodward, David Addicott, Joe Atkinson, David Lewis, Joe Flannaghan, Mark Stanistreet, Paul Moore, Don Storr, Chris Whitehead, Jeffrey Hughes, Adi Jeffery, David Scotland, Mikey Lewis, Bill Benbow, Frank Taylor, Peter

Richards, Elliot Conway, Terry Campbell and Mike Parry. Thanks to you all and the many others who helped.

Wider family and friends, the support I got from all of you after my first book was amazing and inspired me to dust off the keyboard and get writing again. Auntie Jackie and Uncle Ed, I think you're responsible for half the sales of my last one and hope this can fill as many stockings! Thanks for all your help, support and for being there for my dad.

A huge thanks to David Burrows, who was the only man kind enough to take the time to talk to me about his personal experiences of crossing the park. Having that insider knowledge of the event was amazing and really adds to the story within the book, I hope! Having previously spoken with Johnny Morrissey, that was also a huge help too, and his generosity in the past was greatly useful on this project.

Inspiration from people like Jeff Goulding helped me get into writing in the first place and now, thanks to Empire of the Kop, I do this full-time. Farrell Keeling has always been a welcome source of advice and pointers when it comes to writing and I hope there aren't as many spelling mistakes here as in some of my transfer articles! Thanks too to Ste Carson and Rick Elliott for your support. Jeff was also a big help and his book with Kieran Smith, *The Untouchables*, was hugely influential here. Thanks also to Mark Platt and George Chilvers for their brilliant work in *Old Liverpool FC in Colour*, with some of the pictures making it inside the book.

My last book was a lot more about letting other people tell the story for me but this feels like a much more historical venture into the story of both clubs. Thankfully there are plenty of others like me who adore the history of this game and these two teams and it simply wouldn't have been possible without the work of Arnie Baldursson and Gudmundur Magnusson from LFC History, Kjell Hanssen at Play Up, Liverpool, The Everton Collection, James Smith from

Everton Chronicles and some hugely detailed and helpful books by Steve Johnson, John Roberts and John Williams – all of which and more are fully listed in the bibliography.

The work of many others makes it possible that I can sit in a garage in Huyton with my Homer Simpson slippers on and write my second book. Thank you everyone, whether your role has been big or small, I appreciate it a lot. If I've forgotten you, please let me know and I'll make sure you're in the next one!

About the Author

IT FEELS like I just finished writing this chapter for my first book but here we go again for the second, so I'll just reuse a lot from my last effort for *Liddell at One Hundred*.

This whole process has been hard work but ultimately a pleasure and I'm delighted to be able to present you all with my second book. Born in Crosby, Liverpool in 1994, I've been a passionate Liverpool supporter since birth. My first match was against Roma at Anfield in 2001. I was mascot for the club in an FA Cup fourth-round replay loss to Crystal Palace in 2003. The last home match I missed, apart from behind-closed-doors ones at Anfield, was in March 2011 and I've been lucky enough to watch Liverpool across Europe – Champions League finals in Kiev, Madrid and (less so) Paris being the obvious highlights.

My football writing began during my studies at Liverpool Hope University, with my BA dissertation: 'What were the social and cultural roles of football in Liverpool in the interwar period?' and my MA dissertation: 'A Golden Age? A comparative of analysis of Liverpool FC under Bill Shankly and Everton FC under Harry Catterick in the long decade 1959–1974'.

From my dissertations, I was able to write shorter pieces for several Liverpool and Everton fan sites. I tried to then write new articles about the Merseyside clubs before broadening my writing on other clubs and countries. I then tried to make an effort to get my work printed in fanzines, which led to a push to get into official matchday programmes for English Football League clubs.

I was then approached by *Footy Analyst* for some paid opportunities, which was soon followed by a dream opportunity to write in the official Liverpool matchday programme and monthly magazine. From here I've been able to be a paid writer and have been trying to build my portfolio with writing and media appearances. Work for Times Radio, LBC and other football clubs has helped further establish me as a football historian and writer, with over 200 published articles and media appearances.

After writing my first book, I was lucky enough to find a full-time writing role with Empire of the Kop, which means that my dream of being a full-time writer has been realised. The family support from my first book meant I felt a little guilty that I couldn't write something that related to the Blue side. This led to my idea here, touching upon the players to have played on both sides of the park.

Fortunately, Pitch Publishing liked my ideas and writing and now I've written another book. I'm really happy that people are willing to read my work and I hope you enjoy taking the time to go through it.

If you would like to read any of my other published work, it's all available on my website: https://peterkj.wixsite.com/football-historian or my Twitter @PeterKennyJones

I hope you enjoy the book and that there will be many more from me on a bookshelf in your house in the future!

Pete
peter.k.j@hotmail.com
@PeterKennyJones
https://peterkj.wixsite.com/football-historian

Preface

LIVERPOOL AND EVERTON are the two behemoths that hold the foundations for most of normal life in Merseyside. Both so similar, yet so different and evoking such strong reactions from supporters of both clubs. If you're lucky enough to live in the greatest city in the world, then you'll also know how much the mood of your and everyone else's day and week revolves around the football.

There can be a slight glimmer of hope if the others didn't have a good weekend too but there's little worse than watching your team lose and listening to the others gloating if they've won and reminding you all week about the loss that was suffered for yourself. Offices, WhatsApp groups, construction yards, taxis, at 6-a-side, everywhere you look – football is there.

That's not even touching on derby day, when the whole city is crippled with 'derby belly', the fear of losing and the whisper in the back of your head that says, 'How boss would it be if we won today.' There's nothing like it and this drug keeps us all coming back for more, week in, week out.

The thing is though, that all applies the same to whether your seat (or heart) lies in Goodison Park or Anfield, so the rivalry seems almost pointless, yet so self-explanatory.

Much has been made of the tiny differences that have created a huge void in the relationship of the two clubs and how just one park separates a lifetime of decisions, friendships, partners and families. However, there are a few who have managed to bridge the gap between the clubs on a personal level.

That's not to say that they're all adored on both sides of the park but that they've been brave enough to wear both blue and red. This unique list of people, as you may have already guessed, are the focus of what this book will be about.

For supporters, the mere thought of changing allegiances would make most feel sick, but players seem to (sometimes) be allowed to make this change freely. There are the likes of Jamie Carragher, who never wore the colours of both on the pitch but changed their allegiance because of representing them. That's something a fan will never experience, unless you count getting a job as hospitality staff, in a burger van or as a steward for the opposite club, but it's unlikely that would cause as high a percentage to change their club – as playing for the other does.

For this special group of people that this book is being written about, not all were born with the blue or red bug that has infected most of the city, so the thought process and ramifications of their decision will be (hopefully) interesting to further examine.

It's not just naming the 34 (a debatable number that we'll go into much more detail on) men to have crossed the park but also what their legacies are. If a squad player for one club becomes a squad player for another – does that count? If a club legend of one started their career with the enemies, who is the club more affected by that?

There's a whole host of questions and examinations that can (and hopefully will) be covered here and there may not be an overarching question that's set to be answered. Nevertheless, by looking at each of these players on a case-by-case basis, we can see what it takes and what happens when you're brave enough to cross the park.

If You Know Your History

AS MUCH as there will be a focus on individual players, it's important that the start of the story is preceded with a bit of a history lesson.

For many, the foray into the history of both clubs may not provide a tale that's completely new. Yet, in an attempt to remain as neutral as possible and perhaps provide an angle that hasn't been as heavily covered before, this history lesson will be told through the eyes (or walls) of the Sandon Hotel and Public House.

Liverpool Football Club wasn't even a twinkle in the eye of John Houlding when he helped create Everton Football Club and provide their first home at Anfield. Houlding, the original owner of the Sandon Hotel when it was built in 1870, was Lord Mayor of Liverpool and a keen investor for Everton FC. Following the rule that clubs had to play in stadiums with stands or enclosed walls, Everton had to leave Stanley Park, where they were playing for free, and search for a new home.

Houlding made his money through owning breweries and, through his contacts, he managed to agree a rental figure with a fellow brewer to play on the enclosed fields at Anfield, of course the home of Liverpool today. The ground was built up from the pocket of the brewer, and attendances were reaching around 8,000 a match for Everton.

As Everton's reputation grew, so did the Houlding fortune and he managed to purchase Anfield outright.

However, he soon wanted a larger amount of rent from the Blues due to the development he had helped finance on improving the stadium and its stands. After already feeling uneasy about the involvement of a brewer of alcohol, due to the religious roots of St Domingo FC, which then became Everton, the increased rent was enough to further worry the nearly 300 club members who held a vote on what to do next.

The members of Everton voted to leave Anfield and Houlding's control of the club, as they didn't agree with him trying to take advantage of them. The Liverpool-born businessman cut ties with Everton, so was left with a state-of-the-art stadium but no team to play in it. He tried to found Everton Athletic to spite the old tenants of the ground, but the name was rejected by the FA, so he founded Liverpool FC in June 1892.

The team in blue and white were put together within weeks. Most of the city didn't care about the new team, though, and were at Goodison Park, so fewer than 100 people watched Liverpool's first-ever match at Anfield. Houlding triumphantly kicked off the maiden match, where 11 Scottish players represented the 'Team of Macs', led by former Everton captain Andrew Hanner, who won 7-1 against Rotherham, and the rest is history.

The Sandon's complex role in this story is simply that it was owned by Lord Mayor Houlding and used as a pub, hotel and a home for the Anfield branch of the freemasons (with some branding still visible on the building today). The meeting of St Domingo's church members within the pub led to the foundation of St Domingo FC in 1878 and Houlding's involvement in their club increased from that day, up to the split in 1892.

He was president of Everton FC from 1879 when their name change came about, and there were many team meetings held in the Sandon, as well as the pub being used as a dressing room for the Everton players. When the split between Houlding and Everton occurred, it meant that Anfield could now hold sponsorship of Holding Breweries, which helped enhance his brand and fortune.

He also used the site for Liverpool FC meetings and for their dressing room after 1892. Nine years later Liverpool were First Division champions. The Reds' (still playing in their traditional blue and white at this point) success meant that the stadium could continue to be developed and hold its own dressing room and boardrooms, so the need for the Sandon diminished.

Houlding died in 1902 and the pub changed hands, meaning the official ties to the club were cut. From then on the Sandon became a haunt for fans before and after the match for a quick pint and chat. It's a meeting point still today and to be able to say you're stood where Liverpool and Everton players used to get changed before a match is amazing. Although it's so close to the ground, the thought of 11 men trudging down the street in full kit and the sounds of studs clattering off the pavement is unbelievable and must have been a sight to behold for match goers even then.

The building went through a tough period in the 1980s, when it declined into closure and seeming demolition, which would have been a terrible end for such a historic venue for Liverpool and Everton. Thankfully Kate Stewart saved the venue in 2017 and has restored it to a place that match goers can again visit and is hugely popular on every matchday. It's deceivingly big inside, with many bars and rooms and an outside area. It feels like there's always another corner or place to discover and find while you're in there.

The building was recently put up for sale and it would be a massive shame to see it changed or removed from its strong football and drinking connections. It's safe to say, had this pub failed in the late 1800s, there may not have been the wealth for Houlding to get involved with Everton, to rent Anfield, to create Liverpool and so many other events. This could have been a one-club city and the one club may not have been that successful if it wasn't for this one pub.

There are several murals around the building today, the most recent being that of Steven Gerrard, and this again shows how the venue can move with the times and incorporate new fan ideas and traditions, keeping the venue relevant for younger supporters while respecting the great past it has.

Although you may not agree, this isn't a sales pitch for you to go and have a pint at the venue on Oakfield Road – rather a slightly different way to view the rivalry between the two clubs.

* * *

So, we end with two clubs whose history is built upon a falling-out and perhaps there should then be little surprise that the rivalry between the clubs exists today. The unified Merseyside chanting period of supporter history will also be touched upon in the coming pages and chapters, as well as a possible explanation as to why relationships have changed over the years.

For now though, we can tick off several members of our double agents list by examining some of the first years of the Reds (in blue and white). Although the first match of Liverpool was a famous 'Team of Macs', in that all the players were Scottish, there were also several of them who had even more in common – they had represented Everton at Anfield beforehand too.

In the first match in the history of the Reds, there were in fact three Blues within their squad: Andrew Hannah,

Tom Wyllie and Duncan McLean. It then really depends on whether your spectacles have a red or blue tint to them, as to whether you view these players as abandoning Everton or staying loyal to John Houlding.

This seems like a good point to mention that in two home matches during the 2022/23 season, there was a questionnaire handed out to 50 Everton and 50 Liverpool fans at their respective home stadiums and this will be used later in the book. The purpose of this was to get a barometer of how supporters view each individual player and there will be some statistical analysis based on fan reactions. The reason to mention this now is that there aren't any 130-year-old Reds or Blues on Merseyside who can perhaps provide an insight into fan opinion of the time, when it came to the three players to have become the first to represent both clubs.

This doesn't make their impact on Merseyside football any less and they're all indeed trailblazers, achieving a feat that has really not been replicated in the past century and a quarter. What these men have that's also unique for them is that they never played for an Everton team at Goodison Park. With the (at the time of writing) soon departure of the Blues from their second home, they'll soon be joined by other Evertonians to have never played at Goodison Park, but their feat of representing both clubs, although only in one stadium, will surely never be beaten.

The 1800s

SO, THE first game of the red side of the story had been played and that made the most logical place to start the story (again, sorry). That's not to dismiss the indisputable truth that Everton are the birth and origin of the love affair that Merseyside has with football but it's impossible to have a player who represents two clubs when only one existed. The ceremonial introduction of two clubs to the city had begun, everyone from this point on had a real choice between teams. This is the real start of a rivalry.

The start of this tale does feel a little Liverpool heavy but I've mentioned that three former Blues represented the Reds in their maiden match. The rest of the players in this first section of the book also featured in the first 22 years of Everton's history and first eight years of Liverpool's – all certainly worthy of the title of being Merseyside pioneers and the first to experience crossing the park (of sorts).

Now also feels like a good time to mention that the main focus of each player will be purely on their club football with either Liverpool or Everton. That's not to say that other areas of their lives and careers can't or won't be mentioned but, due to the sheer volume of players and history that's set to be covered, this feels like the best way to address each player.

Some individuals have bigger legacies at one club than another and some have done very little for either but certainly still need to be covered. As well as this, we're now going back over 140 years, so the source material isn't always agreed upon, nor is it available at all in some cases. Therefore, the statistical numbers available may need to be taken with a pinch of salt but have been researched heavily to come up with the figures provided.

These early years provided Everton with the 1890/91 First Division title (won at Anfield) and saw Liverpool win the Lancashire League (1892/93) and Second Division title twice (1893/94, 1895/96). These were the first pieces of silverware that were to grace both clubs, with future years providing plenty more joy for both Merseyside teams.

So, without further ado – the book actually starts with the only man to have ever captained both Liverpool and Everton …

Andrew Hannah

Name	Andrew Boyd Hannah
Born	17/09/1864, Renton, Scotland
Died	29/05/1940, Glasgow
Everton stats	44 matches/0 goals (1889–91)
Everton honours	First Division 1890/91
Liverpool stats	69 matches/1 goal (1892–95)
Liverpool honours	Second Division 1893/94
Combined stats	113 matches/1 goal (1889–95)
Direct transfer?	No

RENTON MAY not be a household name for many readers today but it's soon to be one that will become familiar. The small Scottish village in West Dunbartonshire, in the west Central Lowlands of Scotland, today has a population of little over 2,000 people. Back in the late 1800s, the village had closer to 5,000 inhabitants but was still very much punching above its weight in the football world. Winning 16 trophies in a 50-year existence, one of Renton's most notable captains was a certain Andrew Hannah.

During the Scot's (who was born to Irish parents) time at the club, he helped Renton become 'Champions of the World' after beating West Brom at Hampden Park. This was followed up by defeating the Preston North End 'Invincibles' of 1888/89, the Lancashire team that had won the English league and cup double without losing a single match.

Despite being just 5ft 7in and only 12st, Hannah was a robust and feared defender who, in the days of little to no protection for goalkeepers, had the role of blocking opposition attackers from barging into the man between the sticks – who would do so at any given opportunity. When he wasn't putting his body on the line for the 'best team in the world', the moustache-laden right-back also worked as a shipyard detective and owned his own milk business.

Despite the large success in Scotland, the game was still an amateur one, with his average weekly pay in Renton being around 13 shillings, so Hannah made the decision to move to the then second-best team in the world, West Brom. Better-paid (although certainly not handsomely) football in England meant it was a seemingly understandable move for him and any of his peers to make, as they pursued a better life through their football talents. However, selectors of the Scottish international team looked down their nose at any player deciding to leave their home nation and Hannah was never selected for another international fixture in his life. His maiden move to England was relatively short-lived, however, and the homesick defender moved back to Renton briefly before his Merseyside story began.

In March 1889, Renton faced Everton in a friendly, which the Blues won 2-1, but it was clear that the performance of Andrew Hannah had caught the eye of the Everton hierarchy. He was again persuaded to make a move to England, handed £100 for joining the Anfield club and given the lofty wage of £3 per week. If the roughly calculated inflation converters are to be believed, that would equate to around £10,000 up front and £300 per week – something certainly better than the amateur football north of the border. Renton were actually soon thrown out of the league for making illegally high payments to players, when the laws of the game didn't permit that they could do so. These secret financial benefits being outed may help explain how quickly Hannah could forget about how homesick he really was in England.

William Edward Barclay, one of only two managers to have overseen both clubs, had his man and swiftly handed him the honour of being captain. The impact was almost immediate, and Everton followed up an eighth-placed finish in 1888/89 with a second place following the arrival of their new skipper.

During the 1890/91 First Division campaign, Hannah was one of six members of this illustrious list of players for both clubs to win the league with Everton and the first title in Merseyside history. As well as this, the skipper for both clubs was also one of four (to have played for both clubs) to help the Reds win the Second Division three years later.

Because there are so many further opportunities to go into both of these feats soon, there will now be a focus solely on the role of the captain. He became one of the best full-backs in the country with Everton and lived on Oakhill Road, right by the home stadium of his new club. His first season saw him as an ever-present in the team that finished second, just two points behind Preston North End (having achieved their 'Invincibles' feat in the previous campaign).

His role in the ultimately successful 1890/91 league campaign was nothing short of monumental and Hannah missed just two league matches throughout the season, this of course being the days before substitutions too, so it meant that he played over 30 cumulative hours on the pitch. It was a year of football that culminated in a dramatic final day but that will be explored further later. The defensive display in that season saw the team set records for their fewest goals conceded (29), fewest goals conceded at home (12), fewest goals conceded away from home (17) and the longest unbeaten run (7) in the club's short history.

Hannah's role within the club was so respected that he was paid £3.30 in August 1890 because of 'the trouble taken to secure players, etc.'. With the Scot's contract coming to an end in 1891, it's perhaps surprising to see that the right-back didn't have his deal extended but, when minutes from the Everton board meetings are read, it's clear the player wanted to leave. In fact, it was written in February 1891: 'Resolved that the consideration of this player's resignation be left over until the end of the Season.' The club managed to convince the player to play out the rest of the title-winning campaign, so that would have felt like a bonus at the time.

That was all for Hannah, until his departure to Scotland and a Renton return that lasted until May 1982. There was a short period where his football career could have come to an end though, when the fearless defender won a bet by entering an actual lions' den. He walked away with the small, agreed wager and a gold watch worth £5. They certainly don't make them like that anymore! John Houlding's capture of the Scot for Liverpool was a major coup, and Hannah's defensive performances were set to make him a brilliant first captain of the Reds (then in blue and white). Arriving on a wage of £5 per week also meant that he didn't have to endure any more duels with lions.

Due to his success at Renton and Everton, the maiden captain attracted headlines in the press. The *Birmingham Daily Post* wrote: 'Hannah will act as captain and his power of developing players is so well known that the Liverpool club are fortunate in having secured the man who did so much towards improving the all-round play of the Everton team.' The leadership talents he possessed meant that not only was the 27-year-old going to be a great signing as a player but also in terms of getting the best out of those around him.

His spell was initially successful and he helped the new team win the Lancashire League and Second Division in his first two years with the club. The dependable availability of Hannah that had been on show for Everton was also clear at Liverpool, with the defender missing just two matches of the successful unbeaten Second Division-winning campaign.

The next year was much less enjoyable on a personal and club level though. Hannah failed to make an appearance in the final nine months of his Anfield stay due to fitness problems. His final match came in a 5-0 away loss to The Wednesday, and that was when disaster struck. The unforgiving nature of how football was then perceived meant that, despite him playing on with an injury that was to end his Liverpool and English football career, the *Liverpool Mercury* still reported: 'Hannah, for a wonder, was also out of it, his kicking and tackling being as weak as water.' It was this injury, which made him as weak as water, that would go on to end his footballing career in Merseyside.

Although his final Merseyside campaign ended in relegation and another return to Scotland, it is safe to say that his influence was vital in stabilising the new club making its way in English football. Hannah went on to play north of the border until 1897 and continued his work in the dairy business.

Andrew Hannah died in May 1940, at the Western Infirmary in Glasgow. In 2018, the Everton Heritage Society discovered that he had been buried in an unmarked grave. This has now been rightfully marked with a headstone that celebrates his achievements for both clubs and can be found today at Kilbowie Cemetery in Clydebank.

It's hard to rank the importance of players who played in the days before video was available of their performances but it's clear to see that Hannah is a Merseyside great. Fortunately for the format of this book, it's good to know that the first name here can certainly be considered vital for the early success of both clubs and he has the silverware to back this claim up.

An uncompromising defender, a leader, a lion tamer and formidable first entry to this list.

Tom Wyllie

Name	Thomas Graham Wyllie
Born	05/04/1870, Maybole, Scotland
Died	28/07/1943, Glasgow
Everton stats	21 matches/7 goals (1890–92)
Everton honours	First Division 1890/91
Liverpool stats	25 matches/15 goals (1892–93)
Liverpool honours	None
Combined stats	46 matches/22 goals (1890–93)
Direct transfer?	Yes (signed for LFC from EFC in May 1892 for free)

BY ALL means, Tom Wyllie was a real trailblazer, known as the first player to officially sign for Liverpool, but he, like so many others from these early days, saw his career on Merseyside begin with Everton. Another slight Scotsman, Wyllie was a right-winger and stood at 5ft 6in, weighing less than 11st. The Ayrshire-born attacker represented both his hometown club Maybole and Glasgow Rangers before he travelled down the soon-to-be well-trodden road from Scotland to Merseyside.

Much like with Andrew Hannah, a potentially promising international career was sacrificed by a move to England. His solitary performance for his nation was certainly bolstered by the form of 16 goals in 18 matches for Rangers before a move to Anfield. It was a brief, yet influential, maiden campaign with four goals in four matches for the team set to clinch the First Division title.

Despite this brilliant scoring start to his Everton career, the next season saw Wyllie struggle for game time with the first team and he was left to play in the reserves. Only scoring three goals in the reserve team and one for the senior squad didn't seem much of a threat to allow John Houlding to prise the Scot from Everton to Liverpool.

Wyllie joined the blue-and-white Reds on the same day as Jock Smith and Hugh Clifford, although the latter had his contract cancelled before a match was played. Wyllie and Smith lined up in the first official match in Liverpool's history, with the former providing the assist for the latter, proving that the longest-serving players clearly had the edge in the match! The new team went on to beat Higher Walton 8-0 that day, in front of 300 people at Anfield.

His stay at both clubs was brief but was again silverware-laden, as he followed up Everton's First Division title with a Lancashire League triumph with Liverpool. However, Wyllie's golden Merseyside day was easily during the first Merseyside derby.

The attacker had enjoyed a solid maiden and solitary Liverpool campaign, but it was to culminate in the Liverpool Cup Final. It was a game shrouded in controversy after Everton appeals over inept refereeing displays, something that will come up in later Merseyside derbies too!

The first derby between Everton and Liverpool took place on 22 April 1893 at Bootle's ground on Hawthorn Road, in front of 10,000 people. Everton were in the First Division and thus considered more likely to win, but John Houlding was out to prove that he had built the best team in the city once again.

The golden moment for Wyllie was to come just after the half-hour mark. John Miller found his Scottish team-mate, who fired the ball low into the back of Dick Williams's Everton net. Wyllie had put his new team ahead against his old.

The controversy was to follow as Herbie Arthur, from Blackburn Rovers, who had been handed the difficult job of refereeing the match, denied the Blues a penalty. It had been a heated affair, with silverware, bragging rights and the determination to either upset or reward John Houlding all acting as obvious reasons for both sets of players to be determined to claim victory.

The match remained tight after Wyllie's opening goal and in the final moments Everton were awarded a corner. As the ball looped in, a goal-line scramble ensued before the whole Blue side of the city appealed for a penalty after an apparent handball by a Liverpool defender. By all accounts, Arthur lost control of the match and, after consulting his two linesmen, he decided on the bizarre conclusion that a drop ball should be given for the debated infringement.

Liverpool managed to get their boot to the ball first and, as it was cleared up the pitch, the full-time whistle was blown. That was far from the end of the drama though. A beaming Houlding was readying to parade the trophy on a four-horse-drawn carriage from the ground to the Sandon, but he wasn't permitted the chance to gloat in front of his old colleagues.

Everton were so appalled by, as reported by the *Cricket and Football Field*, the 'general incompetency of the referee' that they didn't allow for the trophy ceremonies to begin. They were convinced that either Duncan McLean or Matt McQueen had handled the ball. The ambiguity over which man had done it didn't exactly help their claims, but their complaints didn't allow for the trophy to be given out.

The Liverpool FA met the following Monday to agree on what should be done, with there still being no official winner decided. It was a unanimous decision inside the Neptune Hotel in Clayton Square, where the Reds were named the winners. Andrew Hannah was handed both the Lancashire

League trophy and Liverpool Cup, before Houlding could proudly and finally display them inside the Sandon.

The willingness of the Conservative Party member to show off his riches in the middle of the city was rewarded in quite an unsavoury manner, with both trophies being stolen. In September 1893, as reported by *Daily News*, 'burglars forced open the door of the shop with a jemmy, and took away the prizes, which are of considerable value'. The trophies had been stolen from a pawnbrokers, where they were stored, in Paddington, Liverpool. With the police unable to find the culprits, Houlding had to fork out £127 (around £13,000 in today's money) to replace the two trophies.

As for Wyllie, he stayed in the Lancashire League and moved to Bury. Liverpool's eventual relegation from the First Division was ultimately decided by the Scot's new club, as their victory over the Reds in a test match (play-off) in April 1895 saw Bury promoted in place of the Anfield club. Wyllie played two seasons in the First Division before moving to Bristol City. When he retired from football he became a newsagent in Bedminster, Bristol, then became an insurance agent, before his death in Glasgow in 1943.

Duncan McLean

Name	Duncan McLean
Born	20/01/1868, Renton, Scotland
Died	17/11/1944, Renton, Scotland
Everton stats	26 matches/0 goals (1890–91)
Everton honours	First Division 1890/91
Liverpool stats	82 matches/4 goals (1892–95)
Liverpool honours	Second Division 1893/94
Combined stats	108 matches/4 goals (1890–95)
Direct transfer?	Yes (signed for LFC from EFC in July 1892 for free)

THE LAST member of Liverpool's famous 'Team of Macs' that started the first-ever match in the club's history, who had also played for Everton, is Duncan McLean. Another member of the famous Renton team, the Scot had a similar career to that of Andrew Hannah. He not only represented the hugely successful Scottish outfit and both Merseyside teams but McLean also played in defence with his trusty captain – plying his trade from the left side though. The well-built defender was more than capable of blocking onrushing attackers and wasn't afraid to put his weight about on the pitch.

His departure from north of the border was much like his long-term team-mate, with a snub from the Scotland team (until he returned home in 1895) and illegal payments from Renton. The payments to the players were hidden under the phrase 'Chicken Bree' in the club's accounts, which was a diet that the club's players were fed, consisting of port, mixed egg yolk and egg white on dry toast, but it was complemented on the books by a few illegal pounds. Although McLean didn't quite replicate Andrew Hannah by returning to their shared first club, there's more than enough evidence to suggest that he was also having his palm greased before heading to Merseyside and Everton.

His first season with the Blues ended with a league winners' medal but, after making just six appearances, his role was far from crucial to their success, although the defender did feature in the final two matches of a dramatic campaign. The following year, during the 1891/92 season, the Scot was a much more utilised asset and featured in 20 of the 26 league fixtures, but a fifth-place finish meant it was a year that paled into insignificance when compared with the silverware that had preceded it.

His loyalty to John Houlding was abundantly clear in 1892, as the then 24-year-old made the bold decision to stay with his club president and forgo First Division football to stay with the new team in the Lancashire League. It was a huge decision that wasn't replicated by many, with his last season with Everton showing that he was very much part of their team too. It was a result he probably didn't regret either, with the medals he was soon to win.

Reports of his performances show that he was well ahead of his time too, with complaints about his overzealous desire to join the attack and not sit at the back with the rest of the defence. His attacking desires were perhaps best illustrated by McLean being handed penalty duty for the Reds, and he scored the club's first-ever spot kick in 1894.

Lancashire League and Second Division success was followed up by a disappointing relegation in 1895 and a move to St Bernard's in Edinburgh. Perhaps one of John Houlding's most loyal servants, McLean had a successful five years on Merseyside and returned to Scotland with three different league winners' medals. He went on to captain his new club and was rewarded with a long-awaited call-up to the international set-up.

McLean remained in Scotland up to his death in 1944, aged 76.

Patrick Gordon

Name	Patrick Gordon
Born	19/02/1870, Renton, Scotland
Died	1933, Liverpool
Everton stats	22 matches/5 goals (1890–93)
Everton honours	First Division 1890/91
Liverpool stats	30 matches/8 goals (1893–94)
Liverpool honours	Second Division 1893/94
Combined stats	52 matches/13 goals (1890–94)
Direct transfer?	Yes (signed for LFC from EFC in June 1893 for free)

A SCOT who played for Renton and moved to Everton before joining Liverpool is a story you're all too familiar with by now. Patrick Gordon is another player to have swapped the Scots for Scousers by the end of the 19th century.

The man famed for having an impressive level of fitness and stamina, was slight and the outside-right often seen careering up and down the wings at Anfield. Plying his trade for the Blues, mainly in the reserves, his return of five goals in 23 matches was impressive and he would have been delighted to receive his £2 bonus for winning the league in 1891. He was soon to be offered the opportunity to earn another £5 bonus through a cup final. Gordon's golden time to shine in an Everton shirt was to come at the end of the 1892/93 season with the Scot being handed the chance to start a Merseyside club's first FA Cup Final, against Wolverhampton Wanderers.

The 1893 final was a unique affair as it presented Manchester's Fallowfield Stadium its one and only chance to host the showpiece event. Crowd trouble was to mar the event though, as the 45,000-capacity stadium was heavily overcrowded, with reports suggesting that as many as 15,000 too many attended the final. Barriers were in place around the running track to keep fans off the pitch, but these were broken long before kick-off and fans began to spill on to the edge of the playing field.

It was an otherwise beautiful day and, following a short delay due to the difficulties in policing the crowds, the match finally began. Gordon was involved early on, as he caused havoc on the right, before being swiftly chopped down in full flow. This certainly wasn't the era for tricky and speedy wingers. Alf Milward had the ball in the back of the net for Everton but it was disallowed and welcomed a cagey affair to proceed, with the score remaining 0-0 at half-time.

On the hour mark Harry Allen had a speculative effort for Wolves, which managed to find a way through the hands of Richard Williams in goal, with many bemoaning the fact that he hadn't managed to save a relatively simple shot. Fallowfield erupted as the old gold celebrated what proved to be a vital goal. Despite the best efforts of Prescot-born manager Dick Molyneux's team, he couldn't claim silverware for the Blues as the score remained 1-0.

There was little blame to be placed on Gordon, who had started brightly, but his inability to affect the match perhaps helped the board make their decision on his future. It was decided before the end of the campaign that he wouldn't be needed for the following season and Liverpool were asked to make an offer for the Scot, not something that would be repeated much in the modern era!

The deal was completed in June 1893 and Gordon again repeated the achievements of many others in winning the

Lancashire League and Second Division at Anfield with Liverpool. His involvement in the 1894 test match against Newton Heath was his crowning Merseyside memory though.

After an unbeaten Second Division campaign, which included a 100 per cent home record, the Reds still had to play a further match to secure promotion to the First Division. This was against Newton Heath, the yellow-and-green outfit that would become Manchester United in 1902. The match was played at Ewood Park, a place that Gordon would soon be calling home, in front of 5,000 expectant supporters. The opposition came into the match off the back of a season that saw them finish bottom of the First Division and were playing for their top-division status.

Two familiar names linked up to score the opening goal of the crucial match, with set-piece expert Duncan McLean finding the head of Gordon, who put his team ahead. It ended up being a comfortable victory for the 'new Invincibles' and they were thoroughly deserved winners of the match that saw a place booked in the First Division for the first time. The typically exuberant John Houlding was keen to celebrate this success but he had to wait for the heroes' welcome that awaited the promoted team at Tithebarn Street station and carried players to two separate parties that were held in the Alexandra Hotel and then the Sandon. On-field excellence was rewarded by the board and Gordon had a huge part to play in that.

Things turned a little sour for the Scot, though, as he fell out with team selectors and was dropped to the reserves after he refused to play for the second-string squad and was shown the door. It was a swift move from hero to the reserves to Blackburn Rovers, after one goal in the first five matches of the maiden First Division season. It left a sour taste in the mouth and a swift drop down the leagues, as he ended up representing non-league Liverpool South End. Not the

Merseyside location many thought his footballing story would end at, with a move to Wigan County concluding a strange career.

It was a tumultuous four-year stay in the city that contained snubs and trophies, for and from both clubs. For a player to have recorded just over 50 matches but play in the calibre of matches that he did and win numerous trophies shows that he certainly had some talent and luck on his side. His relationship with the city of Liverpool was strong enough for him to spend his retirement in Everton, and he passed away aged 62 within the city, leaving his wife Caroline, son John and daughter Wilhelmina.

John Whitehead

Name	John Whitehead
Born	1871, Liverpool
Died	1935
Everton stats	2 matches/1 clean sheet (1893–94)
Everton honours	None
Liverpool stats	3 matches/0 clean sheets (1894–96)
Liverpool honours	None
Combined stats	5 matches/1 clean sheet (1893–96)
Direct transfer?	Yes (signed for LFC from EFC in March 1894 for free)

JOHN WHITEHEAD is our first Scouser, first non-Scot, but also the first trophy-less and first bit-part man in this list. The local stopper is the first who will be perhaps more briefly assessed than some others to follow because his legacy is simply not as great as many of his peers.

His Everton career began in the reserves as a young player and the club bolstered his finances by offering him 'employment on the Ground at 20 shillings per week until other job procured' in December 1893. This, of course, also means that Whitehead is the first man on the illustrious list to have played solely for the Blues at Goodison Park. His first-team debut came away to Darwen on New Year's Day in 1894, where a disappointing 3-3 draw with the team that ended the season relegated certainly didn't help the Scouser's claim to Richard Williams's place as the club's No.1.

Although the homegrown stopper held his place for the following home victory against Newton Heath, it was to be his final appearance for the Goodison club and the next time there was an opportunity for a back-up keeper to be handed minutes, the jersey was handed to Scotsman David Jardine. At the end of the season Whitehead wasn't handed a new deal and was out looking for another club, but he didn't have to search far.

Liverpool snapped up the goalkeeper with First Division experience as they sought to find a way to remain in the top tier, with Whitehead set to have a huge say in the fortunes of his new club. After ending the season in 15th place (of 16 teams), another test match awaited, and this time William Edward Barclay's team would have to fight for their place in the division, with Bury standing in the way of the Dubliner's team.

The final league match of the season that preceded the huge match saw Duncan McLean blamed for several of Preston North End's five goals at Anfield. It wasn't just the defeat that affected the home team that day though. Injury was added to insult as Joe McQue, Andrew Hannah, Duncan McLean, John McCartney and Frank Becton were all injured during the match.

Whitehead's debut was therefore almost destined for disaster before it began, and Tom Wyllie's Bury team managed to secure a devastating 1-0 victory that dumped the Reds into the second tier. It was again played at Ewood Park, the location where promotion had been secured a year before. Some solace for the man between the sticks was that he could do little with the goal itself, as a huge deflection wrong-footed him. Even though Bury went down to ten men after their keeper was sent off near the end of the match, it wasn't enough for Liverpool to get back into the match, and relegation soon followed.

Two more appearances came for Whitehead but they weren't quite as important. The 'diminutive goalkeeper', as he was described by the *Liverpool Mercury*, started the Second Division home campaign in goal but was praised for his 'smart' play in a match that ended in an emphatic 5-1 win. Next was what proved to be the final outing for Whitehead, and the scoreline may help explain why. A windy afternoon in Manchester against Newton Heath was one to forget for poor John, as the 24-year-old was bullied by the opposition players and fans alike. He conceded five goals, a further two were scored but ruled out and it was reported by the *Liverpool Mercury* for one finish that 'had Whitehead been in ordinary trim, it might have been saved'.

It was the end of two Merseyside careers after a measly five appearances and a solitary clean sheet but, by all accounts, Whitehead wasn't of the build that was required of late-19th-century goalkeepers. With attackers encouraged to barge the man in goal, being small and seemingly easy to bully weren't the best assets to possess. He was said to be a decent shot-stopper but, perhaps, much like with the attacking tendencies of Duncan McLean, a man before his time.

Fred Geary

Name	Fred Geary
Born	23/01/1868, Hyson Green, Nottingham
Died	08/01/1955
Everton stats	100 matches/85 goals (1889–95)
Everton honours	First Division 1890/91
Liverpool stats	45 matches/14 goals (1895–1900)
Liverpool honours	Second Division 1893/94
Combined stats	145 matches/99 goals (1889–1900)
Direct transfer?	Yes (signed for LFC from EFC in May 1895 for £60)

IF WE label John Whitehead as a man playing in the wrong era because of his size and the poor protection of players by officials of the time, then Fred Geary can very much be the exception to that rule. The forward, who can probably be safe in holding the title of the first Everton legend, wasn't just slight, weighing less than 10st, but he was small in stature too. Standing at just 5ft 2in (or two-and-a-half FA Cups if you like a random measure of height), he's one of the smallest players to have ever represented either club too.

Good things obviously come in small packages though and Geary is very much held in high esteem within the history of Everton, the first real goalscoring hero that graced the club and someone whose achievements in front of goal can stand him alongside many of the future greats that were to follow. The England international was born in Nottingham and moved to Everton from Notts Rangers, in

1889. Perhaps unsurprisingly, given his miniscule stature, one of the key aspects of Geary's game was his electric pace and an unerring eye for goal.

His performances attracted attention from other clubs too, and Everton outright turned down an approach for his services from Notts County in May 1890. He was also selected to play in a 'North vs. South' match in 1891, making the cut alongside fellow Blues Johnny Holt and Edgar Chadwick (where Geary became the first man to score a goal after a net was put between the frames of the goal, an invention by Scouser John Alexander Brodie, who was also the designer of the Mersey Tunnel). He was clearly respected by the club too, being gifted £10 as a wedding present in 1891.

What Geary achieved for Everton on the pitch is nothing short of remarkable. It seemed as though Everton had found themselves a natural goalscorer and he followed up scoring 20 in 27 during the 1889/90 season with the first six matches of the 1890/91 campaign seeing the Blues score 25 times – Geary scoring in each and recording a total of nine. The No.9 ended the season with 19 goals in 23 matches (we'll delve into this campaign soon!) and he was firmly the star of a title-winning team. He was very much the Dixie Dean or Gary Lineker of his era, playing every single fixture in the First Division triumph.

Scoring Everton's first Goodison Park league goal, and a hat-trick on his England debut (on a day when he and Johnny Holt became the first Evertonians to represent England), goalscoring was the major asset of the small and speedy forward. The famed front line of Geary, Edgar Chadwick and Alf Milward brought with it huge success. These first two full seasons were enough to prove to the board that their ace marksman had to stay with the club, something that they may have gone a bit too heavy on ensuring.

Geary's off-field performances were far from what would be considered normal in modern-day standards. Rather comically, when viewed anachronistically, the forward was earning extra money on top of his First Division football with Everton by working in a pub. This caused some understandable concerns for the board, and they requested him to meet with them in May 1892. Minute books from the time summarised the meeting by stating: 'This player appeared & was requested to look out for other employment not in a Public House if possible as members were complaining of same. After several members of Com. had expressed their views the matter was left over for Geary's consideration.'

Seeing as Geary was still working in a public house (the Cabbage Hall Inn in Anfield), not just any pub but one owned by the then much-maligned John Houlding, two years later in April 1894 it doesn't appear that he had taken too much notice of these words. This intervention wasn't just a concern for having their poster boy under the rule of Houlding, Everton knew Geary was their main man and they wanted to ensure he remained at his peak. There's perhaps no greater example of this than in the following 1893/94 season, when he would receive '£3 per week with the nett proceeds of a midweek match as a benefit on that Season'. This was a huge gesture by the club to show how much they valued him, as well as trying to financially convince him to stop working behind a bar.

The first season after the split with Houlding saw Geary choose Everton over his boss and now former football owner. However, there was an incident that led to the ace marksman meeting in front of the board for a second time, after clashing with the supporters. Again, given his stature within the club, this was quickly ironed out. It was soon proposed that Geary would receive shares in the club due to his performances, before being decided that it wasn't 'desirable' for players to have a stake of the business. All more evidence, though, that the club was keen to grease the palm of the striker and keep him at Goodison Park. They allowed him countless visits to Nottingham, trips to Hoylake when injured and to participate in charity matches, certainly not the treatment that was offered to many others within the squad.

Their reward for this was to see Geary ask to be allowed to leave for Nottingham Forest in October 1893; when the club refused the player was soon miraculously too injured to train. An apology soon followed but it was clear that the inflated ego that came from the club's special treatment had been thrown back in their face. He finally accepted to leave the John Houlding-owned pub he worked within in August 1894 but only because the club had agreed to pay him £2 per week until he found a new job.

Two incidents against Sunderland in 1891 have been highlighted by some as moments that saw his career hit a steady decline from there on. In the January, the Nottingham-born speedster careered himself into the post of the opposition goal and the sound of his head colliding with the woodwork echoed around the stadium. No concern for head injuries or concussion protocols saw the forward dragged to his feet and expected to play on. That October then saw Geary injure his right ankle, then being kicked in the ribs before his left ankle was so damaged that he spent the next week in hospital. It seems harsh to label these as *the* moments it started to go wrong for the England international but it certainly shows how injuries affected his game.

Geary remained at Goodison Park for the 1894/95 season but his battles with injuries meant that much of it was spent in the reserves whenever he was fit. He didn't feature in any of the first 17 matches that season, making just eight league appearances in that campaign. It seems as though the board had grown tired of the misdemeanours that came with their talented forward, with their financial and personal benefits for the player not being welcomed with the respect it deserved.

Given the lack of first-team game time offered to Geary, it was perhaps unsurprising to see that Everton had no plans to offer him a new deal for the following season. The club was ready to sell the player but the secretary was under instruction 'not to accept less than £60' for his services. The forward amassed a hugely impressive tally of 85 goals in 100 matches for Everton but his best days were certainly behind him. A sucker punch, or perhaps even a transfer they completed with a wry smile, given the off-field issues, saw the Blues accept £60 from Liverpool and Geary returned to play under John Houlding once again, as the first player to move directly between the two clubs for a fee.

It's important to note that the tragic loss of Geary's child Doris in 1894 would have certainly affected his on-field performances too. Liverpool were very happy to have secured the signature of Fred Geary, and his standing within the game was still strong, despite his run of poor performances. His first goals came in just his third match for the Reds, with a brace against Crewe Alexandra, and it was clear that there was still plenty of talent within the small boots of the 27-year-old, as he built up a strong relationship on the pitch with Scotsman George Allan.

Injuries and a lack of form cost the forward again, although it did seem that he was always capable of glimpses of his old self whenever given the chance to represent the first team. His tally of 14 in 45 career matches for Liverpool, over the span of four seasons, shows that his powers were dwindling, though, and the two-season scoring spree at Goodison was perhaps always destined to be his best days.

Injuries certainly curtailed his career and it does seem as though Geary was quite a complex character. His early success on Merseyside handed him huge (for the timr) financial benefits and it certainly seems as though it affected his ego. It can't be ignored that losing a child would have affected his mental state too, never mind the experiences of cannoning his head off a Sunderland post.

As a struggle for form and fitness followed the lofty heights of his early Everton days, it was destined to see him enter a downward spiral. Ironically, one thing that seems to have benefitted him in later life, though, was his experience behind the bar. Working in and owning several pubs (the Cabbage Hall Inn, the Stanley Arms and the Fountain's Abbey) within the city, Geary spent the rest of his days pulling pints and providing for his wife and children. Enjoying a golden-wedding anniversary with his wife Winifred and retiring to Crosby, Geary would often show off the FA Cup Final ball from 1897 and went on to help out as a part-time groundsman at Goodison Park. By all accounts he enjoyed a long and happy retirement – passing away in 1955, aged 86.

Abe Hartley

Name	Abraham Hartley
Born	08/02/1872, Dumbarton, Scotland
Died	09/10/1909, Southampton
Everton stats	60 matches/28 goals (1892–97)
Everton honours	None
Liverpool stats	12 matches/1 goal (1897–99)
Liverpool honours	None
Combined stats	72 matches/29 goals (1892–99)
Direct transfer?	Yes (signed for LFC from EFC in December 1897 for £175)

YET ANOTHER Scouse Scot, Abe Hartley, arrived at Everton on a wage of £2 per week, after being signed from Dumbarton in December 1892 and made a solitary first-team appearance in his maiden campaign. His time with the Blues never really saw him hold on to a consistent place within the team and perhaps his best opening came through the struggles and subsequent departure of Fred Geary to Liverpool.

During Hartley's time at Goodison Park he never managed to record more than 16 league and cup appearances in a single campaign, across four different seasons. The Scot could play in a variety of forward positions and his return of nearly a goal a game shows that he was more than capable of finding the back of the net whenever he was called upon. The match that will certainly be seen as the defining moment in Hartley's Everton career, though, will undoubtedly be the 1897 FA Cup Final.

Playing alongside Fred Geary, Hartley was handed the start at Crystal Palace (the venue of the final) as he continued to deputise for fellow Scot, John Cameron. The 65,000 spectators created an unforgettable affair as the match against Aston Villa became the highest-attended football match in English football history, many travelling there on horse and cart. Everton had been the first club from Merseyside to experience the final, in 1893, but this time looked set to restore bragging rights in the city after finishing two places below the Reds with a disappointing seventh place at the end of the league campaign.

Villa were about to go on and clinch the league title and thus were big favourites on the day. It was certainly a match that was worthy of the huge crowds, with no fewer than five goals gracing a manic first half. The Birmingham outfit took the lead inside 20 minutes, thanks to a speculative effort from John Campbell, with the wind aiding the ball's pursuit into the back of Bob Menham's goal.

Jack Bell dragged Everton back into the match three minutes later, as he managed to poke the ball and narrowly avoid being flattened – watching his effort roll into the back of the net. Euphoria for the long-travelling Blues was about to be doubled within five minutes, this time Dickie Boyle converting from a free kick to put the Scousers ahead.

With ten minutes of the half remaining, Fred Wheldon got his team back level and in the final minute of a pulsating half Jimmy Crabtree headed home to complete the Villa comeback. The second half was less plentiful in the goals department, with Everton peppering the Villa goal (including a decent effort from Hartley), but it wasn't enough and Dick Molyneux's team again fell to a crushing cup-final defeat. There were some accusations of a poor performance from Bob Menham in goal for the Blues but it was clear they had been beaten by a better team. Results on the day also meant that Aston Villa clinched the First Division title (still the only team to win both trophies on the same day) and it was always going to be a tough task to topple the champions.

Hartley failed to score in the three league matches that followed the final and that seemed to end any real chance of holding down a place in the first team. Despite scoring a hat-trick in his first match of the following season, the Scot was called for a meeting in October 1897 following his poor performances at the start of the campaign, including a 3-1 derby-day loss at Anfield. The following month there was a decision made that the club would 'offer Hartley to Liverpool if they give us a fair price for transfer'. Liverpool offered £175 and a deal was agreed between the two clubs.

It seems again that Everton sold at the right time, receiving a favourable fee for a player who it seemed they may have let go too early but who proved to have a poor Liverpool career. Hartley spent just one season at Anfield, recording only 12 appearances (seven in the league) and scoring once. This came against the formidable William 'Fatty' Foulke, who by all accounts had a brilliant game at Bramall Lane but was beaten by a Hartley winner on a rainy December afternoon.

There isn't much of a Liverpool/Hartley legacy, other than the forward being famed for storing a rolled-up cigarette behind one ear as the match was about to start. He would then somehow keep it safe for 45 minutes and proceed to smoke it at half-time! He's also the first player in this list to join the Reds, with the red strip being introduced in 1896. Other than participating in an unsuccessful cup campaign for the Anfield club, that was that and Hartley was soon sent on his way. There was some redemption in 1900 as the forward scored an Anfield winner for Burnley, celebrating in front of both sets of supporters after he had done so.

Just nine years later, aged 37, it was reported by the *Exeter and Plymouth Gazette*: 'Abe Hartley, formerly a well-known footballer, who played for Dumbarton, Everton, Liverpool, and Southampton, died suddenly, on Saturday, at Southampton Docks, where he was employed. He was standing outside the pay office, when he fell to the ground and expired, apparently from heart failure'.

Certainly not one of the greatest footballing stories for either of these great teams but a tragic end to a life that was so sadly short.

1900 to the Second World War

ALTHOUGH THE turn of the century brought with it a rivalry that had lasted just eight years and seen only nine Merseyside derbies, this was now part of normal life within the city. People would have picked a team and had favourite players, so to see them join the other club would hurt and these players knew what a swap of shirts and loyalties would entail.

Again, as in the previous chapter, there's a severe lack of resources when it comes to this period for both clubs. The turn of the century to the start of the Second World War was a rather uncertain period of Merseyside life itself and these men provided the inhabitants of this great city with an escape from the turmoil many of them were in – or set to be in very soon – given both world wars that occurred.

Each player is as important to this list as the last, so they'll all get a fair mention and representation for their special place in this most unique set of players.

Players from the early years of football's history are often overlooked. There's no doubting that they were likely not of the same quality as players today, with a lack of travel around the world meaning more local men were given a chance at high-quality clubs. However, seeing as there has only been one Scouser mentioned thus far, this may not have been the case on Merseyside.

For any history buffs, mild enthusiasts or non-interested parties, it seems like a good time to have a quick run through the major rule changes that took place in football from the birth of Everton up to the commencement of the Second World War:

- 1878 – Referees introduced to the game
- 1886 – An official football rule book was drawn up
- 1891 – Penalties were introduced to the game and referees were given sole control of a match
- 1902 – Penalties had to be taken from a penalty spot
- 1912 – Goalkeepers were only allowed to handle the ball inside their box
- 1920 – Players could not be offside from a throw-in
- 1925 – Offside rule changed from a three-player to a two-player rule, so you were now onside if there were two players between you and the goal (goalie included) rather than three
- 1937 – The shape of the 18-yard box was agreed upon and the semicircle at the top was added
- 1938 – Stanley Rous, then the secretary of the FA, rewrote the rules of the game to what has been closely adhered to ever since

Whatever your opinion of football in the 19th century, we had now moved into the 20th century and there are goal nets, offsides, referees and penalties aplenty to follow. There may still be the odd story with a pass-back rule and certainly no VAR interruptions, but more modern football was ready to greet Merseyside.

In terms of the silverware that was set to greet the two clubs during this period, this is the honours list that awaited the Reds and Blues in the next 40 (or so) years:

Everton
First Division – 1914/15 (final season before the First World War), 1927/28, 1931/32, 1938/39 (final season before the Second World War)

FA Cup – 1906, 1933
Second Division – 1930/31

Liverpool
First Division – 1900/01, 1905/06, 1921/22, 1922/23, 1946/47 (first season after the Second World War)
Second Division – 1904/05

Despite the first entry of our next group of players still seeing his story start in the late 1800s, the rest of the tales are entirely from the 1900s and we enter that century with both clubs in the First Division and coming off the back of tenth-placed (Liverpool) and 11th-placed (Everton) finishes.

Although 13 trophies were set to greet both clubs, it doesn't mean that every medal will necessarily be covered in painstaking detail, but it's important to recognise how successful the city was on a footballing level. These fruitful moments built the foundations of the modern trophies that were to follow for both and the basis for which both clubs are held in universally high regard today.

Back to the story of the men who dared to cross the park …

Edgar Chadwick

Name	Edgar Wallace Chadwick
Born	14/06/1869, Blackburn
Died	14/02/1942, Blackburn
Everton stats	300 matches/104 goals (1888–99)
Everton honours	First Division 1890/91
Liverpool stats	45 matches/7 goals (1902–04)
Liverpool honours	None
Combined stats	345 matches/111 goals (1888–1904)
Direct transfer?	No

EDGAR CHADWICK is the last of the 1800s stars, but seeing as his entire Liverpool career was played in the 20th century, it felt as though he was the right man to bridge the gap between eras. Each player has been sorted in order of when they crossed the park and played for their second Merseyside club, despite some careers starting earlier than those that are to follow.

As Chadwick was the first man to cross the park in the 1900s, that should help explain why he kicks off this section of the book.

Chadwick arrived at Everton for their maiden Football League campaign in 1888, recruited by W.E. Barclay to play for the Anfield Blues. He was immediately a vital part of the club that was among the first 12 members of professional and organised football within England. It wasn't to be the greatest year for the only team in the city at the time, finishing in eighth place, but they were afforded the special honour of being one of the founding fathers of football.

For Chadwick, he was part of the very first days of football, so it was far from a fruitful venture when he was asked to uproot his family from Blackburn, but the opportunity to join the club alongside his brother Albert was certainly a big convincer. Edgar was also a baker by trade and it took him some years to be convinced to move to the city, with Everton even offering to cover the cost of moving his furniture.

The forward line of Chadwick, Johnny Holt and Alf Milward proved lethal in the early years of Everton, enough to earn Edgar an England call-up (he was only the third Blue to have ever been handed that honour) and a goal to boot. Another small and light player, the tricky and speedy left-winger was much more successful than his stature should have allowed him to be in the era that he played in.

Chadwick and Milward were part of arguably the best left wing in the First Division and for England. Chadwick's friendship with Andrew Hannah and Fred Geary was also somewhat ironic as all three were, of course, set to go on to represent Liverpool too. As well as being part of the 1893 and 1897 FA Cup Final defeats, the 5ft 6in attacker's role in the First Division success during the 1890/91 campaign was crucial.

Chadwick played in all 22 of the First Division fixtures that were played in the vastly successful season, the same season that goal nets and penalties were introduced to the game. The Blues got off to a flying start and won six of their first seven matches, which was swiftly followed by four defeats in five. Inconsistency wasn't something that made it easier for the Anfield club to win the league and it certainly didn't help the nerves across the city.

Everton faced Preston North End at Anfield with just two matches remaining of their season but, due to a fixture pile-up, the visitors had a whopping six left of theirs. The Blues knew that they had to get a victory to maintain their lead over Wolves, Blackburn, Notts County and the visiting Lilywhites, while crossing their fingers that results would go their way in the coming months.

On 3 January 1891 the First Division looked like this (this still being the days of two points being awarded for a victory):

Team	P	W	L	D	Pts
Everton	20	14	5	1	29
Wolves	20	12	6	2	26
Blackburn Rovers	18	11	5	2	24
Notts County	19	9	6	4	22
Preston North End	16	8	6	2	18

The two teams met on 10 January, 16,000 attending, with expectations set on the home team to build their lead at the top. There was snow on the pitch for this fiery encounter, so the turf was covered in 'sawdust, hay seeds, and fine cinders' but it took just 30 minutes for the visitors to stun Anfield. The Blues were frozen in shock and became desperate as the second half commenced. Temperatures boiled over on several occasions but the Prestonian defence remained resolute and they held on for a huge victory.

That put all the pressure on Everton's final match of the season, which wasn't played until 14 March, meaning Everton had over two months of watching all their rivals chip away at their handsome lead at the top. When it came to the last match for the Blues, they had a two-point lead over Preston, so a victory or draw would ensure the first title for Merseyside. Burnley hosted Everton and Sunderland hosted North End, a final day that was set to produce some tremendous drama for all involved.

Everton's superior goal average was also a big plus for their hopes of title success, but they wanted to secure the league on their own terms. Fred Geary certainly turned up on the big day and his double was seemingly title-deciding, as the Blues were two ahead with just ten minutes left of the match. What followed was a meltdown of tremendous proportion and Burnley broke the hearts of the visitors. The hosts, who would ultimately finish the season in eighth place, scored three goals. In the days before wireless radios and mobile phones providing constant updates from the north-east, you can only imagine the fear that must have hit the 2,000 travelling fans.

From ten minutes to glory, to nervously awaiting any updates from the Preston match. Then it arrived. There was no need to worry as Sunderland had emphatically won 3-0 and the league trophy was handed to Everton for the very first time. Despite losing the final two matches of the season and choking in two huge matches, Dick Molyneux's team could hold their heads up high as their earlier form had been enough to deliver success. So that was that and the final league table produced a top two separated by just two points:

Team	P	W	L	D	Pts
Everton	22	14	7	1	29
Preston North End	22	12	7	3	27

Upon hearing the success, the board decided that 'medals & £5 be handed over to each of the original 12 players' and Chadwick was, of course, one of the celebrated players to receive the rewards. This was by no means the end of the wing wizard's Anfield and then Goodison career, as he went on to enjoy another eight years in a blue shirt. Alongside Fred Geary, the pair were certainly right to be considered as two of the best to have ever played for the club and, considering the longevity and loyalty of the Blackburn-born winger, it's seemingly fair to give him the edge as the best.

In May 1899 though, much to the dismay of Chadwick, Everton decided to make him available for a considerable £200 sale, and the 29-year-old was quoted by *Sporting Life* as saying:

> It has been constantly brought under my notice that I am about to retire from the football worlds. This is untrue. Why should I retire when I have good football in me? If I retire it will be because of the big transfer fee placed on me by the Everton directorate, thus hindering me from obtaining a decent situation. I have served the Everton and Liverpool public honourably and faithfully during my stay at Everton, and I think I have been treated unfairly. This will probably surprise my Everton friends.

It's clear that his Goodison Park career came to an end with a sour taste in Chadwick's mouth, but his outburst worked, as he was sold the next week to Burnley for just £40. He left the club having made 300 appearances and scoring 104 goals and, as of the start of the 2022/23 season, only seven players have ever scored more goals for the club. His two FA Cup Final defeats with Everton became a hat-trick with Southampton in 1902, the summer before he joined Liverpool.

Now aged 32, Chadwick was certainly an elder statesman within the Liverpool team and hoped to help them regain the form that saw First Division success in the 1900/01 campaign. With 30 appearances and seven goals in his maiden season, he showed that he was right to claim three years earlier that retirement was a long way away. Following a two-goal performance in a 9-2 Anfield victory over Grimsby Town, the *Lancashire Evening Post* wrote:

I am pleased to say that Chadwick got two of the goals against Grimsby. It was touching to see his pride in his own performance. He was as pleased with the ball as a baby with its rattle, though not, perhaps, for the same reason. The rattle is new to the baby. Now a goal cannot be said to be new to Edgar – he must have got a great many goals in his time – but his performance on Saturday last were an assurance that he has not yet lost his power to get more; hence his juvenile delight.

Chadwick's 14 appearances in the 1903/04 season weren't enough to help Liverpool avoid relegation in what was a disastrous campaign. The Anfield club lost their first five matches and the former Everton man had started four of them, with Tom Watson's team confined to sitting rock bottom. An away match with Wolves during Christmas 1903 proved to be the final league match for the legendary winger, the Reds having climbed only one place by this time. The aged legs of the England international were no longer deemed worthy or capable of high-calibre performances; 11 of his 15 league appearances ended in defeat but things didn't get much better after the 34-year-old's final match.

Chadwick hung around until relegation was confirmed but he parted ways in May 1904. There was a string of moves and appearances for the experienced dribbler to come, before a final appearance as a 47-year-old wartime guest for Blackpool in 1917. He was set to join a German club, but the First World War understandably stood in the way of that move. Then came a successful European managerial journey, as the Blackburn-born baker took on the job as head coach of the Netherlands, winning bronze at the 1908 and 1912 Olympics. Germany wanted him to become their manager, but the untimely death of his father led to a break from the game.

Chadwick triumphantly returned for spells with HVV, HFC, Vitesse and finally a league-winning campaign with Sparta Rotterdam in 1915. Football was now done for the 45-year-old, and he again returned home to Blackpool before retiring in Blackburn. Childless, Edgar saw out his final days alongside his wife Jane and died on Valentine's Day in 1942, aged 72 and in the midst of the Second World War.

There's no doubt that the world in which he died meant that the tributes he should have received were absent. Edgar Chadwick was a legendary Everton player, moving to Liverpool in the twilight of what proved to be an extraordinarily long playing career, before a remarkable managerial experience that few would have ever predicted would follow. A loyal and talented player who was not afraid to speak up for what he thought was right.

David Murray

Name	David Bruce Murray
Born	04/12/1882, Cathcart, Scotland
Died	10/12/1915, Western Front, France
Everton stats	2 matches/0 goals (1903)
Everton honours	None
Liverpool stats	15 matches/0 goals (1904–05)
Liverpool honours	First Division 1904/05, 1905/06
Combined stats	17 matches/0 goals (1903–05)
Direct transfer?	Yes (signed for LFC from EFC in August 1904 for free)

FROM A flagship Merseyside legend to a player who left barely a ripple on the Mersey with his footballing contributions to the city. David Murray was initially invited for a trial with Everton in April 1903, and the 20-year-old clearly impressed enough to be offered a one-year deal with the club and was paid '30 shillings in summer and £2 in winter with £5 for expenses & the engagement'.

Arriving from Scotland, the defender found first-team football hard to come by and, just a month into his life in Liverpool, the Everton board offered the defender to Nottingham Forest for £100.

That was enough to illustrate how sparse the chances were set to be for him. The Scot was handed two league matches for the Blues in the First Division, which both saw the team lose 1-0, against Sheffield Wednesday and Sunderland, respectively. The left-back position of Jack

Crelley was never to be handed to Murray again, after his two November runouts.

The following May saw the Scot placed on the transfer list for £100 and he wouldn't feature for the club again. Everton were interested in signing Liverpool stalwart Jack Cox but the request of £500 and David Murray was deemed 'excessive', so it was decided that unless the Reds could offer a better deal, the move would be off the table.

Cox ultimately stayed at Liverpool for the next six years, but the Anfield club also managed to secure the signature of Murray, as Everton failed to find a buyer for his services and thus allowed him to leave on a free transfer to the other side of Stanley Park.

Although appearances were a little easier to come by in the Second Division with Liverpool, Murray was still a fringe player. His 12 league appearances certainly helped Tom Watson's team achieve promotion back to the First Division at the first time of asking but seeing as his final match in the campaign came on Boxing Day, he wasn't part of the successful run-in. That festive match against Barnsley saw the club programme report:

> Murray took [Billy] Dunlop's place, but did not shine, and he was responsible for Barnsley's goal. He kicked towards [Ned] Doig, who had to run out for the ball, and with a forward on him the goalkeeper only partially cleared, and the ball was in the net just as Doig got back to his place. What he appealed for goodness alone knows, as the goal was absolutely sure. I think he was a bit nettled at Murray's manoeuvre, and felt inclined to talk to him.

This helped make it a mixed season for the Scot but at least he was now back in the First Division. When the 22-year-old was handed his next start it was set to be one of three in September of 1905. Poignantly, his final match for either club came in the Merseyside derby at Goodison Park. Murray was again in for Billy Dunlop, who was ruled out not long before kick-off with a knee injury.

A glance into the rivalry that existed in this era was provided by the *Liverpool Echo*, as it was reported it was 'nothing more serious than a mental reservation on the part of each follower that, come what may, their own side may win. Apart from the dual meeting in League fixtures and a possible English Cup encounter, both sides in these days may easily even sympathise with each other's misfortunes, as they have no grounds for being jealous of each other's successes.'

There were around 40,000 packed inside Anfield, including the Lord Mayor of Liverpool, for the meeting of the two teams. Murray was run ragged by the talented right-wing of Everton and found it particularly difficult to deal with Jimmy Settle, with Ned Doig having to bail out his defender on several occasions. The Scot was 'outwitted once or twice. Ultimately, pressed back by Settle, he passed back rather erratically to Doig, who was unprepared and handed the leather past his goal-line, thus conceding an unnecessary corner, which led to the undoing of the Reds as their ball was nicely placed, and Doig was hemmed in with his backs, who were quite unable to get the leather away, and after several attempts had failed [Walter] Abbot did the trick as he was practically in the goalmouth, and poor Doig was practically helpless.'

This poor first half came to a worrying end, as Sandy Young was brought down early by the nervous defender. Murray was out to make amends for himself in the second half but there was set to be yet more mistakes from the left-back. 'The Blues rushed away in line, circumventing the

Liverpool half-back line completely, and Murray advanced to meet [Jack] Sharp, who was in possession, but he made only a wretched effort to check the cricketer, who beat him easily, and then "Jack" went full steam ahead. At the last moment Doig left his goal, but without altering his course Sharp shot straight, and then found the net.'

Murray was having a day from hell. A poor clearance followed and Young was unfortunate to see his effort sail just over the bar. Thankfully for the Scot, though, his final act was to be a positive one, his cross finding the head of Maurice Parry, who came close to making a nervy end for Everton, but the match ended 4-2 to the Blues and the former Toffee was afforded blame for two of their goals.

Perhaps the greatest day Murray had on Merseyside was his Liverpool performance that benefitted Everton so much and handed them the bragging rights within the city. Fortunes were to soon change for all though. David Murray never played again for the Reds, the Blues went on to finish 11th, while their neighbours won the First Division title.

The Scot left for Leeds United in December of that season and Liverpool received a handsome £130 for his services. Murray went on to captain the club before moves to Mexborough and Burslem Port Vale, exiting the game aged 27 through injury and then becoming a miner in South Yorkshire. September 1914 saw the start of the First World War and, with it, the proud Scot enlisted to join the war effort.

He was posted to the 11th Battalion, Argyll and Sutherland Highlanders and was sent to France for battle in July 1915. Murray was involved in the Battle of Loos, the biggest British attack of 1915, but one that also ended in defeat. A week after his 33rd birthday, the former Merseyside left-back was one of 60,000 to die in the battle. He is buried in an unmarked grave at Loos Memorial in 'Dud Corner'.

Murray is the first of three men in this list whose life was taken during the First World War and acts as a stark reminder of the huge volume of young men that made the ultimate sacrifice for their country. Three of the historic 34 to have ever played for both clubs all dying during the same war shows the unbelievable death toll that greeted the city, country and world at the time. Little did everyone know then that there was set to be another war just 24 years after the death of David Murray.

Don Sloan

Name	Donald Sloan
Born	31/07/1883, Rankinston, Scotland
Died	01/01/1917, Western Front, France
Everton stats	6 matches/0 clean sheets (1906–08)
Everton honours	None
Liverpool stats	6 matches/0 clean sheets (1908–09)
Liverpool honours	None
Combined stats	12 matches/0 clean sheets (1906–09)
Direct transfer?	Yes (signed for LFC from EFC in May 1908 for £300)

FROM A man with a small legacy within the two clubs whose life came to a tragic and heroic early end, to a sadly similar story. Don Sloan was born in Scotland but his footballing life began in Belfast with the club known simply as Distillery, due to being based on Distillery Street within the city. The goalkeeper caught the attention of Everton in October 1905 after impressing in an inter-league match that the Blues had sent scouts to attend.

Distillery initially batted away interest from Goodison Park but the club officials remained confident that, if the Belfast club was 'hard pressed', it would give in to an offer. Distillery remained resolute, and instructions of bidding up to £250 for his services was given by the Everton board. In April 1906 the 22-year-old was finally signed.

Sloan operated mainly for the reserves and had to wait until April of the following year for his maiden first-team appearance, deputising for Billy Scott (Elisha Scott, the legendary Liverpool goalkeeper's elder brother) in consecutive matches, against Blackburn Rovers (2-1 loss) and Woolwich Arsenal (2-1 win). The following season brought with it four sporadic appearances but it was clear that it was going to be an impossible task to displace the man who today remains the holder of the fifth-highest number of clean sheets in Everton history. Three defeats in his four matches and a failure to keep a single clean sheet certainly won't have helped his chances either.

Off-field matters may have also had an impact on Sloan's Goodison Park chances, as he was twice called before the board to explain his 'inattention to training', 'loss of form' and 'absenting himself without reasonable excuse', which led to a caution in January 1907. There was also then a notice published within the dressing room to warn all players over training performances. Failure to break into the first team and a string of training indiscretions meant that the decision to place the keeper on the transfer list in April 1908 may not have come as too much of a surprise to the Scot.

Everton had wanted £350 for their keeper but accepted an offer of £300 from Liverpool, so Sloan made the short journey across the park in May 1908. He was again an understudy but this time for Sam Hardy, another man that it proved impossible to displace from the team, and the Scot's only opportunities came when his team-mate was unavailable.

Sloan was handed six First Division appearances for Liverpool, all between October 1908 and April 1909, and in a string of matches that ended in him having the unwanted stat of never being able to keep a first-team clean sheet for either Merseyside club. His final appearance for either club came against Manchester City and, with the score at 0-0 at half-time, the stopper may have thought he had a chance of securing a shutout.

A fine save at the start of the second half was followed up by an impressive palm over the bar and Sloan looked to be in fine form. The goals did unfortunately start coming though, but it was clear that it wasn't for the want of trying nor effort from the Scot. Two goals went past but a third was chalked off after Tom Holford was adjudged to have impeded the former Distillery man. Joe Dorsett made it 4-0 by the end when, as the *Liverpool Echo* reported, he 'banged both Sloan and the ball into the goal'.

Far from the disastrous farewell that greeted David Murray, Don Sloan's final appearance demonstrated why he had been spotted to play at this level, but no clean sheets in 12 First Division matches isn't great for a keeper. The end of the season brought with it a move back to Distillery as the 25-year-old was offered the chance to become player-manager of his former club. From there came a return to Scotland with Bathgate and East Stirlingshire, before his football came to an end in 1914 because of the start of the First World War.

Private Don Sloan of the Black Watch was killed in action following heavy German mortar fire near Saint-Laurent-Blangy on New Year's Day in 1917. He's one of nearly 3,000 that are buried in Faubourg-d'Amiens Cemetery and even more heart-wrenching is the fact that he was one of four Sloan brothers to die during the war. It's hard to imagine the toll this had on his elderly parents and lone remaining Sloan brother, who lived in Edinburgh, and the wife and three children he left in Glasgow.

Another man who may not have had the greatest Merseyside football career but made the ultimate sacrifice for his nation, at just 33 years old.

Arthur Berry

Name	Arthur Berry
Born	03/01/1888, Liverpool
Died	15/03/1953, Liverpool
Liverpool stats	4 matches/0 goals (1906–09 & 1912)
Liverpool honours	None
Everton stats	29 matches/8 goals (1909–10)
Everton honours	None
Combined stats	33 matches/8 goals (1906–12)
Direct transfer?	No

A NEW first for the list, finally a player whose career began at Anfield, but with the Red half of the city. Scouser, Olympian and an all-round sportsman, Arthur Berry had a career that's quite unlike any of the men who have come before, or will come after him here.

Despite being born within the city, Berry was educated at the prestigious Denstone College in Uttoxeter and it was there that he found and displayed his talents in a smorgasbord of different sports. In 1908 the club programme wrote that 'he gained a reputation for excellency in nearly every branch of athletics. Tennis, sprinting, and Rugby football occupied his attention chiefly, and in each he represented his school.'

Berry went on to attend Oxford University and finally his attention turned to what he's being recognised for here – football. It was the end of his university studies that helped see a return to his home city and, thanks to some help from his father Edwin Berry, who happened to be Liverpool's chairman from 1904–09, he managed to find himself given a chance at Anfield.

Perhaps the fact that he was so talented in other fields and that the opportunity to represent Liverpool was favourably handed to him meant that there were some accusations that Berry never had his full focus on being a footballer. He joined the Reds in April 1906 but it took him two years to break into the first team, away to Newcastle in a First Division clash. The 'Oxonian and amateur', as he was introduced, started at inside-right and his performance was described in the matchday programme: 'It would be unfair to judge Berry on his initial League appearance, but he did sufficient to show that if he cares to take to the game seriously he will be an excellent forward.'

It didn't look as if he was taking football too seriously though, as it wasn't until he was a 20-year-old that he was given a second first-team runout, against Leicester City and Woolwich Arsenal in the October of 1908. The latter match saw Berry record an assist for Ronald Orr with a 'sweet pass', which was partnered with a decent chance that was 'interfered' by his own captain Joe Hewitt. It wasn't the best (nor worst) of displays in a match that ended 2-2 at Anfield, and the assessment of his game read: 'Berry is too easily knocked off the ball for an inside man, and although he did give [Arthur] Goddard several nice passes, he was too dainty in his movements very frequently.'

It seemed as though the board agreed with this assessment as it proved to be the final goal of his first spell of representing Liverpool. Berry left soon after and began to enjoy the freedom of being able to move freely between clubs, representing Wrexham in no fewer than six separate stints, playing for the aptly named Northern Nomads and even remaining to live in Merseyside but commuting to play for Fulham. It was clear that the forward had talent but he seemed to prefer to keep his fingers in several pies, rather than focusing on what could have been a rather successful Scouse pie at home.

Despite making a solitary England appearance at senior level, his amateur status and career is what granted him the opportunity to move clubs so frequently and also represent the amateur Great Britain side in the Olympics. In London 1908 and Stockholm 1912, Berry helped secure a gold medal for his nation and scored in both competitions – including the fourth in a 4-2 final win against Denmark in 1912. Only he and Vivian Woodward represented their nation in both tournaments and this was a real testament to the clear talent the West Derby-born forward had. He was clearly committed to the sport but enjoyed the benefits of moving between clubs and competing in the Olympic Games that remaining an amateur player provided him.

Following his uninspiring Liverpool career then, it's somewhat of a surprise that he received a senior England call-up in 1909, while a Fulham player. It's likely that the squad selectors looked to celebrate some of the Olympic heroes in the match against Ireland, as he and Woodward were both played on the day.

In August 1909 it was brought to the attention of the Everton board that 'Mr. A. Berry son of the Exchairman of L'pool F.C. would be glad to play with us if we thought him good enough'. Berry was intermittently representing Wrexham at this point but looked as though he wanted to return to playing at a consistently high level. What followed was a (ultimately short-lived) first indication of a possible worsening relationship between both Merseyside clubs.

Up to this stage the only real point of controversy or angst between the two clubs was John Houlding but he had died seven years earlier in Nice. We had seen with David

Murray's unfortunate derby display in 1905 that the only real competition was when playing each other and the rivalry was 'nothing more serious than a mental reservation on the part of each follower that, come what may, their own side may win'. However, Everton's minute books noted that 'Mr. A. Berry had decided not to proceed with his application fearing that his action might create ill feeling between the two clubs'.

The forward made the decision to reject the Everton advances and made his move to Fulham, in an attempt to not fan any flames of hatred on Merseyside. In January 1910, with the commute to London for fixtures at Craven Cottage proving a logistical nightmare for Berry, it became clear that he wanted to return to playing a little closer to home. The Scouser again came up in board meetings for the Goodison club: 'It being reported that Mr. Arthur Berry, the Amateur, outside right of Fulham, being desirous of a change & of coming to our Club and the Secretary having reported that he believed that Fulham would transfer him to us he was instructed to write Fulham requesting such transfer & too see Mr. A. Berry and offer him the outside right position in the Combination team with a view to his proving his worth for inclusion in the League team.'

It certainly didn't appear that Everton had any motives behind signing Berry other than wanting to add a talented forward to their ranks and hope that he could break into their first-team set-up eventually. The following month the Olympian gave way to his worries of antagonising the Reds and became the first man to cross the park in the opposite direction.

The Berry name wasn't just tied into the Red side of the city though, as Edwin Berry was also the co-founder of St Domingo FC and went on to represent Everton as a player too in their early days. There seemed to be little controversy when he went on to become chairman of the Reds and, in truth, there was little for Arthur to worry about with his transfer to Goodison Park.

Off-field is certainly more interesting when it comes to Berry but he had a much better spell in a blue shirt than he did in a red one. He again had to bide his time for a first-team appearance, which finally came in February 1910, when Berry impressed enough to play six of the final 17 league matches in a campaign where the Blues finished tenth in the First Division. He scored two goals in his first season, both coming in his final appearance of the campaign, at home to Manchester United.

Despite interest from Blackpool and Manchester City, Everton wanted to keep Berry at the club for the following season after the successful end to his maiden one, but he looked to be getting itchy feet yet again. In August 1911 the forward submitted a letter 'expressing the fear that he would be unable to play for us this season as he seriously considered giving up the game'. It's certainly not something that people will feel too sorry about but as an Oxford graduate with wealthy and successful parents, Berry's sporting ambitions were never ones that he made for financial gain.

Arthur Berry was a law student who lived at home with his parents but they were very wealthy, owning large houses in West Derby (on Fairfield Crescent and Prescot Drive) before moving to Wrexham, where his father worked in the Supreme Court and the family home had two servants. He had been sent off to school as a child and had no want for money, so his sporting talents enabled him to move around the country with ease and he always had an impressive home to return to. This worry about giving up the game didn't last but this flaky move between major decisions seemed to be in the nature of the privileged, skilled and confused then 23-year-old.

After missing the first three matches of the 1910/11 season, Berry started the next nine in a row and looked to be finally settling and maturing into life as a top-level footballer. Six goals in 23 matches was enough to attract more attention, and again from Liverpool in March 1911, but Everton declined to listen to an offer. The forward took part in a Merseyside derby at Anfield in October 1910 and helped assist the opening goal for the Blues in a 2-0 win, where, as reported in the Liverpool matchday programme, 'Everton have again demonstrated their superiority over us when they come to Anfield.' The report went on to say, 'One thing we can all congratulate ourselves upon, and that is the bitterness which used to characterise these matches has gone. No cleaner games take place anywhere than between these keen rivals, and I believe the people of Liverpool themselves have much more to do with the spirit of sportsmanship which prevails.'

Berry's nomadic tendencies returned in May of that year, though, and he asked to be allowed to leave the club. The board asked for a meeting but the player declined, and on the same day the Reds submitted another offer. Whether a huge coincidence or a more seemingly well-orchestrated double attack from player and new club, the Blues had little option but to allow him to leave. His exit actually ended up being back to Oxford though, another short spell before a return to Liverpool.

His return to Anfield in 1912 was certainly not spectacular, as Berry again looked to concentrate on his ability to change field as often as possible and he made a solitary first-team appearance in the six months he spent back with Liverpool. The *Dundee Courier* reported when the 24-year-old re-signed for the club that 'Berry is reading for the Bar, and expects to be called shortly'. Another interest was set to take over his life. October 1912 and a 4-1 loss to

Sheffield United was the end of Berry's Liverpool story but he still had time for one more return to Everton.

The man with more clubs than Tiger Woods was unable to break back into the Everton team in 1912, after transferring from Liverpool. Berry refused to represent the Blues at any level other than first team though, and despite the club offering to 'play him in the League team whenever possible', he never did make another league appearance for either Merseyside club.

From Liverpool, to Everton, to Liverpool and back to Everton – Arthur Berry is certainly a unique character within the book. In 1913 the 25-year-old retired from the game and moved to London after being called to the bar at Gray's Inn. He then joined the war effort with the Lancashire Fusiliers, serving on the major fronts. He's fortunately not one of the men who died while doing so. His reward for a chaotic first 30 years of his life was the safe haven of his family's law firm, where he went on to become a barrister and worked in Liverpool (Edwin Berry and Company, solicitors, 21 Old Hall Street).

His tendencies to move around finally ended when he settled down in law and lived with his wife Irene until he died suddenly in 1953, aged 65, before being buried in Allerton Cemetery. Truly a unique character and life lived by an interesting and complex man, who was the first to swap red for blue and will surely never be beaten in signing for both clubs twice.

Harold Uren

Name	Harold John Uren
Born	23/08/1885, Clifton
Died	07/04/1955, West Kirkby
Liverpool stats	45 matches/2 goals (1906–12)
Liverpool honours	None
Everton stats	24 matches/3 goals (1911–12)
Everton honours	None
Combined stats	69 matches/5 goals (1906–12)
Direct transfer?	Yes (transferred from LFC to EFC in February 1912 as part of a swap deal)

GROWING UP in Bristol, Harold Uren repeated Arthur Berry's feat of representing Liverpool before Everton. His family moved to the Wirral after John Uren, his father, founded a food provision business. The versatile winger moved up the ranks of the lower leagues, and when he was signed by Liverpool in 1906 as a 20-year-old amateur, it was agreed he could still represent Wrexham at the same time.

The speedy youngster was handed just two appearances in his first season at Anfield, a draw away to Manchester City and a home defeat to Preston in November 1907. The latter, although 'a weak team and a weak display' produced a disappointing result, saw Uren impress the writers of the matchday programme enough for them to write: 'Uren, the amateur who took [Jack] Cox's place, is on the other hand a man to persevere with.'

Uren was built like an athlete and looked destined to break into the first team one day, with his pace, trickery and passing causing a constant menace on the wing. He wouldn't have expected his next match to be nearly 18 months later and in a record-breaking derby-day defeat for his team. Good Friday of 1909 saw 50,000 fans cram themselves into Goodison Park, and the *Liverpool Courier* reported: 'The struggles of Everton and Liverpool are always a source of unbounded interest, and on these occasions partisanship runs exceedingly high, but when the meeting occurs on Good Friday; football excitement in the city is at an unusually high pitch.'

Uren was in at outside-left for the away team and, despite the disaster that unfolded around him, on a personal level he was said to have given 'a good display and centred effectively'. By all accounts he was the major outlet for Liverpool on the day as he continued to test the Everton defence and Billy Scott in goal. It was a day for the Blues though, and a Bertie Freeman brace was combined with goals by Bob Turner, Wattie White and Tim Coleman to make it a triumphant 5-0 victory.

After reading match reports of Uren's performances, although Liverpool failed to win in any of his first-team matches in his first three years with the club, it does seem strange that it took him so long to break into the team consistently. It wasn't until the 1910/11 campaign that he was allowed to make more than three appearances in a season and his best run was playing 24 times and scoring his only two goals in the following year.

Rather ironically, in Uren's 45 matches for Tom Watson's Reds, he played against no team more than Everton. In fact, in the five times he played against the Blues, the winger only recorded one victory, with four defeats – failing to score in any. By the February of the 1911/12 season, though, the 26-year-old had played in 26 of 29 Liverpool matches that season and was firmly part of the first team until a lucrative offer was put on the table.

What followed was a decision that affected the careers of Uren and the two following players in this unique list of men. Liverpool wanted to acquire the services of both Tom Gracie and Bill Lacey from Everton and, in order to do so, were willing to offer £300 (the same fee spent on Don Sloan four years earlier and around £27,000 in today's money) as well as throwing in Harold Uren as part of the deal.

It seems strange that Liverpool would be willing to part with a player who looked to have worked his way up from an amateur to a mainstay of the team. Not only that, but offer money on top to capture two Evertonians for Anfield. Gracie and Lacey, a poetically named transfer duo who will, of course, be examined further, were a pair that had made little over 50 appearances between them for the Blues. Yet the Reds had seen enough to part ways with a promising player who had played 26 times in the past five months. Everton minute books read: 'The transfer of Thos. Gracie & Wm. Lacey to Liverpool in consideration of £300 & the transfer of H. J. Uren to us was confirmed as was the engagement of Uren at £4 per week with a bonus of £10. The Secretary's action in making application to the League for consent to pay Lacey £150 was confirmed.'

This transfer also highlighted the good spirit that was clearly present between the clubs. The initial offer from Liverpool was for Jack Parkinson to leave the club in place of Lacey but the negotiations rumbled on for several weeks, until this outcome was achieved. The *Liverpool Echo* reported on this deal by stating, 'The transfers I announce today have been possible through the sensible and somewhat new friendly feeling between the two clubs. Liverpool citizens can support two first-class clubs, and if ill feeling is eradicated the clubs can help each other.'

As for Uren, the same report summarised that his Liverpool life thus far and had some suggestions as to how he may fare in blue:

> Uren is a clever player, who has been a misfit. He has style peculiarly his own, and sometimes aye many times, he has played in a manner that suggested he was out of football sympathy with the other members and that the other forwards could not make headway from his ideas. It is an oft-quoted axiom that a player may be unworthy inclusion in one club's second team, and yet when transferred he finds new life and becomes an international player.
>
> He began with New Brighton Wesleyans, then travelled to West Kirby, later assisted Wrexham, and finally joined Liverpool with which club he has been a professional for three years, and all told has served them on and off for five years.
>
> He needs to curb his excessive dribbling, and needs to be 'hearty' at times. Still he is a player whose style should fit Everton, and the club has done a good stroke of business in gaining his transfer.

Uren became the first man to transfer directly from Anfield to Goodison Park and was thrust straight into the first team for Everton. It was just four days after his final Liverpool appearance that he made his debut at Goodison Park. The Reds ended the season in 17th place, while the Blues were runners-up to Blackburn Rovers.

The following campaign looked to provide Uren a platform to kick on, and he was handed the opportunity to feature in the first six matches of the new season. However, his campaign became a little stop-start due to injuries and a lack of form, leading to some doubting the talents of the now 27-year-old winger.

In April 1913, Everton took the decision to list Uren for transfer at £500. The verdict was met with some competition within the board though, and they twice changed their mind. This shows that he still had some fans but his failure to score more than three times in two seasons at Goodison Park may have had something to do with the lack of trust in his ability.

Uren was a player who looked great, even often playing well, but his end product left a little to be desired. A speedy winger who could beat a man and put a cross in was often all that was required in this era of football but perhaps the early 20th-century statisticians would have analysed his lack of goal involvements, akin to a Stewart Downing or Theo Walcott of his day.

Much like with his early days at Liverpool, Uren was allowed to play for Wrexham following the end of the 1913/14 season while Everton attempted to recoup some money for his services. The start of the following season was, of course, set to bring with it the start of the First World War, meaning the Blues never had the opportunity to sell their winger, as he was sent off to help the war effort.

As part of the British Army, Uren rose to the rank of 2nd lieutenant but was sent back to Britain after health issues meant he could no longer fight on the front line. He returned to join the home front. It was a decision that was likely to have upset the man but certainly helped ensure the fact that he saw the war out and didn't have to make the ultimate sacrifice.

Whether disenfranchised or no longer able, Uren stopped playing football after the war and joined the family business on the Wirral. Uren Food Group is still in existence today, thanks to the work of the three generations of John, Harold and Harold Jr. His two sons also went on to represent England in rugby and his daughter was a competitive yachter. The former footballer became a successful businessman and was elected president of the Liverpool Provision Trade Association.

Uren maintained a keen interest in sport, with his friends on both sides of the park, as well as being a generous beneficiary of the Royal School for the Blind on Hope Street in Liverpool. He and his wife Annie had six children, and when Uren fell ill in 1955 the world of sport and business flocked to visit his West Kirkby home and pay their respects during his two-month illness before his death aged 69.

Another first for the list, as he directly moved from Liverpool to Everton, Uren's career always seemed set to take off but never reached the heights that many seemed to predict it could during his early Anfield days. His success in business, though, set up what proved to be a happy and fruitful life after football.

Tom Gracie

Name	Thomas Gracie
Born	12/06/1889, Glasgow
Died	23/10/1915, Glasgow
Everton stats	13 matches/1 goal (1910–12)
Everton honours	None
Liverpool stats	34 matches/5 goals (1912–14)
Liverpool honours	None
Combined stats	47 matches/6 goals (1910–14)
Direct transfer?	Yes (signed for LFC from EFC in February 1912 for £150)

YOU ALREADY know his name and the story of the transfer but here's the second member of a three-man swap deal that unified Merseyside. Tom Gracie sees a return to the traditional members of this list, with a Scot moving from Everton to Liverpool once again.

The Glasgow-born forward was impressive during his early days north of the border and starred for a host of Scottish clubs before attracting the attention of Everton. Gracie studied to be a bookkeeper and worked as a meat salesman during his early playing days but it was a call-up as a reserve for a Scotland fixture that helped start his life on Merseyside.

Everton had been aware of Gracie and had considered a move for the player on several occasions but were never thoroughly convinced enough to make an approach for him. While he was in England for the match of his nation, members of the board spoke with the forward and were convinced that he could be a good fit for Goodison Park.

With the struggling goalscoring form of James Gourlay, Gracie was given a chance to shine and played in all of the final seven First Division fixtures in the 1910/11 season. It showed that there was clearly a level of both belief in the talents of the Scot and patience for him to find his feet at the top level of English football. The No.9 then started the first two matches of the new season but one goal in his nine appearances so far seemed to affect the confidence of both club and player.

It turned out that a goal scored by Gracie in his third appearance for Everton was to be his only one in 13 matches, and an eight-month spell in the first-team limelight for the forward. Clearly this wasn't a return that was desired by the club and they were greeted by possible suitors in the form of Clyde, Celtic and Partick Thistle. The year before saw the club knock back offers of £650, before placing him on the transfer list and asking for £750 for his signature. This was all, of course, before the deal that was eventually agreed as part of the Harold Uren transfer.

With the initial transfer negotiations, as mentioned, being centred around Liverpool's interest in Bill Lacey, it's clear that Gracie was used as somewhat of a makeweight in the move to Anfield. Seemingly not entirely wanted by either club at this point then, it's perhaps no surprise that his career in red was little better than his days in blue. One shining light for him, though, was that he arrived with Lacey, and the pair had a strong bond off the pitch.

It was to be a stay of just two years and two months for Gracie at Anfield but a move that got off to the best possible start. He was handed his debut two days after signing for the club, bizarrely alongside Uren, as his deal to move to Everton wasn't completed yet, and managed to get himself on the scoresheet. The Blues must have been worried at the sight of their now former striker equalling his goal tally for them in his first match for the Reds, and while watching their new signing unable to get himself in on the act too.

Gracie appeared to ride the crest of this wave and started six matches in two months of his first season but failed to register another goal after his debut. The forward was handed a further seven starts between September and October of the following season too but he was to only score a further solitary goal. His late and ultimately match-winning finish against Chelsea in a 2-1 victory was recalled in the matchday programme alongside the comment, 'I was glad to see Gracie score; the success may give him that encouragement for which he has been longing.'

Again, though, this was to be a solitary moment of brilliance from the forward. The following weeks saw further comments like this in the matchday programme, which read: 'The centre forward berth will require strengthening, for Gracie seems unable to infuse any life into the attacks, and in the match under notice was seldom seen.' It was soon evaluated that Gracie was 'by no means a deadly forward when near goal', but there still seemed to be some fans of his at the top of the club, so a move to inside-left soon followed.

This became a new position for the Scot, where he continued to be deployed for the rest of the 1912/13 season and into the next too. Despite being the reason why he was first brought into the top English division, Gracie wasn't a goalscoring machine, and he only managed a total of five in three Anfield seasons. He was still being regularly played in the First Division but his position at inside-left was soon taken by Bill Lacey, and Gracie's appearance in February 1914 proved to be his final one before leaving the club and returning to Scotland, with Hearts.

His form dipped to such a low standard that, following a defeat to Chelsea, the Liverpool fans accused Gracie and several other players of deliberately playing badly. Manager John McKenna was forced to release a statement that debunked this theory but the fact that the Scot was removed from the starting line-up (alongside Bill Lacey and Jack Parkinson) for the next match with Manchester United meant that there must have been some thought that he wasn't performing at the level that the club had expected when he was signed.

He managed to achieve the feat of being joint-top goalscorer in the division upon his return to Scotland with Hearts but a rejuvenated football career was met with two life-altering events for Gracie. The first was the war that interrupted so many careers in this era and the second was to be a reason that stopped him from being able to fight.

Gracie signed up with the majority of the Hearts squad and they were set to be sent to join the war effort, but it was soon discovered that the forward had been diagnosed with leukaemia. He had managed to climb the ranks to becoming a corporal in the Royal Scots, while still shining in front of goal as a player, but he wasn't allowed to partake in overseas operations because of his illness.

Gracie wanted to keep playing football, and Hearts allowed him to do so, but it was an understandably short-lived affair, as eight months after his diagnosis he had a sudden decline that ended with him passing away aged 27. His death was met with more family sadness, as his brother John was killed in the same battle that took the life of David Murray in Loos. Following the outpouring of love that came to the family and from Liverpool in particular, his mother wrote an open letter to the *Liverpool Echo*:

> I have to thank you most sincerely for your article regarding my dear son, Tom. Tokens of respect

such as you have written help to lighten the burden the loss of him is to us who loved him so much. Only God knows what I have lost in my darling boy, and when I state that another loved son of mine fell in battle on September 28, only three and a half weeks before Tom died, you will understand what my loss is, and how much I appreciate any little words of praise, especially coming from such an unlooked for source as yours did. They who have gone have left pleasant memories behind them to others outside their own private circle. I would like to thank all Liverpool sympathisers. – Mrs. Gracie.

Despite not dying in battle, both Liverpool and Everton consider him a player who died in the war effort and, had it not been for his untimely diagnosis, he certainly would have been involved overseas. The loss of his friend deeply affected Lacey too, with the family still keeping a picture of him to this day and ensuring that his legacy is remembered. Thankfully Gracie is the last of the men here to have died during the First World War.

Bill Lacey

Name	William Lacey
Born	24/09/1889, Enniscorthy, Ireland
Died	30/05/1969, Bootle
Everton stats	40 matches/11 goals (1908–12)
Everton honours	None
Liverpool stats	260 matches/29 goals (1912–24)
Liverpool honours	First Division 1921/22, 1922/23
Combined stats	300 matches/40 goals (1908–24)
Direct transfer?	Yes (signed for LFC from EFC in February 1912 for £150)

SIGNING FIVE days after Tom Gracie and part of the now-famed Harold Uren deal, Bill Lacey was perhaps the biggest and only winner from the whole affair. An Englishman, a Scotsman and now our first Irishman. The formidable winger and half-back shone at Shelbourne in Dublin before being spotted by Everton and being asked to play for the club.

Gracie was signed in May 1908 to help fill the void of Harold Hardman and Jimmy Settle on the left wing. He became the third Irishman at the club, alongside Billy Scott and Val Harris. The 5ft 8in winger was robust and certainly not an easy opponent for anyone to have to deal with. His three-and-a-half-year stay at Goodison Park didn't bring with it any silverware but did provide him with a rare opportunity to travel to Argentina.

It was a quite remarkable plan that saw 13 Everton players board a train from Lime Street to London, where a bus took them to Southampton and they set sail for Buenos Aires. They spent 20 days in Argentina, facing Tottenham Hotspur in seven different matches. You have read that right. It took no less than 21 days to reach Argentina, via stops in Cherbourg in France, Vigo in Spain, Lisbon in Portugal, Madeira, Saint Vincent in the Caribbean, Pernambuco, Rio de Janeiro and Santos in Brazil, before finally arriving in their destination country. In what sounds like a dream cruise, the Everton and Spurs players enjoyed a holiday of epic proportions and were there to 'show the Argentine people how first-class football should be played'.

The wishes of Everton director Edward Askew Bainbridge in his diary for the *Liverpool Echo* were certainly fulfilled and the Blues won six and drew one of the seven matches. Lacey managed to get himself on the scoresheet during a 4-0 victory.

Despite being shipped around the world by his club, Lacey was only entrusted with one start in the 1908/09 season, his performances in the reserves having impressed enough for a start as centre-forward for the first team. Despite playing out of position and failing to score in a 1-0 loss, it showed to the player that there was clearly some trust in him and that the club was trying to find a way to integrate him into their line-up. A cash-strapped Shelbourne had asked the Blues whether they could provide any more money for the Irishman's services but the Goodison club claimed they wanted to wait for the winger to further prove his value.

This showed that he was in their thoughts but by no means a first-team player. The following season saw Lacey fill in for an injured Tim Coleman at inside-right for four successive matches in October 1909 but the 20-year-old again failed to score. This wasn't his only job, of course, but he was rewarded with only two further appearances during the season. His final match did see him score his first goal though, and that set him up for the most successful period of his Everton career in the 1910/11 season.

Much like with Uren at Anfield, Lacey had to bide his time but he was finally rewarded. He took the place of Wattie White at inside-right, before going on to end the campaign on the left wing. The Blues finished the season in fourth place and the Irishman played in 24 of a possible 38 First Division matches, showing how he had become a pivotal part of the team. What followed was a rather strange turn of fate though, and the Irishman quickly turned from hero to zero.

It's not known exactly why, but after a successful year filling in across three different positions and helping the team to achieve a decent finish in the table, Lacey was replaced in the starting line-up by Willie Davidson. He had played in three of the first four matches but then in just three of the next 23. The December of that season saw the proposed swap of the Irishman for Jack Parkinson of Liverpool, the three-month long negotiations, of course, ending in a deal we're all well versed in now.

Lacey was very much on the back of having a similar time to Harold Uren and Tom Gracie. They all showed glimpses of brilliance but a lack of consistency. What Liverpool had seen was enough for them to make a move for a man who was now seemingly out of favour, and it turned out to be a remarkably wise decision.

Lacey was to go on to spend the next 12 years at Anfield and becomes our first member of the back-to-back title-winning teams that were set to greet Liverpool in the 1920s. His longevity at the club makes this three-way transfer certainly one of great value to the Reds. The fact that he was still playing in the 1920s shows that the Irishman also made it through the war. He returned home to help the war effort and featured for Belfast United and Linfield during the period.

The efforts of this amazing Liverpool team will be covered further later, with another member of the so-called 'Untouchables' still to come. With Lacey playing 43 and then 44 matches in each title-winning campaign, though, it just goes to show how important he was to the conquering Reds. He also had the unexpected honour of being in goal on the day that the second title was presented, after Elisha Scott was taken off injured, so, with this being the days of no substitutes, it was the job of the Irishman to take his place between the sticks and keep a clean sheet to boot.

At Anfield though, he swiftly found a new home, although admittedly not too far from his previous one. The trip across the park did his confidence and performances the world of good, although some weren't too surprised to see him thrive. As reported in the matchday programme: 'I have always an idea that Lacey would make a better man for Liverpool than Everton. He has, it is true, been more than useful to the Blues, but he is the type of player that has always been associated with Liverpool than Everton. We as a rule play more robust football, due to the fact that our forwards have been bigger men. And Lacey while he is capable of clever work is also a dashing, fearless forward.'

Much like the two others who were involved in the transfer, Lacey was never a man who was known for finding the back of the net. His return of 29 goals in 260 appearances is perhaps the best illustration of that. However, he was better known for causing havoc out wide and creating chances for his team-mates. Players like him are certainly robbed of the adulation they deserve from this era of football.

The earliest footage of a Merseyside derby comes from a match in September 1902 at Goodison Park but that was by no means when footage from this era became available. Even when replays of matches began to be shared on the likes of Movietone and British Pathé, they didn't give a full idea of how the play actually turned out. Goals have always been rather consistently reported in the press, so these numbers are pretty much correct across the board; however, assists aren't always something that are recorded. Because of this, many great wingers of the day who may have struggled to find the back of the net, such as Lacey, have had their involvements within matches denied them.

Due to the success that followed, there's little need to dwell too much on the pre-First World War days of Lacey, other than to say he recorded consistent appearances for Tom Watson's team from his arrival and up to the pause of football following the end of the 1914/15 campaign. Everton were the team that lifted the final league title that preceded the pause. Although the former Blue may have regretted his departure when he watched that piece of silverware being clinched, he was soon to taste success himself, although that had to wait until after Liverpool had experienced their first FA Cup Final.

Crystal Palace in 1914 saw the last final to be held in the stadium, the first to be attended by a reigning monarch (George V) and a first cup-final appearance for the Reds. Tom Watson's team fell to defeat at the hands (or feet) of former Blue Bertie Freeman. Over 70,000 supporters witnessed a day that failed to live up to the hype for those who had travelled from Merseyside. After waiting 22 years to reach the final and being set to wait another 51 before they actually won one, had everyone present that day known how long it would be before a return to the FA Cup Final, the mood may have been even more sombre. However, one more year was set to follow before the war stopped football, and then the Reds were about to become very used to clinching silverware.

For those perhaps unaware, the First World War officially lasted from July 1914 to November 1918, and football in England was halted from April 1915 to August

1919. The period in between did see football played but only in unofficial regional competitions, a period that allowed players to represent any club they were asked to, which was often teams centred around where they were based at the time. This is similar to what later happened during the Second World War, and, of course, opened the door to yet more unofficial instances of players crossing the park. These will be covered later.

Lacey returned from Ireland following the end of the war and re-signed for the club after having been formally released so that he could return home during the conflict. He was immediately thrust back into the Anfield first team and found himself being deployed as part of the defence, a position he had played before the war. He made his mark as a solid and dependable member of the team in defence, which also helped account for the lack of goals in his career! His robustness at the back was perhaps thanks to his physicality, which led to one match report reading, 'As for kicking Lacey as a hobby, I can assure you it's a waste of time, the boy is made from Solid Rock. Dynamite could not shift him off the ball.'

This was a position he enjoyed for the next couple of seasons before a return to the wing was presented for Lacey. He soon became part of the team that went on to win the league in consecutive seasons. Now operating on the right, the Irishman ended the 1922/23 campaign as a 33-year-old who had played 77 matches in the last two seasons and won the league title in each. Longevity, versatility and an infectious personality made him a hero within the team, and a player adored by supporters. Images of him putting golf balls into the corner-flag holes during Anfield training sessions show his team-mates thoroughly enjoying his company. He was a man who embodied the spirit of the team and his adopted city, perhaps best exemplified by him spending the rest of his days within Liverpool.

All good stories come to an end though, and his glory days of winning the two league titles will be further assessed later. Lacey had watched nearly the whole squad change around him during his 12-year stay at Anfield, which saw the whole nation change considerably too. Rather aptly, one of the nine matches that he played in his final season with the club came against Everton at Goodison Park. Only five more appearances in a Liverpool shirt followed what was to be a disappointing day against his old employers.

In a trend that certainly hasn't caught on, the *Liverpool Echo* reported the event as 'the "Liverton" Derby game'. There were over 50,000 packed into Goodison Park and the impact this had on traffic within the city was also reported upon: 'Have you ever seen a real tramcar procession? No? Then you ought to stray into Scotland-road on a Saturday afternoon when there is a Derby day in the immediate offing.' It was clear, though, that Lacey's powers were dwindling and, on a disappointing day, the Liverpool attack was described as follows: 'The Reds' forwards had so far failed to get moving and Lacey in particular had no sort of a show.'

It's always sad to see a hero come to the end of a successful career, particularly if their stay stretches on long enough for their adoring fans to witness a drop in performance and talent. Thankfully for Lacey it seemed to be a quick drop from league winner to no longer being able to shine for the Reds. His final appearance came in March 1924 and his contract came to an end three months later. He had already been rewarded with a benefit match to aid his finances and give thanks for the many years of brilliant service for the Reds. A move over the water to New Brighton followed but this was by no means the end of his career.

Two further clubs in Ireland were set to welcome the services of Lacey to their ranks and he ultimately retired in 1931 with Cork Bohemians, aged 42. He represented the Irish

Free State (modern Republic of Ireland) as a 41-year-old and went on to coach the team for several years, including during World Cup qualifiers for France 1938. This was combined with successful spells as manager of Shelbourne and then Cork Bohemians, where he clinched the FAI Cup in 1935.

His retirement from football management saw a return to Liverpool, where he was still adored by his supporters. A vote of Liverpool's greatest-ever player was held in 1939 and Lacey was among the 16 shortlisted (as well as Fred Geary). Even up to his 70s, the legendary figure was giving talks in schools about his footballing memories and inspiring the next generation on Merseyside. He has a plaque outside his family home in Ireland, such was his impact on the sport as a whole. Lacey lived in Bootle up to his death in 1969, aged 79, leaving a wife and son. The family remains in the city and, although having a red allegiance, they remain respectful of his achievements and memories in blue – much like how the Irishman spent his retirement years.

He was a true character and by far the best piece of transfer business Liverpool had ever managed to complete with Everton. Successful, versatile and long-lasting – Lacey was a much-loved and talented member of a hugely successful team.

Frank Mitchell

Name	Francis William Grant Mitchell
Born	25/05/1890, Elgin, Scotland
Died	18/01/1958, Chester
Everton stats	24 matches/8 clean sheets (1913–21)
Everton honours	First Division 1914/15
Liverpool stats	18 matches/8 clean sheets (1921–23)
Liverpool honours	First Division 1921/22
Combined stats	42 matches/16 clean sheets (1913–23)
Direct transfer?	Yes (signed for LFC from EFC in February 1921 for £1,250)

NO MORE mention of Harold Uren and his transfer from hereon in. Now we move to a keeper whose best days were denied by the war. Frank Mitchell is the only member of this esteemed list to have been part of Everton's second First Division title success in 1914/15 but, as he only made two appearances in the campaign, it feels a little unfair to attribute too much success to him.

Everton signed Mitchell from Motherwell for £100 (after bartering down from £300) in May 1913, the Scot being brought in to fill the position of Jimmy Caldwell, who had left for Woolwich Arsenal. The 23-year-old was immediately handed the No.1 shirt and was selected to start the first nine matches of the season. With the Blues winning just four, though, a change was about to be made. The stopper was set to share the role with William Hodge, until Tommy Fern took over and made the position his own. The Leicestershireborn keeper was to keep a tight grip on the jersey from then on, eventually making 219 appearances for the club.

Mitchell played in those first nine matches available to him at Everton but only recorded a further 14 appearances over the next eight years, although the pausing of football due to the war had a lot to do with the longevity of this. The Scot actually played most of his football for Everton during the war years, stats that aren't attributed to his official record. These were clearly impressive enough performances for him to be again handed the No.1 shirt at the end of the war though.

This was again short-lived, however, starting seven of the first eight matches but making just one further appearance in the 1919/20 season. Mitchell remained at Goodison Park for half of the next campaign too but never played another match. Nine wins and eight clean sheets in his 24 appearances is certainly not a terrible record for a stopper, and he was part of a title-winning team.

As mentioned above, his war efforts were by far his best years. Between 1915 and 1919 Mitchell amassed 99 appearances for Everton, which made him the fifth-highest for the club during this period. Much like during the Second World War, it's very unfortunate for such players that they had huge parts of their careers erased. Despite putting their lives on the line by even taking part in the sport, everyone's efforts are ignored in history. The Scot even represented other clubs during this period too, including his former club Motherwell.

Despite the increased game time for Everton, times were understandably tough for Mitchell during the war and there are several reports of him asking for increased wages and loans from the club. The wages were never increased but he did successfully repay multiple loans. In January 1921, after not being played in a match since November

1919, the Scot asked whether he could be placed on the transfer list.

Later that month Liverpool offered £750 to take the keeper, and after a month of tough negotiations between the neighbours, Everton agreed to sell Mitchell for £1,250, so off he headed across the park. The Scot was thrown in at the deep end once again and it's not known whether it was through injury or form but he displaced the legendary Elisha Scott immediately, featuring 15 times in two months. It was only upon losing the final match (the only one that ended in defeat during the run) that his place was given back to the Northern Irishman. Mitchell did get to enjoy being part of a pre-season tour of Italy, where the two keepers shared the responsibility of guarding the Reds' net.

The next season began and the 31-year-old was now firmly behind Scott in the running to play in goal for the Reds. He made just three appearances in what was another title-winning campaign. These were all due to the first-choice option being on international duty and also following Scott being knocked out by a Bob Pender shot at Middlesbrough. The report in the *Derby Daily Telegraph* after the incident that saw Elisha Scott knocked out wrote how Mitchell would be coming into the team, and also said he 'has no peer in the art of saving penalties, and one of the amusements of the Liverpool boys when training is to test their shooting powers from the spot – with Frank in goal'.

A win, a draw and a loss in what was to be a successful season for the Reds showed that Mitchell was a capable understudy but wouldn't be breaking into the team. During a reserves match in January 1923 though, the Scot broke his wrist against Port Vale, which seemed to halt his progress further. The stopper never recorded another appearance at Anfield or Goodison Park but his Merseyside career continued with Tranmere Rovers.

The Wirral-based club have offered a home to several men from either side of the park, and one man, Dave Hickson, who like Mitchell had also played for both Everton and Liverpool, will follow in this list too. It didn't seem quite as good a book title to say crossing the park and then over the water, so I've just stuck with Liverpool and Everton players. It would have been a much quicker book to write though!

As for Mitchell, after his football career came to an end, he moved into the brewery industry and lived in Chester. The Scot passed away in 1958 aged 67. He was a man who was present for two of the biggest successes of this era for each club but always seemed to be on the perimeter of silverware. The keeper proved he was good enough to feature for either club at their best but his chances came just before he could be truly appreciated or, as in the case of the war, when no footballer was able to be appreciated for their skills.

A nearly man by all accounts and our first three-club Merseyside hero.

Dick Forshaw

Name	Richard Forshaw
Born	20/08/1895, Preston
Died	26/08/1963, Brighton
Liverpool stats	288 matches/123 goals (1919–27)
Liverpool honours	First Division 1921/22, 1922/23
Everton stats	42 matches/8 goals (1927–29)
Everton honours	First Division 1927/28
Combined stats	330 matches/131 goals (1919–29)
Direct transfer?	Yes (signed for EFC from LFC in March 1927 for £3,750)

DICK FORSHAW came to Liverpool after the end of the First World War and proved from inside-right that he was a more than capable goalscorer. His arrival at the club was reported by the *Liverpool Echo*: 'Dick Forshaw, Liverpool's soldier recruit, is an enthusiast at hockey and tennis. He is considered a player who will develop into a top-notcher.' This 1919 prediction proved true, and the Preston-born finisher was certainly top-notch.

The 24-year-old had been robbed of the opportunity of playing football while serving in the British Army during the war but was now ready to make an immediate impact in the First Division. Manager George Patterson handed chances to Tom Miller and Harry Lewis in the first few matches of the 1919/20 season but, when the chance was handed to the 5ft 8in attacker Forshaw, he grasped it. It took three matches to get himself on the scoresheet but his overall performances showed that the No.10 shirt at inside-right was his.

The major success was set to follow in the coming years, but proving useful across the forward line, playing in 23 of 42 possible league fixtures and scoring seven goals was enough to prove that Forshaw would be an important member of the squad for the coming years. His maiden Anfield year was to end with a fourth-placed finish and that feat was repeated in the following campaign, this time having scored nine in 27 appearances.

What was to follow was a success for the ages and Forshaw was an integral member of the band of brothers known as 'The Untouchables'. Not only is this era one of the most successful and important in Liverpool's history, certainly within the formative years of the club, but the goalscoring traits of their Preston-born forward was invaluable. This whole era is of huge interest and importance and is best covered by Jeff Goulding and Kieran Smith in their book entitled *The Untouchables*.

Getting his chance to consistently shine came through injury to Dick Johnson and, as written in the above-mentioned title, 'Forshaw's 17 league goals made a major contribution to Liverpool's eventual championship triumph.' His involvement in the first title success of the double culminated in a league-clinching goal at Anfield. David Ashworth's team faced the champions, third-placed Burnley, and a win for the Reds and a loss for second-placed Tottenham would hand the title to Liverpool.

As written by Goulding and Smith:

With the game heading towards the last ten minutes, one such pass from [Ephraim] Longworth found Dick Forshaw who raced towards the goal. As the crowd held its breath, he let loose a shot that

103

flew past Dawson. The net bulged and Anfield had rarely sounded louder.

The resultant cacophony could be heard in the streets surrounding the stadium and beyond. Anfield's glee at Forshaw's winner would soon turn to elation as supporters later discovered that Tottenham had been beaten 1-0 by David Ashworth's former club, Oldham Athletic. The Reds were champions again, at long last.

It was to be a first league triumph in 16 years but the Anfield faithful wouldn't have to wait quite as long for Forshaw and the rest to win another. He and Harry Chambers proved to be a potent strike force and the Reds carried their form into the new campaign. When Matt McQueen took the top job partway through the season, it was over to the Preston-born scorer to give him the perfect welcome present, a hat-trick in a 3-0 win over Blackburn Rovers that put Liverpool four points clear with 13 matches to go.

Although Forshaw wasn't to be the man who delivered the next golden moment, his tally of 19 goals in 42 matches was the second-highest number of goals and certainly helped clinch a successive league title. Festivities for the second success would see none other than Bill Lacey leading a celebration evening at the Adelphi Hotel, alongside several other members of the prestigious team in a sing-song.

The feat achieved by this team has certainly not been given enough credit here, but Lacey and Forshaw were two of the most crucial members of a star-studded squad of players. The gulf in time between the silverware that preceded and what was to follow shows that this was a unique bunch of lads and they deserve their place in the history of football within the city.

This success was certainly the pinnacle of Forshaw's Anfield career, as it was for any member of that team, with it being 24 years until any further silverware was clinched. Forshaw by no means swapped a 1923 winners' medal for an early retirement though, going on to spend the following four seasons with the Reds, making 132 more appearances and scoring 64 times in the league. The 1925/26 season was his final full one at the club but also his best scoring return with 29 in 35, showing that the forward was far from past his best.

The Prestonian played 27 times during the following campaign before Everton made him a transfer target, meeting with Liverpool representatives in March 1927. It was then agreed that a fee of £3,750 was enough to prize a bona fide legend from the club and across the park.

Everton had endured and were set to continue to suffer some of the most erratic league finishes imaginable. The signing of Forshaw came as a massive shock to many, as the *Liverpool Echo* reported: 'The deal was completed last night and will come as a great surprise to the followers of both clubs fans, it is a big move on the part of the Everton to strengthen their attack ... The signing of Forshaw recalls the deal when Everton transferred William Lacey and Tom Gracie to Liverpool for Harold Uren.'

It appears, though, that no one was more surprised than Mrs Forshaw. Neither man nor wife knew that the transfer was being negotiated until Everton club officials arrived at the family home and convinced the forward to change his allegiances. The *Liverpool Daily Post* reported that his wife said, 'I have never been an Evertonian, and I don't know what I shall do about it.'

When Forshaw arrived, the Blues were 21st, second bottom of the table, putting their ever-present position in the First Division at serious risk. Thomas H. McIntosh's team had 12 matches to save themselves and were willing to splash the cash in order to do so. As reported in the *Liverpool Echo*:

> Everton have paid on £20,000 within recent weeks for new men, and doubtless they will count it worthwhile if the club retains its position in the first division.
>
> The payment made by Everton have been made possible owing to the loyal following of their crowd. It is no secret that the attendances at Goodison Park this season have been abnormally large, and possibly constitute a record for league games.
>
> All these signing go to increase the attendance for the remaining home matches, of which there are five.

Forshaw played in all of the final ten matches of the season, scoring on his debut and helping the Blues win four and draw three, thus securing their place in the top tier. This newly revamped team were set to enter the new campaign with a spring in their step and a deadly weapon in the shape of a 21-year-old Dixie Dean.

Rarely can one man be attributed with the success of an entire season, but seeing as Alec Troup was the club's second-highest scorer with ten league goals and was the only other man who managed to reach double figures, Dean's return of a record 60 goals was easily the key reason why the Blues went on to win the league. Forshaw played 23 of the 42 matches, so his league-winning contribution was certainly not as large as when he played in red. The 32-year-old was still part of the first title win since the start of the First World War, the third of Everton's history.

The forward's progress was certainly halted by a serious knee injury that saw him sidelined for several months after surgery. Forshaw played in the first 21 matches of the league-winning campaign but only made a further 11 appearances in their next 67 fixtures. His effort for the Everton cause was still hugely important and, although success still came without him, it's fair to assume that he would have played all if not most of the famous season if not for injury.

Dixie Dean will take all the plaudits for what was a ridiculously impressive feat of goalscoring and, of course, a number that still stands as the best ever seen in England, but there's enough room for a small portion of credit to be handed to the experienced Forshaw. However, his injury was a major stumbling block and spelled the end of his Merseyside career.

It was clear that his chances at Goodison Park were dwindling, and the offers started to come in for the influential Forshaw. Bury, Tottenham, Bristol City and finally Wolves all showed interest, and it was the latter who managed to get the deal over the line, for £750 in August 1929. This came after a season that saw Everton follow up their title win with an 18th-placed finish, and the forward was lucky to get out of the club ahead of a season that ultimately saw them relegated.

For Forshaw though, there was an understandable drop down the football ladder. After just two months with Wolves he asked to be placed on the transfer list, so the end of the season saw a move to Waterford Celtic, Hednesford Town a year later, before playing for Rhyl as a 35-year-old. Everything looked set for a triumphant retirement from the game and a legendary status on Merseyside for Forshaw but he somewhat ruined his legacy. Despite being in his mid-30s when he retired from the game through injury, the aged forward had clearly not thought about how he would continue to make money once his football days came to an end.

Forshaw moved back to Liverpool with his wife and three children (his then second child tragically passing away at birth) and worked as a commission agent, but he mysteriously disappeared following a bet he was commissioned to make by a local bookmaker on a horse race in Ascot. It was then discovered that he and his wife had been running a fish and chip shop in London, before police tracked him down following the missing £100 that was supposed to have been bet on the race. Forshaw had run off with the money and now faced prison time.

With it being clear that Forshaw was in need of retirement finances, which was the ultimate reason for his actions, despite the 'particular meanness' with which he had acted, he was sentenced to 17 months hard labour. This was far from the end of his criminality though. By 1944, the now 49-year-old had spent most of his retired footballing life in prison. Forshaw was a common thief and not a very good one. Stealing suitcases from train stations and hotels was a trademark, as well as stealing clothes from shops. One crime was committed two hours after he was released from prison and it seemed that the former hero couldn't stop himself. He blamed drinking and gambling for his 'hobby' and often pleaded for support, but it's hard to know what to believe.

It's clear that the financial benefits from football weren't fruitful enough to set Forshaw up for the rest of his life, but that gives little excuse for him to start thieving. Had Forshaw played in the modern era, he certainly would have been in a much better position to be set up for the rest of his life, but addictions such as alcoholism and gambling can strike anyone and at any time. It's a sad end to what should have been a triumphant career on Merseyside, which, on a purely footballing basis, it certainly was.

It appears that both clubs were a little reluctant to be publicly attached to Forshaw, and his later life and death was not marked by either. Forshaw moved to Brighton after his career in crime and passed away less than a week after his 68th birthday. His life ended in disgrace after a hugely successful ten-year spell on Merseyside.

Neil McBain

Name	Neil McBain
Born	15/11/1895, Campbeltown, Scotland
Died	13/05/1974, Ayr
Everton stats	103 matches/1 goal (1923–26)
Everton honours	None
Liverpool stats	12 matches/0 goals (1928)
Liverpool honours	None
Combined stats	115 matches/1 goal (1923–28)
Direct transfer?	No

FROM THREE league titles and a lengthy Merseyside career to a reasonable amount of appearances but certainly less success. Our tenth Scotsman in 17 players thus far, and quite surprisingly the last (if Don Hutchison being born in England counts, despite his Scottish international career). It appears there was an initial reliance on the footballing talents of those north of the border (something that was still present in the late 1920s) during the early years of both clubs. There's also a factor worth considering that the players weren't from the city or the country, so would have felt less guilt about changing allegiances, as shown by the apprehension of Arthur Berry.

Now though, by the time Neil McBain arrived at Everton in 1923, both clubs were well established in the football world and the influence of the sport had transferred into exciting local players taking the fore. From here there's an influx of

Scouse players to come, something that may be a surprise, as it would be assumed that the people who are least likely to change which side of the park their ideologies are based are those who were born with a blue or red heart. These will all be covered as and when we come across them but, for now, we have McBain, who is also the first man to have also represented a club that few will like to hear mentioned at this point – Manchester United.

McBain was a defender who spent his pre- and post-First World War years north of the border, before moving to United in 1921. The Old Trafford club were relegated from the First Division at the end of 1921/22 and Everton saw an opportunity to sign the 27-year-old, although he was reluctant to move from Manchester. A fee of £4,000 was paid, with the board agreeing to cover his travel expenses until an apartment was found within the city. His now former club's supporters were furious with the decision to allow such an important player to leave.

McBain's performances on the pitch didn't reach more of a high than during one Merseyside derby. The *Liverpool Echo* reported: 'McBain hasn't played a better game this season. He was artist, schemer, and passer de luxe … McBain, [Danny] Shone, and [Tom] Bromilow the stars of the day.' It was a record-breaking day in terms of attendance for the derby at Goodison Park, as 'fever raged in Liverpool to-day. It was a fervest fever, centred on Everton and Liverpool.' The match ended 1-0 to Liverpool but was overshadowed by the death of a spectator 'who was taken on a stretcher from the ground and died in the dressing room'.

McBain was a consistent starter for an Everton team that failed to capture the imagination and were in somewhat of a transition period. The worrying 20th-placed finish in 1926/27 came two years after the Scot's departure, but the Blues were on their way downhill during his time at the club. He did have a brief experience as a forward, filling in for Bobby Irvine and Joe Peacock, and managed to get himself on the scoresheet against Arsenal. The defender proved that he had more to his game when he, as written in the *Liverpool Echo*, 'tricked two of the Arsenal defenders and scored a wonderful goal which left the home keeper guessing'.

The defender was a consistent and dependable member of the team on the pitch but did come with some off-field issues that clearly upset the board. In the spirit of Fred Geary 30 years before him, McBain had wanted to take over management of a pub but a vote by the club officials voted unanimously against allowing him to do so. In April 1924 he requested to be put on the transfer list but the club refused. They then also refused to help him with expenditure when travelling from Seacombe on the Wirral but they clearly had trust in his talents, as he was named vice-captain.

Throughout his entire career at Goodison Park, the defender seemed to be constantly trying to find a way to leave the club. There seemed to be an ever-present to and fro over the player asking to leave, the club convincing him to stay, and then repeat. Everton did offer his services to the likes of Newcastle, Sunderland, Aston Villa, Manchester City, Wolves, Bristol City, Cowdenbeath, Rangers, Leicester City, Airdrie, Swansea Town and finally St Johnstone but the requested fee of £3,000 put most clubs off. Even lowering to £2,000 didn't work, but the Blues finally had a buyer.

Despite initially requesting to leave in 1924, the Scot didn't get his wish until over two years later but remained an ultimate professional at the club. St Johnstone finally got the defender for just £1,000 and the 30-year-old headed back to the nation of his birth. It was only to be a two-year stay though, before McBain was heading back to Merseyside.

St Johnstone faced Liverpool in a friendly at Anfield in February 1928, something that was a big crowd-puller at the time. This was because the home supporters were eager to witness 'the "carpet" game ... good scientific football' of the Scots. The *Sunday Post* went on to praise the former Everton man: 'Neil McBain showed up well at right half, playing his forwards with good openings.'

Less than a month later the 32-year-old was signed by Liverpool and it was clear that his performance in the friendly was hugely influential in this decision. It was only set to be a short stay in McBain's career, as he called Anfield home for just two seasons and 12 appearances. The 1927/28 campaign and the one that followed were less than exciting First Division seasons for the home crowd, and the Scot was certainly not a huge part of them.

The defender's first ten appearances all came within the first three months of his arrival, as he filled the void of Harry Chambers, who had recently departed to West Brom. This initial run culminated in a crushing 6-1 defeat at Old Trafford against McBain's former club on the final day of the season, the same afternoon that saw Dixie Dean score his 60th goal and clinch the Blues their league title.

McBain's penultimate appearance in red saw mixed fortunes in a 4-4 draw with Arsenal in which he gave away a penalty, helped join the attack in a late search for a goal and showcased his impressive passing ability. Ultimately his performance was described as him being 'Liverpool's best half-back'. It was clear that McBain still had talents but he again found himself in a team that was transitioning between dismantling the back-to-back league winners and breathing some fresh life into the squad.

McBain was now in his early 30s and was clearly not looking for a role as a squad player. When Watford came in for him he was happy to depart on a new journey in November 1928 and by the end of the season he had impressed enough to become player-manager. He spent nine seasons with the

London club before managing Luton and Leyton Orient and finally an exciting venture as manager of La Plata in Argentina.

His return to Britain saw him take charge of New Brighton, where McBain became both the 'oldest man to appear in League football' and 'the one whose career spanned the longest gap – 32 years', when he filled in as a 51-year-old goalkeeper in an emergency in 1947. His obituary in the *Liverpool Echo* showed that he was well respected across Merseyside.

McBain passed away in Scotland aged 78, as a very well-respected man in the football world. Playing for and managing clubs in three countries across a 30-year career, the Scot may not have had the best or most influential time on Merseyside but his value to football wasn't lost on anyone inside or outside of the city.

Tommy Johnson

Name	Thomas Clark Fisher Johnson
Born	19/08/1901, Dalton-in-Furness
Died	28/01/1973, Manchester
Everton stats	161 matches/65 goals (1930–34)
Everton honours	First Division 1931/32, Second Division 1930/31, FA Cup 1931/33
Liverpool stats	38 matches/8 goals (1934–36)
Liverpool honours	None
Combined stats	199 matches/73 goals (1930–36)
Direct transfer?	Yes (signed for LFC from EFC in March 1934 for free)

TOMMY JOHNSON will forever be best known for his achievements in a Manchester City shirt but his three winners' medals that he took from his four-year stay with Everton show that he still had plenty of happy days after departing Manchester.

At the time of writing, no player has scored more goals in a single season for Manchester City than Tommy Johnson (in the season before he moved to Merseyside), and his return of 166 goals is the third-highest tally in the club's history. Fondly known as 'Tosh', the ace marksman only managed to win the Second Division title with the Citizens but, by the time he arrived at Goodison Park in 1930, the first man in the list to have been born in the 20th century was a seasoned pro and ready to help the Blues. The fee of £6,250 was enough to prise the 28-year-old away from City but not from Manchester itself. Given the prestige of the player, though, the Everton board were a lot more accommodating than we saw with Neil McBain. They did not push for Johnson to move to Liverpool but were not willing to pay for his travel, despite an application from the player for this to be refunded to him.

In 161 appearances for the club, Johnson achieved a lot. He was part of the Everton team relegated two months after his arrival, bouncing back successfully from their relegation in 1930 by winning the Second Division the following season. This was then followed up with a First Division winners' medal in 1932 and an FA Cup one to match in the following year. His spell touched five different campaigns but each of the full ones that he played in ended in silverware.

The goalscoring burden that he had been placed under at Manchester City was very much with Dixie Dean at Everton. Although the Birkenhead-born finisher never repeated his feat of 60 goals from 1927/28, he was the club's top scorer in eight consecutive years, including the entire time that his forward partner Johnson was at the club.

As has been mentioned, Johnson's arrival for the final nine matches of the 1929/30 season couldn't stop a bottom-placed finish and the indignity of relegation to the Second Division for the first time. Arriving so late and scoring four times did show that it wasn't his fault though. Everton met the challenge of the lower division with consummate ease, the experienced forward being a key cog in the machine that steamrolled the substandard opposition.

Johnson played 41 times that season, his 18 goals not only helping the Blues finish seven points clear at the top of the Second Division, winning the league by early March, but even reaching the semi-finals of the FA Cup for the first time since 1915. Although the humiliation of dropping down a division really hurt the club, it helped restore a winning mentality and free-scoring spirit of just three seasons before, but this felt like an age ago when they were in the division below.

Everton's confidence was so high that they repeated their performances from the Second Division when promoted to the First. There were only two changes to the squad between seasons, Archie Clark at right-half and teenage keeper Ted Sagar given a first-team chance. No player played more than Johnson in the title success, and only Dean (45) scored more than his 22 in the league.

Johnson's role in the 1931/32 season was that he at last received the winners' medal that his career had warranted to this point. The 30-year-old was rewarded with three England call-ups during his time with Everton, having only been handed two when he was with Manchester City, so it shows that his performances had gone up a level and he was being recognised for this.

The Blues having both him and Dixie Dean in attack was a strike force that was so potent that it delivered the biggest prize. Despite the league success and finishing nine places above their local rivals, the Reds restored some local pride in that season's FA Cup. Over 57,000 packed into Goodison for the 'greatest cup tie of the city', in which Liverpool provided a shock with a 2-1 victory in the lions' den. Following the match though, the words of Dean illustrated the state of the rivalry of the time. Speaking to the *Liverpool Echo*, the Everton captain said, 'In my heart I wish Liverpool the best of luck, and I hope they go forward to win as good a game at Wembley as they have done today.' When viewed through the prism of modern-day rivalries of the two clubs, it's quite sad to see how much this feeling of city unity has dwindled away. Despite Dean's well-wishes though, Liverpool were knocked out in the quarter-finals, but his team were set to do much better in the following campaign.

It wasn't to be three successive table-topping seasons for Everton but the culmination of Thomas H. McIntosh's three campaigns of success was to be the 1933 FA Cup Final. Johnson had already scored in the Charity Shield against Newcastle and his four goals en route to the showpiece Wembley meeting had again proved his standing within the team. In a strange twist of fate, in the final the England international was set to face the club for which he had so many happy memories – Manchester City.

It was a unique match in which City wore red and all the players had numbers on their backs for the first time in English football. It was a strange decision, though, to see Everton handed numbers 1 to 11 and the Manchester club having 12 to 22. Johnson was the only member of the team from Goodison Park who had ever played in the final before, during the 1926 defeat to Bolton for the club he was now set to face, while being their all-time top scorer.

This day was a happy one for all attached to Everton, and the unlikely hat-trick of Second Division, First Division and FA Cup was completed against the odds. Although he didn't get on the scoresheet in the final, Johnson was part of all three successes and it was a vital role he played too. That's what makes it all the more surprising that Man City ever let their star man go.

Johnson left City as their top scorer and still went on to have three tremendous campaigns, even when all the goalscoring focus (and pressure) at Everton was on Dixie Dean. The England caps that Johnson went on to win also showed that there was still so much more left for him to achieve in the game. The club who had nurtured him for 12 years watched him spend his best (or at least most successful) days on Merseyside.

Signs that Johnson's powers were finally fading were on show in the month before the FA Cup Final though, as the *Evening Express* wrote: 'The Everton forwards were particularly poor. Johnson has not had such a bad day since joining the club from Manchester City three seasons ago.' Although he would still spend a further ten months at Goodison Park, the FA Cup Final was the last golden day before he headed across Stanley Park to join Liverpool on a free transfer.

The *Liverpool Post and Mercury* broke the news: 'The Liverpool Football Club, secure the signing of Tosh Johnson of Everton ... who had rendered the Goodison Club, splendid service, both at centre-forward and inside-left.' Again though, the lack of controversy around this deal shows the amicable relationship that was in place between the clubs.

His Anfield arrival in March 1934 was to lead to a much less eventful and successful stay for the 32-year-old, when compared to his feats at both Manchester City and Everton. Much like when he first arrived at Goodison Park, Johnson's immediate job was to help turn around poor results and help create a run of form that would avoid relegation. Liverpool won three of their last six matches of the season with the help of Johnson, after having won just one of the previous 17. The Reds finished in 17th place and were able to give a triumphant farewell to the legendary Elisha Scott, following a final-day victory over Manchester City. The job of the England international was to add some experience to the squad and improve the immediate results, something he did successfully.

Johnson's second season saw him in and out of the first team but one match he did receive a senior appearance for was the Merseyside derby. The former Blue shared some niceties with his old team-mate Jimmy Stein before kick-off and both old-timers were surprise additions for the derby. The Reds came out on top and the experienced striker was to play nine more times in the 1934/35 season.

Although his playing time and powers weren't what they had been, Liverpool knew that the England international was so respected within the game that he was a useful asset for the club, even off the pitch. The club's officials had to select a host of players to showcase the new FA school scheme of throw-ins and several other tactics, as well as the new 'tip-up seats' that had been installed. The *Liverpool Echo* confirmed that the players present were 'Ernest Blenkinsop, Tosh Johnson, Tom Bradshaw, Arthur Riley, Jack Tennant, and others'.

Three seasons, 38 appearances and eight goals shows that 'Tosh' wasn't the most influential player to have ever walked on the famous Anfield turf, but his role was significant despite being short. Johnson left the club in 1936, before joining non-league Darwen as their player-manager. He held the role up to the start of the Second World War, when football paused again, the legendary striker volunteering for the Royal Artillery, where he was made a corporal and sent to an anti-aircraft battery in Scotland.

The 39-year-old penned a letter to the *Evening Express* that read: 'I have lost the superfluous flesh and, believe it or not, I am still playing football and doing my stuff. I am fitter now than I have been for some years.' The war may have helped improve the fitness of Johnson but it was also thankfully not something that saw him drawn into battle or harm's way. Following the end of the conflict he moved into working in and owning pubs in Manchester. Several young City players would frequent his place of work and Johnson would be seen offering advice to the likes of Bert Trautmann. He would also attend matches at Maine Road, and seeing former Everton team-mate Joe Mercer become a successful manager was a real thrill for him.

Johnson passed away in January 1973 at the age of 71 after developing pneumonia while caring for his wife Annie.

Such was the influence of the free-scorer that there was a street named after him on Moss Side – Tommy Johnson Walk – and an induction to the Manchester City Hall of Fame. He had such a huge influence on Manchester City that his football legacy has very much been attached to them, but what he achieved in four Everton years is up there with the accomplishments of some who spent their entire careers at the club.

Billy Hartill

Name	William John Hartill
Born	18/07/1905, Wolverhampton
Died	12/08/1980, Wolverhampton
Everton stats	5 matches/1 goal (1935)
Everton honours	None
Liverpool stats	4 matches/0 goals (1936)
Liverpool honours	None
Combined stats	9 matches/1 goal (1935–36)
Direct transfer?	Yes (signed for LFC from EFC in January 1936 for £3,000)

IT REALLY is quite remarkable that, for a group of footballers that's so relatively small in comparison to the reams of players that have played for either club, these men so far have all had such interesting careers. Tommy Johnson won everything he could in a short stay with Everton but next comes a man who didn't achieve too much in fewer than ten matches in the city.

Billy Hartill was another man whose career was best known for his time outside of Merseyside and in particular his seven years with Wolves. The forward amassed 170 goals for the Midlands club and left them as their all-time top goalscorer, still holding the record for the most goals scored in a match with five finishes being recorded on two separate occasions. His wartime introduction to life at Molineux led to him being known as 'Hartillery' and it's a name that stuck for the rest of his career.

Everton had deliberated whether to sign Hartill for a long time, with interest from some board members starting in April 1930, but the forward wasn't officially signed until July 1935, for £3,250. The Wolverhampton-born goalscorer got off to a brilliant start with the Blues, scoring twice in a practice match between players within the squad a month after his arrival. The *Evening Express* wrote: 'Hartill has impressed far more than any other of the newcomers. He was ever ready to essay a shot.'

Being an understudy to Dixie Dean meant that the 30-year-old was never destined to be a hero at Goodison Park due to the obvious priority of the club's record scorer. However, the Birkenhead-born legend did have a poor run with injuries, so it was worth finding someone who could cover his goals during any possible absence. Hartill didn't have to wait long for the first opportunity to arise, with Dean suffering from a broken toe. Hartill's chance came against Portsmouth in September of 1935. Ahead of the match the *Evening Express* wrote: 'Hartill, the quick shooting leader from the Wolves, takes over the leadership from Dean and his debut with the Blues will be watched with interest.' It was to be an interesting watch too, Hartill scoring the third goal in a 3-0 win on his debut and filling the void at centre-forward in the best way possible.

The post-match write-up in the *Liverpool Echo* showed why the forward was not going to have a long career with Everton, was never going to score another goal and would only record four more appearances: 'Everton can be termed all-round interesting and effective. Everton's reserve strength has been given its chance and has continued the good work shown in the Central League games.' No one would ever replace Everton's famous No.9 but, after leaving Wolves as their Dixie Dean, why should the 30-year-old settle to be an understudy?

This makes the move a strange one in the first case, though, but when Hartill failed to score in the next four matches, the writing may have been on the wall. Another twist of irony saw his final appearance in blue against his former club Wolves, and the forward was even selected as captain of the team. He was given a hero's welcome at Molineux and the *Liverpool Echo* even wrote: 'Certainly Hartill played his best game this season at his old ground.' It doesn't sound like the description of a final appearance for the club but a 4-0 loss will certainly not have helped his claim to a starting role.

Hartill dropped back into the reserves, and when Aston Villa showed interest in November, Everton were willing to listen to offers, which illustrated their stance on the forward. Grimsby and Swansea Town also soon showed interest before Liverpool bid £1,500 in January 1936.

Everton managed to get £3,000 for a player that had spent just six months at the club but he certainly hadn't filled the role they thought he would. Initially brought in at Anfield to fill the void of the departing Gordon Hodgson, Hartill became the fourth former Everton player within the squad at the time, alongside Tommy Johnson and two others who will be covered at the very end of the book – Jack Balmer and Alf Hanson.

It was somewhat of a surprise deal but again showed the approachable relationship that was in place between the clubs. If Hartill's Goodison Park stay was brief though, then his winless four-match and 65-day tenure as a Liverpool player was almost meaningless. His debut in a 0-0 draw away to Grimsby almost ended in disaster as he gave away a 90th-minute penalty, but the Mariners failed to convert from the spot.

There is very little to report on the rest of his career other than Bristol Rovers being interested in making Hartill part of the deal when Liverpool enquired about their player Phil Taylor. Seeing as the half-back would go on to both captain and manage the Reds, perhaps the former Wolves forward's biggest role was helping negotiations be completed for an important man in the club's history.

Hartill went on to spend a year with Bristol Rovers before finishing with three years as a non-league player for a team named Street – retiring in 1940 as a 34-year-old. After the end of the war, the forward moved into the pub market himself and became a landlord in Wolverhampton before passing away aged 75 in 1980.

The final man whose career on Merseyside ended before the start of the Second World War and, although it certainly wasn't a hugely significant one, it was good to end this era with two club legends and proven goalscorers – even if it wasn't during their time on either side of Stanley Park.

Wartime

WARTIME IN football is a peculiar period. As aforementioned, records of matches and goals from this period don't count towards the official statistics of any player. This same rule applies for both World Wars, so there are several players who represented the 'other' Merseyside team but only during these two strange periods of football history. The sacrifices these players made to play football while aiding the war efforts shouldn't be ignored and the four-year pause for the First World War and six years for the Second World War deserve at the very least to be recognised in this book.

Rather than assessing each player on a case-by-case basis as above, there will be a brief mention of their name and role in Merseyside football before, during and after either war:

Liverpool players to have played for Everton:
First World War
- Harold Wadsworth: LFC 1919–1924
- Albert Pearson: LFC 1919–1921
- (J Murphy): Listed as playing for Liverpool by Everton when they faced Stockport on 3 November 1917

Second World War
- (Billy Hall): Listed as playing for Liverpool by Everton when they faced Wrexham on 5 February1944
- Norman Low: LFC 1933–1936

Everton players to have played for Liverpool:

First World War
- Billy Scott: EFC 1904–1912

Second World War
- Cliff Britton: EFC 1930–39

Unsurprisingly, the reporting of football statistics during the wartime period is also surrounded in scepticism, so this may not be a complete list but it's still an idea of how many players crossed the park in these unofficial matches. Due to the close vicinity of both clubs too, there would have been little need for them to have represented the other in either era.

There will also be several players that would have guested for both Liverpool and Everton during the war but never officially signed for either club. Because of this they have not been included. While the sacrifice of these players deserves the utmost respect, there's no doubt that rivalries were very much pushed aside at this point, so there wouldn't have been any controversy around any of the above representing the other.

As we have seen so far, there hasn't been too much in the way of a nasty rivalry between clubs, so this good relationship would have been present during both wars too. Instances of immense significance within the city often bring people together, and it's likely that, as wartime left Europe, the city of Liverpool had never been more united. The resilience, shared heartache and huge loss that everyone had experienced meant that the maiden campaign after the Second World War saw both clubs perhaps more together than they had ever been.

Over the next 60, 70, 80 years though, this relationship slowly started to diminish, so this story will be told through the players who moved between the clubs from postwar, to modern to Premier League football.

Jimmy Payne

Name	James Bolcherson Payne
Born	10/03/1926, Bootle
Died	23/01/2013, Kendal
Liverpool stats	243 matches/43 goals (1948–56)
Liverpool honours	None
Everton stats	6 matches/2 goals (1956)
Everton honours	None
Combined stats	249 matches/45 goals (1948–56)
Direct transfer?	Yes (contract expiry 18/04/1956)
Remembered (%)	LFC 33%/EFC 15%/Ave. 24%
Legend (out of 10)	LFC 6.5/EFC 7/Ave. 6.8
Traitor (out of 10)	LFC 5

FIRST UP in this new era of football is Jimmy Payne. The Scouser was part of one of the least successful Liverpool teams before having a career swansong with Everton. Now feels like the good time to remind everyone of the questionnaire that was handed out to both sets of supporters during a home match in the 2022/23 season. Each supporter was asked whether they had heard of the player in question. If they had heard of them, they were then asked to score them 1 to 10 on how much of a club legend they were (10 being Dixie Dean or Sir Kenny Dalglish). Finally, if the player had then moved to the other Merseyside club after first playing at the supporter's team (for example, for Payne, a Liverpool fan would be asked this about him because he played for Everton second), they were then asked to score them 1 to 10 on how much of a traitor they thought they were (1 being not at all and 10 being the biggest traitor imaginable).

The point of reintroducing this idea now is that the earliest member of this illustrious list that modern-day supporters were asked about was Jimmy Payne. Using the end of the Second World War as a cutoff point felt like the most logical way of ascertaining how well remembered a player is, and how much they are respected and hated by each set of supporters. Some quotes from those interviewed will also be used, which should hopefully add a different dimension of analysis for this second part of the book.

The scores awarded will be included at the start of each section but, to help solidify what the 'man on the street' thinks about Jimmy Payne, an average 24 per cent of Merseyside supporters had heard of him. The Blues on average gave him a club-legend rating of 7/10, whereas the Reds awarded him 6.5 and thought he was a 5/10 traitor for moving to Goodison Park after his Anfield career. It's by no means a scientific confirmation of what every Red and Blue thinks but hopefully these measurements will help further demonstrate the legacy of each man from here onwards.

Now that lengthy introduction has been completed, back to Payne, and it makes sense why some fans today won't have heard of him as his first senior appearance on Merseyside occurred nearly three quarters of a century before these questionnaires were completed. The Scouser broke through into a team that had won the league just two seasons before and was sharing a dressing room with such legendary Anfield figures as Billy Liddell, Albert Stubbins, Bob Paisley and Phil Taylor.

There weren't many better in England during this time than Stanley Matthews, and when a young Payne was first making his way in the team, he was instantly compared to the winger of Stoke and Blackpool fame. As written by John Williams in *Red Men*: 'Jimmy Payne, a crowd-pleasing Bootle-born right-winger, emerging to offer guile and threat on the touchline as the putative "Merseyside Matthews".' The boyhood Evertonian fitted the Liverpool team like a glove and, from his senior debut as a 22-year-old (after joining the club six years earlier), the winger's appearances in a season never dipped below 30 until 1954.

However, this was not the greatest era in the club's history and his first five seasons of mid-table mediocrity was followed up with relegation to the Second Division, which lasted longer than anyone of a Liverpool persuasion ever could have expected it to. There was one brief chance of success for Payne in the midst of this though, as he was handed the opportunity to start in the FA Cup Final of 1950.

The wing wizard had played a significant role in helping his side reach that stage too. A fourth-round tie set up the arrival of Third Division Exeter City. The late January Merseyside rain played havoc with the playing surface, causing a soggy affair, where most of the players found that their feet could not get going in the thick mud. Goals from Kevin Baron, Willie Fagan and the 'Merseyside Matthews' saw Liverpool through.

Liverpool welcomed their first top-tier opposition, Blackpool, for the quarter-final. Hordes of Blackpool fans travelled in fancy dress to watch their Stanley Matthews-less team, this being the same team that went on to reach three FA Cup finals in six seasons from 1947. They were accompanied by a duck that had been dyed orange and had its own pail of water; the Tangerines' travelling supporters were out for a party. An initially tight affair saw the game stuck at 1-1, causing manager George Kay to switch Liddell and Payne in hope of securing a win without a replay. The two, now on different wings, linked up superbly as Payne set

Liddell up on the edge of the box. He expertly curled the ball into the top-right corner and sent the crowd into delirium. There was a nervy concluding ten minutes before the final whistle relieved the tension. The news over the tannoy that Everton had also progressed to the semi-final was met with cheers, as the prospect of an all-Merseyside final loomed, but it was to be red vs. blue in the semi-final instead.

Merseyside travelled to Manchester for the big match at Maine Road. The last time the pair had met in the semis saw Everton not just win but go on to clinch the cup, in 1906. This match being played on the same day as the Grand National meant it was a festival for Merseyside sport.

Liverpool went into the match as favourites, with their potent attack. The opening goal came through Payne's wing play, his cross finding its way to Paisley, who lofted the ball back towards goal. Liddell jumped with the Toffees' keeper George Burnett, causing him to lose flight of the ball, and Paisley's effort looped into the goal. Over 70,000 supporters were in attendance and the Red side went ballistic in jubilation as their team went 1-0 up.

Liverpool lived up to pre-match predictions, and the final whistle was greeted with an explosion of excitement. The Reds were off to Wembley for the first time, to face Arsenal. However, that day wasn't to be what it promised for Payne and the rest of his team-mates. The Gunners marked all of the key men from Anfield out of the game, including Walley Barnes stifling the Merseyside Matthews, and they left Wembley with the cup in their hands.

Payne was part of a Liverpool team that went through a decline that wasn't as sudden as had happened with Everton after Dixie Dean's 60-goal heroics, but was much more long-lasting. Although it would be unfair to attribute too much blame to the winger, he was still part of a team that fell from the heights of nearly winning the league and FA Cup in 1950 to finishing a club-record lowest-ever 11th in the Second Division in the 1954/55 campaign.

Injuries hindered Payne's progress in the final three years of his Anfield stay, and his drop in appearances led to a decline in ability and thus an increase in criticism from the Liverpool fans and press. Don Welsh tried to tinker with his team, using the Bootle-born winger as an inside-forward, but it only seemed to make performances and confidence worse for him. He was one of the better performers in a poor Liverpool team, though. Not just that but he was judged against the great Billy Liddell, and with the team being known as 'Liddellpool' it was clear who the Anfield crowd would side with out of the two. It was by no means years of hostility for the Scouser but he always played second fiddle to the man who dominated the other wing at the club. In his final season at Anfield, the *Liverpool Echo* wrote: 'Payne did not let the side down, though – much to the disappointment of his rabid following – he did not see a great deal of the ball.'

Everton perhaps could see this growing angst, and the increasing injury problems meant that Liverpool were prepared to listen to offers. The Blues decided to offer £3,500 for the local lad, which was accepted, leading to the boyhood fan signing for his club after 14 years on the other side of the park. The 30-year-old was not set for a long stay at Goodison Park, though, and his fitness issues continued.

Payne featured in one match in the 1955/56 campaign, the final day of the season against Blackpool, with the Goodison crowd hopeful of what he could bring to the team. The *Liverpool Echo* reported: 'Although Payne has not been up to his best form during the last season or two, not entirely due to himself. He is still a clever player, and the change of surrounding may bring him back to the best.' It was clear, though, that he wasn't the man he used to be. Troubles with a blood clot led to an operation and a long comeback, before he was able to make a second appearance for the Blues, ten months after his first. Payne was handed the chance to play five matches in a row as he covered the position of sidelined Tony McNamara.

By all accounts, the lengthy time out didn't hinder Payne's abilities too much and that's why he was trusted to deputise five times over. The *Liverpool Daily Post* wrote, 'Payne did as well as could have been expected after his long lay-off ', perhaps showing the point that the 30-year-old was at in his career. His second appearance of the run brought a first goal, described by the *Liverpool Echo*: 'Payne, at inside left who cracked in a shot which left Duff helpless. This was Payne's first goal to Everton, and it was a good one, too.'

The five-match spell in blue came to an end with a Goodison appearance against Preston. It ended in a perfect and sad way for Payne though, as he scored Everton's only goal but in a 4-1 defeat. He was never selected again. The Merseyside Matthews had completed a dream of playing for his boyhood club but he was always set to play second fiddle once his injury issues again proved that he was no longer as dependable as he used to be.

His talents and longevity at Liverpool have probably been unfairly remembered but, as has been mentioned, this is probably because he was compared to Billy Liddell. A loyal local lad would normally garner the lion's share of the Kop's affection but poor performances from the team as a whole, and being compared to a legend, means Payne's career has been somewhat forgotten. The Second Division days have largely been wiped from the history of the Reds and many assume that Bill Shankly started the story of LFC in 1959. However, there were many years that came before, and the darkest days were often brightened by the wing play of a homegrown talent.

The move to his boyhood club perhaps provided an opportunity to achieve some dreams but little else in the six matches he played. Payne's legacy is unfairly small, although the Merseyside Matthews failed to live up to the potential of some glittering and consistent early days, probably weighed down by an overly optimistic nickname. Retiring as a 31-year-old through injury shows that it was a career that curtailed too soon.

Payne moved into the family newsagent business and then became a hotel owner in the Lake District. He lived his final days in Kendal, Cumbria, leaving a wife and two children when he passed away in 2013, aged 86. A career of what could have been, in the shadows of others and a poor team, cut short by a cruel string of injuries.

Tony McNamara

Name	Tony McNamara
Born	03/10/1929, Liverpool
Died	30/05/2015, Liverpool
Everton stats	113 matches/22 goals (1951–57)
Everton honours	None
Liverpool stats	10 matches/3 goals (1957–58)
Liverpool honours	None
Combined stats	123 matches/25 goals (1951–58)
Direct transfer?	Yes (signed for LFC from EFC for £4,000 on 21/12/1957)
Remembered (%)	LFC 42%/EFC 38%/Ave. 40%
Legend (out of 10)	LFC 3.3/EFC 4.5/Ave. 3.9
Traitor (out of 10)	EFC 3.5

A RETURN to the traditional relationship between the two clubs, as the story again starts at Goodison Park. It's our first entry to the tale that begins with football in the 1950s. Although occurring three years into Tony McNamara's time with Everton, an open letter from Billy Liddell to the Liverpool fans, via the *Liverpool Echo* after the Reds were confirmed to have been relegated, shows the state of the relationship between the clubs at this time:

> I would like to add my congratulations to Everton on achieving promotion to the First Division. We at Liverpool are glad that this city will still have

a representative in the premier division and we
sincerely hope that Everton will have as successful
a season next year as they had this year.

Tony McNamara was part of this Second Division success for
the Blues and it may seem strange to start in the middle of
his career, but to give more insight into how both clubs were
interacting at this point, the *Liverpool Daily Post* reported on the
victory against Oldham that secured promotion in April 1954:

> It all ended happily – for Merseyside – and
> news of Everton's victory was quickly flashed
> round the area. Crowds of people waited for the
> special editions of evening papers the *Daily Post*
> switchboard was jammed by hundreds of telephone
> calls and the result of the match was announced
> in city cinemas, public house licensees reported
> excellent business. And last night came this
> tribute from Mr. Don Welsh manager of relegated
> Liverpool F.C. 'That's good news I congratulate
> Everton and hope that we'll meet them the season
> after next.' It was a tired – but very happy – Everton
> team which arrived home at Goodison Park late
> last night. A handful of faithful supporters who
> had not been fortunate enough to see their team
> in action mobbed the players and cheered them
> through the club entrance. The team had enough
> celebration for one night at Manchester – and they
> contented themselves with a toast in orangeade to
> skipper [Peter] Farrell. Then they made straight
> for home and a much-needed rest.

If the purpose of this book is not just assessing the influence
of each player but also the state of the relationship between

the clubs, this era of Everton being the solitary First Division team in the city for eight successive years (after Liverpool had carried the torch during Everton's three-year drop to the division below) shows that a clear bond was strong, even if the quality of football wasn't. With the successes that are set to come, perhaps the relative mediocrity within the city may have had a part to play in the amicable relationship.

Back to Tony McNamara though. The Scouser was given his chance as Everton were dumped into the Second Division, and his debut as a 21-year-old was to be the first of 34 appearances in 1951/52. The local lad was described by John Roberts as 'a tall, graceful right-winger who later moved to Anfield, [and] added a touch of class to the proceedings'. He also made his debut for the Blues alongside Dave Hickson, and the pair had a big influence on the maiden season in the second tier but were unable to get their team promoted at the first time of asking, as had happened in 1931.

Joe Harris, George Cummins, Eddie Wainwright and Derek Mayers proved competition for McNamara on the right wing in Cliff Britton's team during the next season though, and he only managed seven league matches in a disappointing 16th-placed finish in the Second Division. He was selected to start the campaign on the right but it appeared that the supporters weren't too enamoured by his maiden campaign's performance, and the *Liverpool Daily Post* described his treatment: 'do not care how badly he performs he is still entitled to a fair deal from people who oddly describe themselves as supporters. Stanley Matthews, Finney and other leaders of winging art would wilt if every time the ball came their way 20,000 nicotine-scratched lungs "advised" them on how best to use it.'

Pressure on the player from an understandably disenfranchised supporter base meant that the board began listening to offers for McNamara from the likes of

Workington Town, Blackburn Rovers, Notts County and Sheffield United but they decided to stand by the winger, for now at least. On top of criticism he received from the fans, though, the Scouser also experienced several injury issues and in December 1953 had surgery, with cartilage removed from his knee. It was an injury that kept him out of action from the first team for nine months. This meant that he wasn't in the squad when promotion back to the big time was assured.

It was back in the First Division that McNamara restored his place in the Everton line-up. Such was the gulf in talent of the two Merseyside clubs during this era that the Scouser never actually played against Liverpool during his five seasons at Goodison Park. He was given an extended run in the team from February to the end of the first campaign back at England's top table and he proved to Cliff Britton that he was a better option than Wainwright on the wing. Goals against Chelsea and Huddersfield certainly helped his claim to the No.7 shirt too, but injuries were set to again interrupt his career.

Another season on the sidelines saw him make just seven league appearances in the 1955/56 campaign and ensured another battle with Harris and Mayers, before the arrival of Jimmy Payne provided McNamara another opponent to displace on the wing. A lack of confidence in McNamara out wide saw the arrival of his Liverpool counterpart, but it was a short-lived spell out of the team before McNamara won the battle and ended the 1956/57 season as first choice.

The 27-year-old had proven that he was the best option for Everton but also not a player that the club could trust in terms of fitness, as well as not being overly enamoured by the level of performance from him or his peers. Jimmy Harris was about to make the Goodison Park right wing his own, so when it became clear that McNamara was only going to play second fiddle to the Birkenhead-born winger, Liverpool made a bid of £3,500 and the Blues were ready to listen.

It nearly presented another Harold Uren-type deal between the clubs, as Everton asked whether a deal for McNamara could also include left-winger and Welshman Graham Williams both leaving Goodison Park in a deal that would see Johnny Morrissey head the other way. The 17-year-old had just signed professional contacts with Liverpool and the Blues were clearly admirers, but the deal was not one that the Anfield club was willing to entertain (for now), so an improved bid of £4,00 was eventually accepted for McNamara alone.

Over 113 appearances and seven years, McNamara had struggled to maintain a place in the Everton team but had proved in spells that he was certainly capable of flashes of brilliance. So the drop down to a Second Division club could provide a platform on which he could compete more consistently, if he could keep his injury concerns at bay. The fact that the Scouser had asked to leave the club also shows that he may have thought he deserved more opportunities. The *Liverpool Echo* reported the transfer by writing:

> Liverpool F.C. today signed Tony McNamara, Everton's outside right who was put on the transfer list by the Goodison Park club at his own request on Tuesday evening. I understand the fee is around £4,000. Whether McNamara is likely to provide the answer to Liverpool's outside right problem is a matter upon which there will be considerable cleavage of opinion among the club's supporters and though the majority are most likely to be unduly impressed, in fairness to the player judgement must obviously be deferred. McNamara has had spells

when he has been regular choice for Everton, but in between have been periods when he has frequently been in and out of the side.. He has however often been harshly treated by a section of the Goodison supporters, some of whom refused to see any good in him, and this did not help him to produce his best. If he finds Liverpool's style of play more suitable he may reach the heights which Everton had once hoped.

Liverpool made their first approach to Everton on Tuesday evening as soon as they learned the request had been granted. The figure they were asked was more than they were inclined to pay, but agreement was reached today after Everton had reduced their original estimate. Manager Phil Taylor and chief coach Bob Paisley interviewed the player at Goodison Park this morning, and after McNamara had indicated his willingness to join Liverpool the three went over to Anfield to complete the deal ...

This signing recalls the last deal between the clubs two years ago which also involved an outside right Jimmy Payne at a slightly less figure. Payne did not prove a good investment for Everton, due to injuries and other causes and played only six first-team games for them.

Comparison to the transfer of Jimmy Payne was set to be a correct one, with McNamara having a comparable career in blue as the Merseyside Matthews did in red. Signing in December 1957, he made all ten of his Liverpool appearances over the next three months. The 28-year-old made front-page news in the *Evening Express Sports Special* following the surprise signing, which went on to say, 'Crowd encouragement today can help McNamara. I have great hopes that at last he might find his real place and confirm the views, many, including myself, have formed about his ability.'

Scoring on his debut in a 4-3 win at Anfield over Bristol City looked to be the perfect start. In fact, three goals in his first five outings couldn't have made for a much better start for the new No.7 but his place in the team was again shared, between himself, Billy Liddell, Brian Jackson and Louis Bimpson. Perhaps the biggest problem that faced McNamara was the FA Cup. Phil Taylor, either out of loyalty or squad rotation, changed his team in the cup, which reduced the former Evertonian's stranglehold on a position in the team.

Failure to make much of an impact in his final five appearances as a Liverpool player spelled the end for McNamara. He and Jimmy Payne ultimately swapped roles within the two clubs. Because Payne preceded McNamara at Anfield, and vice versa, both clubs seemed reluctant to give their new man an extended run in the team. Inconsistent performances, past injury concerns and a lack of real trust or opportunity from either club meant that both had a similarly unimpressive second Merseyside spell.

McNamara was just not the player that Liverpool needed, or at least not one that Phil Taylor could afford to wait for, as his position at the club became less secure with each day his team remained in the Second Division. Moves to Crewe, Bury and Runcorn followed McNamara's Anfield departure in July 1958. This fall down the leagues actually handed him the unwanted feat of being the first player to play in all four English divisions within a calendar year. After his footballing career came to an end, the Scouser stayed local and would often frequent Everton matches at Goodison Park in later life. He passed away in 2015, aged 85.

Another nearly man who was forged on one side of the park but for whom an attempt to recapture a career he could have had didn't work when he swapped blue for red. McNamara was certainly a proud Scouser and custodian of Everton but never managed to achieve what he might have, had injuries and luck gone his way.

Dave Hickson

Name	David Hickson
Born	30/10/1929, Salford
Died	08/07/2013, Liverpool
Everton stats	243 matches/109 goals (1951–55 & 1957–59)
Everton honours	None
Liverpool stats	67 matches/38 goals (1959–61)
Liverpool honours	None
Combined stats	310 matches/147 goals (1951–61)
Direct transfer?	Yes (signed for LFC from EFC for £12,000 on 06/11/1959)
Remembered (%)	LFC 75%/EFC 92%/Ave. 84%
Legend (out of 10)	LFC 6.8/EFC 8.6/Ave. 7.7
Traitor (out of 10)	EFC 2.7

DAVE HICKSON was the third player to transfer between the two clubs in the space of four years but there's no doubting that his career is much more respected and appreciated at Goodison Park. Two spells at Everton, a transfer to Anfield and a later move to Tranmere Rovers makes him one of the most well-respected and capped players in Merseyside history.

There's no doubting, though, that he's an Everton legend, and the only thing more consistent than his performance level for the Blues was his haircut, which remained consistently in place throughout his life. His answerphone message in his retirement played: 'I'm sorry I can't get to the phone, I'm busy combing my quiff!' Coined the 'Cannonball Kid', there's not much that hasn't already been said about the great Hickson, and his whole life and career is perhaps best summed up with a very famous quote: 'I'd have broken bones for all the clubs I played for but I'd have died for Everton.'

Born in Salford and raised on the Wirral, he was a Manchester United fan as a child before Everton signed him from Ellesmere Port Town as a 14-year-old. He was perhaps helped by their Second Division status as it gave him quicker access to first-team football. Described by Stephen F. Kelly as 'a tall, powerful, old-fashioned centre-forward who scored more through aggression than skill', his first season in blue was a roaring success.

Handed his debut as a 21-year-old, Hickson was set to play 31 matches in his and Everton's maiden campaign in the Second Division, and his return of 14 goals made him the club's second-highest scorer for the 1951/52 season. A seventh-place finish wasn't enough to get the Blues back in the big time but the supporters were now safe in the knowledge that they had a new hero in their midst. In a line of prolific forwards that had represented the club, dating back to Fred Geary, the youngster was set to make his legacy better than most who had come before him. Being coached by Dixie Dean while he was an army cadet also meant that he was destined to impress at Goodison Park.

His chaotic style of play meant that he was often disliked by referees as much as opposing defenders, and he was certainly a great character for diehard Evertonians to enjoy. His seven-year spell as the key man up front for the Blues can often be summed up by one match in February 1953 against Manchester United in the FA Cup, where the cut on his head was as big as his performance on the day. The Old Trafford team were champions from the division above, with John Carey as part of their experienced squad, and close to

70,000 supporters flocked to Goodison Park for the meeting. Thanks to goals from Jack Rowley for the away team and then Tommy Eglington for the home team, the match was set to reach the half-time break at 1-1. That was until, as written in the *Liverpool Echo*:

> Five minutes before the interval Everton suffered a blow when Hickson had to go off with a badly cut right eye. He had made a valiant effort to connect with a ball from Lindsay which had dropped near the penalty spot. Hickson flung himself at it in a praiseworthy effort to score, but in the act of falling appearing to come in contact with an opponent's out-stretched foot and blood poured from his eyebrow. He was led off by trainer Harry Cooke with a pad of cotton wool held to his face.

Both the end of the first half and start of the second passed without Hickson returning to the pitch and, with this still being before the days of substitutions, it looked set to be an uphill battle for Everton. However, the sight of their star man running out of the tunnel minutes after the start of the second half had Everton fans at Goodison Park rising to their feet. With a handkerchief in hand to wipe the blood from his brow, their forward barged past the referee and on to the pitch amid a cacophony of noise, looking like a man possessed.

One of his first actions, after being brought down by the United defence that looked flustered by the 23-year-old's unexpected return, was to cannon a header off the post after a brilliant corner. There was clearly no fear from the player for the gash on his head, although the heavy leather ball evidently took its toll and caused him to reopen the substantial wound. The referee tried to get Hickson to leave the pitch for further treatment but he was duly waved away – he already had a handkerchief, what else could he possibly need? Blood continued to gush down his face but the fighting spirit of Hickson embodied an uncharacteristically resolute performance from the whole team. Then, according to the *Liverpool Echo*:

> Everton took the lead at the 63rd minute through Hickson, who all the second half, with blood streaming from his face, had played a hero's part. The move began with a long ball from Clinton near the half way line which went over to Eglington who wasted no time in squaring it to Hickson. He appeared to have little chance with two men in attendance but he was a Liddell-like persistency about going for every possible chance. Chasing the ball he beat one man, side-stepped another and then screwed back an oblique shot which Wood failed to reach.

You can only imagine the atmosphere as Everton chased down every ball, put in huge tackles and Hickson continued to terrorise the United defence. He may have only been able to see out of one eye but the opposition must have felt there were two of him on the pitch. The final whistle blew and Goodison Park knew that they had witnessed not just a major cup upset but one of the best, or at least most determined and influential, individual performances the famous turf had ever seen, and the Salford-born forward had delivered it. Keeper Jimmy O'Neill ran the length of the pitch to thank him after the match and everyone inside the stadium would have loved to have done the same.

This wasn't a one-off for the striker but a moment that perhaps best described his role at Goodison Park. Hickson was always attracting attention from other clubs during this period (including one offer from Torino in 1953) but Everton were always stern in their response, that he was their man for the future, and they often pushed interested parties on to the possibility of signing Tony McNamara instead.

However, Hickson's return of 13 goals in 41 matches during the 1954/55 First Division season saw a surprise call for James Harris to take his place in the starting line-up in the third match of the following season. Hickson made the swift and surprise decision to request a transfer, three days after being dropped for the first time. Manager Cliff Britton was given the power to make a decision on what to do with the player. A week later he was sold to Aston Villa for £20,000, the player telling the *Liverpool Echo* upon his exit, 'I am relieved it is all over. Now I can concentrate on football again.'

He was to return to Goodison Park the following month, receiving a hero's welcome when the second-largest home gate of the season thanked him for his service in blue. It was only to be a 12-match stay at Villa Park, though, for the much-loved forward, as he was soon making a move to Huddersfield Town, where he made a huge impression during his relatively short spell – netting 31 goals in 60 appearances during 1955/56 and 1956/57. At Huddersfield, Hickson played under Bill Shankly and finished as his top scorer during his maiden campaign as manager of the club.

Harris's goals had dried up, Everton were back in the market for a forward and the board decided that Hickson was again their man. Some shrewd negotiating from Shankly and Huddersfield led to several emergency meetings for the Goodison Park board as they toyed over deadlines, interest from West Ham and an increased fee requested from the parent club. The Blues may have parted with more money than they had first anticipated but it was a signing welcomed with open arms by the supporters.

One major reason for the 26-year-old also wanting a return was said to be the failure of his wife to settle in Huddersfield. One can only imagine how she coped, being just over an hour away from Liverpool. Hickson was said to have been contacted by Liverpool for a transfer too, but his heart lay at Goodison Park, and he wrote in the *Liverpool Echo*:

> The past week has been one of the happiest in my life. I won't say it has been the happiest of all, because nothing will ever match the wonderful feeling I got when, as an ambitious and impressionable youngster, I first signed for Everton nearly ten years ago. I was thrilled to bits then, and although I have been again ever since I re-signed for Everton a week ago today, there has been a vital difference. Ten years ago I was young, the world was at my feet, and my one ambition in life, to play in the Blue shirt of the famous Goodison Park club, looked likely eventually to be realized. That was the thrill of my life, and always will be whatever the future may hold.

The future was set to hold two and a half more seasons of Hickson in a blue shirt, 92 further appearances and 40 more goals. By the end of this spell he was now 30 years old and Everton were set to become the 'Mersey Millionaires' after being bankrolled by new owner John Moores. Although being a consistent performer for the Blues, manager Johnny Carey was ready to start a new era at the club, so offers were again welcomed for the striker. Liverpool offered £7,000 in October 1959 but Everton refused to sell. The next week Hickson put in a transfer request. The Blues wanted £15,000, their neighbours offered £10,000, a deal of £112,000 was eventually agreed. The club readied a thank you statement for his services and gave the player a month to move out of the club-owned house that had been provided for him on Mostyn Avenue in Old Roan. Neither club was ready for the backlash that was set to follow.

The deal itself had shown that at board level both clubs were more than friendly with each other and it was obvious that remaining in the city would be the best for Hickson, so Everton were happy to help the player and their neighbours by accepting an offer below their valuation of him. The Cannonball Kid was a player who frustrated rival players and supporters alike, meaning that the red half of the city was quick to protest the deal – as too was the blue. Merseyside supporters wrote in their thousands to both clubs and the press to plead for the deal not to be completed and it felt like a move destined for failure.

Phil Taylor eyed Hickson as the man who could take Liverpool back to the First Division, now at the sixth time of asking. The former Blue was set to help youngster Roger Hunt find his feet and take some scoring pressure away from him, as well as fill the void of the recently dropped and now aged Billy Liddell. Despite it being just one day after signing for the club, the new forward was ready to make his debut, and any ill feeling was quickly forgotten by an adoring Anfield crowd. The 30-year-old wrote in the *Liverpool Echo*: 'I was a bit embarrassed when the fan ran on the pitch before the game and jumped into my arms. He kissed me first and said: "You're a Liverpudlian now," and kept on repeating it. What a welcome!' If the welcome was fit for a new hero, then scoring twice against Aston Villa at Anfield to secure a 2-1 win was the perfect way to ensure a perfect day. Hickson went on to write: 'At the end, every Liverpool player shook my hand

and most of the Villa boys too. It was a wonderful moment for me, one I will never forget. The rest of the players stood back and to my surprise I found myself first off the pitch. The cheers were really most moving and just before I went into the tunnel, I scratched my head in amazement, feeling: "Gosh, just listen to that.'"

The significance of this being the first transfer between clubs that was met with disapproval of the supporters shouldn't be ignored. At the highest level both Liverpool and Everton were on good terms but the idea of seeing a Goodison Park darling in a red shirt turned the collective stomach of the city. In fairness to the Anfield fans though (with a gate that was the highest in 18 months to welcome their new signing), they were clearly happy to turn initial distaste into a welcome 'which only Liddell could previously command', as written by the *Liverpool Daily Post*. That's quite a U-turn from the Kopites and one that illustrates the level at which they decided to back their new man – even before he produced a two-goal debut performance.

As for the Evertonians, their upset is a lot easier to understand. Hickson never wanted to leave Everton but he had shown in 1955 that his priority was playing football, so the slightest sniff that his club was willing to listen to offers was enough for him to be ready to depart again. The strange thing for the player and supporters, though, was that he had been playing *and* scoring. New ownership and management may have produced a two-pronged attack for something fresh but it felt like an unnecessary risk to lose a real fan hero and consistent performer. Although the two clubs were friendly at the highest level, they should have seen the upset his crossing of the park would cause.

Back to his story in red though, Hickson's role off the pitch meant that he, Liddell and Ronnie Moran were the most experienced members of the squad. On the dawn of

Shankly's Anfield arrival, this trio of players was set to help nurture the talented youth players coming through – such as Ian Callaghan. Taylor was still trying to find his best team, and found it difficult to juggle the attacking prowess he had within his squad. A month after capturing the controversial signature of his new forward, though, the former Liverpool captain was replaced by the legendary Scottish manager.

Shankly's Reds weren't exactly off to a flying start but, having played with Liddell in Scotland and worked with Hickson at Huddersfield, the new boss was keen to bring them both back to their former glory and get Liverpool out of the Second Division. Hickson's 15 goals in 15 matches from February to April of 1960 helped secure a third-placed finish but not promotion.

The following season saw Shankly again rely on Hickson; however, Liverpool again finished third, but 16 goals in 33 league matches showed that the 31-year-old's powers were dwindling, so he was placed on a transfer list, as Ian St John was eyed to take his place within the team. The following season was to be the one when Second Division football finally left Merseyside but Liverpool achieved this without the Cannonball Kid.

Hickson went on playing up to the late 1960s, and his time at Tranmere Rovers saw him join Frank Mitchell as playing for the three major Merseyside clubs. Continuing to create attention in his later career, the Salford-born striker became one of the first in the country to wear white boots, and his Ellesmere Port Town team were handed a loss in a match when their player-manager refused to leave the pitch after being sent off. Work for the council on the Wirral followed professional football playing and management, but he continued to play local football and in charity matches up to the impressive age of 77.

There's no doubting where Hickson's Merseyside allegiances lay. Despite huge respect and admiration for his days as a Red, Hickson had royal-blue blood. He remained friends with Billy Liddell and Ian Callaghan on the red side of the city though. Bill Kenwright later asked him to return to Everton as a tour guide and member of the hospitality staff when he was 65. It was a thrill for so many Blues to be greeted by a real club legend and he was even awarded the honour of having a suite named after him inside Goodison Park. He worked for the club up to his death in July 2013, aged 83.

Hickson is one of the later players in this list whose achievements will be forgotten in time due to the lack of televised footage of his glory days in blue. One can only imagine the thrill of watching that FA Cup performance against United and the atmosphere that he produced inside the famous old stadium. His Anfield welcome as a Red was also special and helps to show how much of a likeable man he was. To also be the first transfer that evoked any kind of negative reaction shows how well loved he was too, and how important he was to football in Merseyside.

There's no doubting that Dave Hickson is an Everton legend and his alias as the Cannonball Kid perhaps took away from the footballing talents he clearly possessed. Although certainly a no-nonsense battering ram of a player, he was also a skilled goalscorer and by all accounts a well-mannered, principled and much-loved man too.

Johnny Morrissey

Name	John Morrissey
Born	18/04/1940, Liverpool
Liverpool stats	37 matches/6 goals (1957–62)
Liverpool honours	None
Everton stats	315 matches/50 goals (1962–72)
Everton honours	First Division 1962/63, 1969/70
Combined stats	352 matches/56 goals (1957–1972)
Direct transfer?	Yes (signed for EFC from LFC for £10,000 on 23/08/1962)
Remembered (%)	LFC 50%/EFC 77%/Ave. 64%
Legend (out of 10)	LFC 5.6/EFC 8/Ave. 6.8
Traitor (out of 10)	LFC 3.8

FROM A set of players who were dealt the rough hand of enduring Merseyside's Second Division days, a phoenix was about to rise from the ashes. From the birth of both clubs to the end of the 1950s, each had won five league titles – ten within the city since 1891. From 1960 to 1990 though, Everton won four more and Liverpool 13. This was set to be a golden era for both clubs, with further silverware also added in domestic and European cup competitions.

Up to this point, many of the major moments in terms of trophies have been individually covered. Now though, due to the volume of accolades to come and by entering a period of living memory where these achievements are more commonly known, this won't be covered in the same way. Where necessary, major wins will still be covered but the

Dave Hickson transfer showed that there were some subtle undertones of a rivalry brewing between the supporters within the city, so the public reaction to each deal will be focused on more from this point too.

Johnny Morrissey, as mentioned above, was an early target of Everton as a 17-year-old, when Liverpool showed interest in Tony McNamara, but his career began with the Reds and Anfield was his first home in football. The local lad was a boyhood Red too and, in my exclusive and previously un-used interview for *Liddell at One Hundred: A Family Portrait of a Liverpool Icon*, he explained his early love for the club and his hero:

> I was a Red. I was a left-winger because of Billy Liddell. My father used to take me to the football and as I got older I used to go to the boys pen. It was 'Liddellpool' then because he sat prominent in the team and as a young kid I used to admire him, he just seemed to be scoring every week. You could say he was my idol, and he played left-wing.
>
> He was the biggest name at the club and the best player at the club. The first time I met him was when I signed for Liverpool. I know when I was about 15 I used to be dying to get in the dressing room to see him but he was quiet, a bit introverted. At football a lot of banter goes on and mickey-taking in the dressing room but he was never part of that; he was a quieter man, and to say he was such a big figure on the field and off the field and a great player, he wasn't forward in any way at all. I was overawed but after a few weeks the strange becomes the norm and watching him getting his kit and his boots out and training with him …

Liddell was a bit introverted. There were players like Laurie Hughes who were very outspoken or taking the mickey out of each other but Billy was never part of that, he was part of the dressing room but didn't get involved in the mickey-taking. I mean, it was unbelievable to be honest, if the public even knew what was going on, it was unbelievable. He sat quite central in the changing room and he did speak but he wasn't outlandish like some of them. Ray Lambert was a mickey-taker but it was a dream world for me, to be honest.

Obviously I couldn't get in the team on the left wing while Billy was playing, and Alan A'Court played for England, so my chances got limited you see, but we were playing against Sunderland one year and I was about 18, very young, it was at Sunderland, Alan A'Court was on the right and he was on the edge of the penalty area on the wing and I remember him dragging the ball back like a right-winger does with his left foot, and he's hit this ball over and I'm looking at it. It was a bit too high, so I'm thinking I'll chest it because it was a bit too high, and I shouted, 'My ball,' and I was just about to get it and Billy Liddell, I don't know where he came from, and I can still see the bulge in his neck and he headed this ball and, honest to god, I couldn't have hit it harder with my foot. It bulleted into the net. It was amazing, at Sunderland Roker Park. I can remember that to this day.

The Liverpool fans loved him, the Anfield roar now was the same then. I mean, you would get goose pimples when you were playing. They would cheer the team but, although there was no chanting or anything then, there was a roar when he got the ball. I think Liverpool's crowds have always been very passionate. There was always a full house, it was about half a crown to get in and there was always big gates. They were as passionate then as they are now and they are very passionate now aren't they?

One of my greatest memories was Billy's testimonial at Anfield and I had a photograph taken with him because I was supposed to be the new left-winger, but of course Alan A'Court was there so I wasn't, but the press wanted that photo and I had this big photograph with me and him shaking hands at his testimonial game.

At the game I was on the left wing and Tom Finney was on the right wing for the other team, which was quite something for me. I was in the background, I can just remember being star-struck because of all the big players there. I remember Jimmy Armfield, Nat Lofthouse and the likes playing and it was a great day for me to play in that game.

Football really improved from the late 50s to the early 60s. We won the World Cup in 1966 didn't we, so it really improved. We were probably fitter with new training techniques. Billy had gone by then. I was still in the reserves. I think they spoiled my career, to be honest, playing in them too long. You were not challenged enough. But there would be players playing the reserves I would say were good enough to play in the Championship today.

The manager was Phil Taylor and he was a lovely man, a gentleman. I can remember him calling me in his office and they used to have board meetings on a Thursday night. So he called me into his office on the Friday, showed me his team and said, 'This is the team I gave to the board last night but the board want Billy instead of you,' and so I didn't play. So although he was manager, the directors had players they liked more than others and influenced the selection, that is just what went on in football then. In those days it was surf-like, you didn't question it. Nowadays the agent would be on the phone wouldn't they!

Bob Paisley was very similar to Billy, he wasn't a show off or anything. Bob gave me a lot of advice. I could imagine Bob as a manager was very good to the players. You didn't see the managers on the training ground then, the coaches took the training. Managers didn't get in tracksuits or anything like that, and Taylor would be in his office.

I didn't know the circumstances that saw him lose his job but I think the club started getting more ambitious because when Shanks came he put Liverpool on the map. They were in the Second Division for a long time and Shanks was the catalyst for everything. When Phil was there I don't think too much was expected from the Liverpool side. You know you won your home games, maybe draw away, it was just accepted. When Shanks came he brought the success and it has never stopped has it?

Shankly gave the board a list of players he wanted to get rid of and Billy was on the list because he was getting on, and on high wages. High wages! £20. I wouldn't have been on that list though, because Shanks was going to resign over me.

I was training at Melwood and you used to get taken to Melwood by coach and brought back by coach. I was getting off the coach one day, I think it was a Thursday, and the Chairman Mr T. V. Williams met me and said, 'John I want a word with you. I have got Harry Catterick in the boss's office, go in and see him.' So I went in to see him and he said, 'John, we have agreed to sign you,' and gave me all the details. So I said okay, yes, I will sign and he told me to come across to Goodison for the press and all that. I think it was about 3pm.

So I went home to tell my mum because my father was at work. When I got there, Shanks, who was in Scotland, I think, checking out a player or something like that on the Wednesday night, scouting, and Ruben Bennett took the training. Anyway, the boss, I still call him the boss because I respect him that much, Shanks was on the phone, he said, 'John what have you said?' So I told him I had said yes. 'No, you can't son,' and he went on and on calling Catterick and all that kind of thing. Anyway, he said this is not the end of it and I put the phone down.

I was thinking, *What do I do?* So I phoned Everton and spoke to Catterick and said, 'Mr Catterick, Mr Shankly has been on and said I have got to go and see him at Anfield and I can't go to Goodison.' Catterick said, 'No, no, no,' and I was told to wait for another call. This time it was from T. V. Williams, and he said, 'John, you report to Goodison, you haven't got to go to Anfield.' So I said, 'Okay.'

Then the phone goes again. This time it was Shanks, and he said, 'Come and see me here,' and I said, 'Boss, I've got to go, it's three o'clock.' He said,

'Come and see me before you go then,' so I went to
see him and he took me down to the old dugout by
the pitch and he was complimenting me, saying I
was part of his set-up and all that. I was on about
£17 per week then, I think, and Everton were on
£35, so I was thinking, *I'm going to be a millionaire!*
So I said, 'Sorry, no boss, I'm limited here,' and he
called Catterick a gangster and shook my hand and
said, 'You are going to be successful son.'

I had a great relationship with him and
then Shanks went to the board and put his
resignation in. Bob Paisley saw it on his desk
and held it back from the board and didn't let
it go before the directors. That's the best thing
Paisley ever did for the club, because Shanks put
Liverpool on the map.

It was best to hear the intriguing Anfield career of Morrissey
from his own mouth but it was one that started with a
boyhood supporter struggling to displace the likes of Billy
Liddell, Alan A'Court, Ian Callaghan, Kevin Lewis and Fred
Morris for a place in Phil Taylor's team. The diminutive wing
man won over the Kop with his tenacious efforts, tricky play
and powerful shot, and being a Scouser helped them associate
with him – he was one of them.

Despite signing as a 15-year-old and spending seven years
with the Reds, he only managed to record 37 appearances.
Seeing as 24 of those matches came in the 1960/61 campaign
under Bill Shankly, though, it was clear that the Scot had
big plans for Morrissey's future at Anfield. The 21-year-old
held down a role on the right wing but the board had decided
that the position was to be filled by Callaghan, much to the
dismay of the manager. The decision to not hand any first-
team games to the Scouser during the promotion campaign,

may have proved costly to the boss, as the board and the player may have thought there was no future for him at the club. An offer of £10,000 was accepted behind his back but it's fair to say that the fury this time was more from the manager than the supporters.

In Becky Tallentire's *Real Footballers' Wives*, Celia Morrissey did provide a different insight into some abuse that her husband received from Liverpool supporters: 'John became a Blue that afternoon. For the next few years, whenever he played against Liverpool, the fans would shout "Traitor" and "Judas" but it was nothing he couldn't handle.'

Dave Hickson left Everton after building a legacy, which is certainly similar to what Morrissey was set to go on to achieve. Shankly realised that this could happen for him at Anfield but the Liverpool supporters hadn't had enough opportunity to witness this yet. When the move was completed, although it was a surprise to see the player arrive at Goodison, there was no real heartache from the Reds nor jubilation from the Blues – although the years and successes that were set to follow perhaps suggests there certainly should have been.

Morrissey arrived at the start of the 1962/63 season and his first match was, of course, the Merseyside derby, the first league meeting between the teams for 11 years. Harry Catterick had splashed the cash on a new team that he thought was ready to win the league, and his new winger was part of that, ready to prove Liverpool's board wrong for allowing him to leave the club. No one in red or blue that day had ever experienced a derby, so the boyhood Red perhaps had the greatest understanding of what the match could entail.

There were 73,000 tightly packed into Goodison Park, nearly double the modern-day all-seater capacity of the ground, to watch a memorable match-up. James Holland painted a picture of the day in *The Guardian*:

Everton squad picture 1889/90, taken outside The Sandon– featuring Andrew Hannah (back row one in from left) and Fred Geary (bottom row centre). Courtesy of and colourised by George Chilvers.

Liverpool squad picture 1892/93 – featuring Andrew Hannah (back row three in from the left), Duncan McLean (back row three in from the right) and Tom Wyllie (front row far left). Courtesy of 'Old Liverpool FC in Colour'.

Andrew Hannah, the first man to ever captain both Everton and Liverpool.

Tom Wyllie, scorer in the first Merseyside derby in 1893.

Duncan McLean, one of John Houlding's most loyal servants.

Patrick Gordon. Courtesy of 'Old Liverpool FC in Colour'.

(Liverpool squad picture 1899/00, Geary bottom row far left).
Fred Geary, the first great Everton goalscorer.

Edgar Chadwick, a key member of
Everton's first title-winning squad in
1891.

Abe Hartley, 29 goals in seven years on
Merseyside but a life cut tragically short.

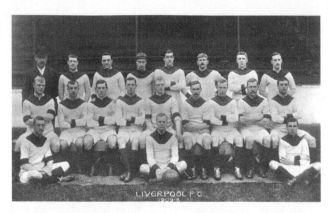

(Liverpool squad picture 1905/06, Murray middle row three in from the left). David Murray, Scottish defender who sadly lost his life during World War One.

(Great Britain Olympic squad picture 1912, Berry back row three in from the left). Arthur Berry, the only player to transfer to each club on two separate occasions.

(Liverpool squad picture 1910/11, Uren back row four in from the right) Harold Uren enjoyed a promising youth career at Anfield but failed to live up to the hype either side of his part in the three-man transfer between clubs.

Tom Gracie, part of the three-man deal in 1912 between the clubs, lifelong friend of Bill Lacey and sadly passed away during World War One.

(Pictured for Liverpool in 1913) Bill Lacey, Irish international turned staunch Red after back-to-back titles in the 1920s.

(Everton squad picture 1919/20, bottom row three in from the right) Frank Mitchell, the first player to play for Everton, Liverpool and Tranmere Rovers.

(Liverpool squad picture 1926/27, Forshaw back row one in from the left).
Dick Forshaw, goalscoring hero turned disgraced criminal.

(Pictured for Everton in 1925) Neil McBain, longest spanning career in football
when he retired after 32 years between his first and final performances as a player.

(Pictured for Everton in 1931) Tommy Johnson, Manchester City goalscoring legend with a hugely successful spell at Goodison Park.

(Pictured for Liverpool vs. Everton in 1950) Jimmy Payne, the 'Merseyside Matthews' who occupied the opposite wing to Billy Liddell during Liverpool's Second Division days.

(Liverpool squad picture 1935/36, Hartill bottom row one in from the right). Billy Hartill, Wolverhampton Wanderers club legend with a brief stay at both Merseyside clubs.

(Pictured for Everton in 1954) Tony McNamara, the first player to appear in all four divisions of the Football League within 12 months, between 1957 and 1958.

(Pictured for Everton vs. Hull City in 1952) Dave Hickson, the 'Cannonball Kid' is an Everton legend and another player to have represented all three Merseyside clubs.

Dave Hickson (Pictured for Liverpool vs. Charlton Athletic in 1960).

Before the game this vast blue and red mosaic of humanity, the colour pattern being formed by the blue of the Everton faithful and the red by the followers of Liverpool, enlivened proceedings by chanting in great volume and approved Continental fashion EV-ER-TON or LIV-ER-POOL as the mood or fancy took them, so that was undoubtedly high, but it is pleasing to record that throughout the citizens of Liverpool conducted themselves admirably.

No bottles were thrown, no stones, no orange peel, and for once even the goalmouths were not bestrewn with plebeian toilet paper. True, Liverpool's senior mascot at one point was pelted with apples – not all of them bad for that worthy picked one up and ate it – but that is one of the hazards of excessive loyalty.

'Excessive loyalty' was one way to describe an enthusiastic, orange peel-less and expectant crowd. The apple-throwing incident seems to have not been too severe and there was certainly more of a party atmosphere than one that seemed ready to turn into violence and anger. Gerry Byrne marshalled Morrissey well during the match but when a chance fell to him on the hour mark, thanks to a block from Ron Yeats that landed at his feet, he duly accepted the opportunity to score his first of 50 career goals in blue. It was an enthralling match and one where Roger Hunt managed to score a 90th-minute equaliser to see it end 2-2. The visitors would have been happier with the result but the home team were set to have much bigger things to cheer about.

The reaction to the match showed that there was no angst about Morrissey's move to the Blues. He was just a former Liverpool youth player who now represented the other side. He was still making his way at Goodison Park but 33 appearances across the campaign showed that he was part of Catterick's team. The rivalry between the clubs was perhaps best depicted by a cartoon drawn by Stan Jones for the *Liverpool Echo* after the match. It showed two men walking down the street together and one says: 'I can't understand these people who only see one colour – they miss a lot. To see the beautiful control of Alex Young, and the genius of Jimmy Melia is equally delightful. The anticipation of Brian Harris and the industry of Gordon Milne can bring tears of joy to my eyes. The artistry of –' The pair walk past another man selling rosettes. 'You don't deserve to sell any wearing that thing!!' There was a mutual respect and appreciation between supporters, but they did pick a side on derby day and the subtle undertones of distaste for your foe was clearly growing.

Harry Catterick was manager of an Everton team that accrued more First Division league points than anyone else in the 1960s. Considering the Darlington-born boss was up against the likes of Don Revie, Matt Busby, Bill Nicholson, Joe Mercer and Bill Shankly during this era, it shows how good he and his teams were. His first league title came in Morrissey's first season with them, and the Blues were buoyed by the increased finances pumped into the club. However, homegrown and nurtured talents such as Roy Vernon, Brian Labone, Alex Young and Alex Parker were also crucial.

The 1962/63 season had the winter known as the 'Big Freeze', and from the 12 January to 2 February there were only four matches played in England. Everton didn't play at all from late December to mid-February and their form was severely hampered by this break. They didn't win in their first four matches after the hiatus, yet their title-winning form was soon rediscovered. Catterick's team were far from cold in their performances for the rest of the season and ran out league winners by six points. After the Blues won the league, the board treated the players to a two-week holiday in Torremolinos, with the players getting closer and more hungry for future success.

When Everton lifted the First Division title in 1963, the fans were optimistic that this was to begin a period of success under the stewardship of Catterick. They didn't have to wait long for more silverware to come to Goodison Park, and finishing thirrd and fourth in the following two seasons showed that further success wasn't far away. In fact, it was only three years after their winning the league that they were winning a trophy once again, when 1966 brought Everton FA Cup success. However, Morrissey was no longer holding down his starting role (partly due to an ankle injury sustained that season) and had to watch Derek Temple start ahead of him in the league, receive the call-up to the final at Wembley, then score the winning goal in the famous victory over Sheffield Wednesday.

The Scouser did manage to get back into the team on the left wing but the headlines and plaudits were centred around the famous 'Holy Trinity' of Howard Kendall, Colin Harvey and fan favourite Alan Ball. Signed from Arsenal, World Cup winner with England in 1966, Ball would light up Goodison Park with his flair and ability. Morrissey wasn't akin to a usual wing man of the time though. Defenders were usually sent out to intimidate and flatten the quick feet and speed of the wingers they came up against, but it was the other way round with the boyhood Red. His no-nonsense style of play would often mean that he was the one flooring the opposition, with his fearless strength and unerring aerial ability for his size proving a tough task for anyone to put up with.

In Ball, Morrissey, Royle, Jimmy Husband and John Hurst, Catterick had built a forward line that complemented each other and would again make his team champions of England in 1970. In October the Blues were already eight points clear but many continued to use John Moore's millions against the qualities of the manager and his team. They won the league by a healthy nine points and looked set for a period of dominance at the top but it was relatively short-lived.

Catterick didn't win another trophy in his next seven years with the club and the surprise sale of Ball in December 1971 looked to slowly derail and dismantle his team. Morrissey's final two years with the club saw them fall from league champions to 15th and 17th in the division. He was definitely still an important player but a drop in confidence and playing time for him would certainly not have helped his claim to start more matches. Having been part of some of the greatest teams Goodison Park had ever seen, his role was not forgotten by the fans, although his place in the team was never as the poster boy.

Morrissey juggled his football with running a newsagents in Bootle, as he worked hard on and off the pitch to ensure a better life for his family after his retirement from the game. The removal of the wage cap in the country during his playing days meant that he ended up earning as much as £100 per week towards the end of his career.

Morrissey had been with the team that enjoyed their first experience of European football, the 1966 FA Cup triumph, two Charity Shields and two league titles but, come the end of the 1972/73 season, the Blues were in decline and their local hero was 33 years old. After winning the league in his first season and scoring in the derby in his first match, it was always going to be hard to top that. Scoring a penalty in the 1968 FA Cup semi-final helped take the team to the final against West Brom but he was unlucky that they lost that match and instead tasted victory in the year that he was sat on the sidelines. However, 1969/70 wasn't about Morrissey, as other members of Catterick's team drew more attention, but playing in 41 of a possible 42 league matches illustrates the role he had in such a talented team.

In over 300 appearances it's hard to argue that his legacy at Goodison Park is nothing short of great. Merseyside supporters love to resonate with a player, and when one worked as hard, remained as loyal and came from the same city as them, it's easy to understand why Morrissey was and is so loved today. A tough opponent who made life hell for opposition defenders, he had to fight on several occasions to win back his starting role in the team, which was testament to the resolute nature within him and his love for Everton.

Dave Hickson was quick to part ways when his place in the starting line-up was taken but Morrissey was different. Such was his love for the club that he remained a Blue even after his playing days – despite his boyhood love for Liverpool. Then Johnny Morrissey Jr also represented Everton in the mid-1980s, before forging a long career with Tranmere Rovers, and the family continue to frequent Goodison Park.

After the former Red ended his career with the Blues, he went on to play a solitary season for Oldham Athletic before retiring. Moving into the property business proved lucrative and has become a family trait to this day too. Morrissey remains a keen follower of Everton today and divides his time between living in the city and in Florida, where the family go to escape the English weather for four months of each year.

Morrissey and Hickson will be held in similarly high esteem by Everton supporters, and the presence of the former in some of the greatest teams of his era shows his talents within the game. Supporters understood him and the move from Liverpool never affected him, because it came so early in his career. Had the board had the same confidence that Shankly did in the player, he may have been an equally important part of Anfield successes, but perhaps also the decision not to play the winger during his final season in red didn't help either. Regardless, Morrissey had an easy decision to make, and it's fair to assume that whether it be in red or blue he would have gone on to win silverware and become a firm fan favourite on either side of the park.

Thankfully too, at the time of writing Morrissey is the first man on this list to still be living. Speaking from first-hand experience, he's certainly a man who is generous with his time and seems to be enjoying a lovely retirement with his wife and two children.

David Johnson

Name	David Edward Johnson
Born	23/10/1951, Liverpool
Died	23/11/2022, Liverpool
Everton Stats	105 matches/20 goals (1969–72 & 1982–84)
Everton honours	None
Liverpool stats	213 matches/78 goals (1976–82)
Liverpool honours	First Division 1976/77, 1978/79, 1979/80, 1981/82, League Cup 1982, European Cup 1977, 1981, European Super Cup 1977
Combined stats	318 matches/98 goals (1969–84)
Direct transfer?	Yes (Signed for EFC from LFC for £100,000 on 10/08/1982)
Remembered (%)	LFC 100%/EFC 85%/Ave. 93%
Legend (out of 10)	LFC 7.5/EFC 5.6/Ave. 6.6
Traitor (out of 10)	LFC 5.6/EFC 6.5

NOT QUITE at Arthur Berry levels of switching teams but David Johnson's two spells with Everton and one with Liverpool made him the first-ever person to record over 100 appearances for both clubs. Despite this, though, many within the city only associate the Scouser with wearing a red shirt, which may be down to the ridiculous haul of trophies he secured during his Anfield tenure.

Johnson described his pre-football playing days within the city during an interview with The Asian Kop: 'I'm from

Liverpool, Merseyside born and bred, and if you come from this area it's normally Dad or your brothers who determine who you support. My brothers took me to Anfield, that was my team, my idol obviously was Bill Shankly and I believed him when he stood on the steps and said, "I'm going to make Liverpool into a bastion of invincibility." I stood on the Kop with my brothers and watched the 60s side, my heroes were Ian St John and more so Roger Hunt. I dreamt a dream of playing for them.'

In a later interview with Liverpool's matchday programme, Johnson went on to add, 'I was an ardent Liverpool supporter as a schoolboy.' However, his break was to come with Everton. He said, 'They came in for me, and it just seemed to happen that way. I was still at school, and I suppose it happened at a time when I was wondering how I was going to break into professional football. Everton were throwing youngsters into their side, and I reckoned I must be in with a chance. As it turned out, it was a good move, too, because I got into their first team and did fairly well.'

There's no doubt that one of those youngsters initially given a chance was Johnny Morrissey, with Harry Catterick also being an advocate of allowing youth prospects to break through into his successful team. Morrissey's penultimate campaign as an Everton player was Johnson's first and he certainly would have fed off the experience that was present, in what had been a successful team.

Bill Shankly was a long-term admirer of Johnson too, despite not being able to sign him for Liverpool. He tried on several occasions to prise him away from Goodison Park and later Ipswich. Speaking with The Asian Kop, the boyhood Red described how this was one of the greatest regrets in his career: 'I haven't got many disappointments in football but professionally that's one of them ... when some of the 60s lads talk about Shanks and how he was, I'm so envious because I missed that opportunity of actually being managed by Shanks.'

Johnson made his decision though, and as a 15-year-old he was to forge his way in football at Goodison. He impressed at the younger age groups and was making a big impression for the reserves as a 17-year-old. Those were the days when playing in the Central League saw young players tested a lot more than they are in youth set-ups today. Brian Labone, Gordon West, Sandy Brown and Jimmy Husband were all at the tail end of their careers but their teen team-mate was attracting all the right attention on the pitch.

The small matter of displacing Joe Royle as centre-forward was the task at hand for the youngster but Catterick could no longer ignore him and handed a debut to Johnson in January 1971. Injury to their usual No.9 meant that Burnley were set to deal with the exciting striker, who was about to score on his debut. The *Liverpool Echo* wrote: 'Johnson added to a remarkable debut day by putting Everton ahead with yet another fine shot. It was [Tommy] Wright's accurate pass down the line which found Johnson unmarked 10 yards outside the penalty area. Johnson took it on, delayed a shot or pass obviously waiting for [Jimmy] Husband to run into position, but then decided to go it alone. He closed in and from a very narrow angle smashed the ball into the roof of the net past [Tony] Waiters.'

This was to become a trait in Johnson's career, scoring in his maiden Central League, First Division, FA Cup, League Cup and European appearance for the Blues. Not just that but his first Merseyside derby too. Johnson was again handed a chance thanks to fitness issues with Royle and Morrissey, and lined up as part of a struggling Everton team in November 1971. It was described in *The Guardian* as a 'donkey derby', with the further description of 'the stubbornness of both teams in continuing to treat the ball as though it were impregnated with bubonic plague was the main factor in making the game the mediocre spectacle it was' showing what type of match it was. Not that the 20-year-old minded though, as his header past Ray Clemence was enough to win the match.

Johnson's first stint at Everton is often billed as unimpressive, especially in comparison with what his future held elsewhere. The Scouser managed just 55 appearances in his three first-team seasons with the Blues, with Catterick struggling to find him a consistent role in the starting line-up. There was also the tough job of replacing the club legend Joe Royle, but seeing as Johnson finished 1971/72 as top goalscorer for the club, it's fair to say he was well on the way to doing so. It's hard to know what more a 21-year-old youth product can do to show a team that he's worthy of being given a chance.

Instead, Everton saw Rod Belfitt, a 27-year-old with fewer goals for Ipswich Town than Johnson had scored for the Blues, as the perfect replacement for Royle, agreeing to a deal that saw the young Scouser leave the club and adding £50,000 to sweeten the deal. Belfitt scored two goals in his 14-month Everton career, and by the time Johnson returned to the club ten years later he had won every trophy possible in the club game.

Ipswich were the initial benefactors of this decision though, and Johnson spent four successful years with the club. Playing under Bobby Robson, he helped his new team win the Texaco Cup and was an influential member of the European football that blessed Portman Road. Performances in East Anglia earned him an England call-up and interest grew in the forward. Tottenham tried to sign the Scouser but he didn't want to relocate. An offer from Bob Paisley at Liverpool, though, was soon to change his mind.

The collection of trophies that Johnson was set to assemble at Anfield means that each award won't be covered here but, as already mentioned, he won the lot in his six years with the club. Despite this, he found it difficult to break into a team that was on the cusp of domestic and European dominance. He was settled at Ipswich and wouldn't have left but for the lure of his boyhood club, which was too hard to ignore. This may have provided him with the patience needed to try to break into the team.

Slight injury concerns and a wealth of attacking options for Paisley to select from meant that 'Doc' Johnson was not a guaranteed starter, often finding himself coming off the bench and featuring on the wing. His nickname came from the wide array of painkillers that the Scouser always had on his person, especially cough sweets due to his perennial sore throat. First competing with Kevin Keegan and John Toshack (the latter for whom he was deemed to be a long-term replacement for), it was always going to be a tough task to be a regular part of the squad that was to win the club's first European Cup, in 1977. However, seeing as he managed 38 appearances in his maiden Anfield campaign, he certainly didn't do too badly (despite not featuring in the squad for the final in Rome).

With the two aforementioned forwards leaving the club soon after, new competition came in the form of Kenny Dalglish and David Fairclough. The Scot went on to be one of, if not the, very best Anfield has ever seen, so it was between two local lads to fight for the role alongside him. The 'bionic carrot' Fairclough was given the early nod before Johnson finally forced his way into the team. That was until a serious knee injury curtailed his season and again saw him miss out on European Cup success.

His comeback was set to be emphatic though. From 1978 to 1980, Johnson enjoyed two prolific seasons with Dalglish – scoring 45 goals in 91 matches and finishing the second season as the club's top scorer. He and Kenny scored

55 goals between them in a single season and the confidence the pair played with was unerring. With the Reds winning no less than two First Division titles and their third European Cup in this period too, Doc was a crucial part of Paisley's winning machine.

Despite going on to make a further 67 appearances in the following two seasons, Johnson's scoring return of 20 goals was enough for fresh options to be handed more opportunities in the limelight – one of these was Ian Rush. The Welshman was set to go on to become the club's all-time record scorer, so it wasn't a surprise to see Johnson gradually faded out of the team. However, Paris in 1981 was finally an opportunity for the Scouser to taste European Cup Final success first-hand, as he played the full match against Real Madrid.

There were, of course, plenty of individual highlights on this journey, one of which came against Everton in 1978 when Doc became the first man to score a winner for both clubs in the Merseyside derby. In an interview with James Pearce, the Scouser described the historic moment:

> I had gone full circle and that day I was playing in the derby wearing the red of Liverpool – the club I had supported as a kid and travelled all over the country to watch. I must admit that goal in front of the Gwladys Street was far sweeter than the one I got for Everton against Liverpool.
>
> It's difficult to put into words what it felt like. Scoring goals in cup finals or derbies is what kids dream about when they are kicking a ball around in the streets and I was able to fulfil that dream. The fact that I had played for Everton and then gone back there to score a winner for Liverpool made the stick I got that day even worse. I still

don't think Evertonians have forgiven me but I was pleased to get some stick because it meant I had done something right.

One thing that would have done little to ease the stick that was headed Johnson's way was a rendition of 'Thank you very much for David Johnson!' (sung to the tune of 'Thank U Very Much' by The Scaffold) that was echoed from the Liverpool supporters inside Goodison Park that day.

Another personal highlight came in May 1980 when Liverpool needed a victory to secure a second successive league title. Johnson scored two, and his left-footed effort that flew into the Kop end goal ended with the commentary line of 'that's the championship' from John Motson and is a moment that provided great pride for a homegrown lad.

Johnson's tireless and free-scoring years at Anfield may have been set to come to an end but he wasn't ready to leave Merseyside again, as £100,000 was enough to see both clubs shake hands on their first direct transfer for 20 years. Johnson joined an Everton managed by Howard Kendall and called the likes of Graeme Sharp, Mark Higgins and Steve McMahon his team-mates. The same summer saw Andy King return to the club, while Kevin Sheedy arrived from across the park too.

Johnson was to spend only one more year at Goodison Park, making 29 further appearances in blue. One of those saw him suffer the humiliation of a 5-0 loss against his former club as Ian Rush scored four and became the first man since Fred Howe in 1935 to score a hat-trick in a league match between the clubs. Now a 31-year-old though, the former red and blue forward didn't set the world alight like he had before. After the match, he said, 'Everton are a Rolls-Royce raring to go, only we are driving in first and second gear and we have got to use third and fourth.'

No doubt previous injuries had a part to play in the moustache-wearing striker's slightly premature drop in quality, but he failed to win over the Everton fans, many of whom felt he never left first gear himself. They had witnessed the start of his promising career but watching his increasing levels of success and performance level from afar meant that they rued the lack of finances that came their way for him and the fact that the silverware he won wasn't in a blue shirt. Although it may have felt as if Johnson could ease back into Goodison Park, the supporters felt they were watching an unwanted Liverpool player represent their club.

Speaking with Everton supporters about him, descriptions of the player being 'rubbish' certainly don't align with the statistics on offer for his days as a Blue, either side of his Anfield career. There was certainly a drop in performance from those for Paisley's all-conquering team, so perhaps Johnson was unfairly judged against his heyday across the park. Feelings that his best days were in an Ipswich shirt, that his allegiances were always to Liverpool and being lucky to be part of a winning team were also shared.

Everton wasn't the move that Johnson had hoped it would be, as he failed to win over the supporters and reach a consistent level of performance, leading to a loan move away from the club and a gradual climb down the footballing ladder. His final clubs included Barnsley, Manchester City, Tulsa Roughnecks, Preston and Barrow, where he was the player-manager for a short time. The last dance for Johnson was with the Naxxar Lions in Malta in 1987.

A move into insurance, radio, coaching and working in Anfield's hospitality lounges were set to follow after his retirement from football as a 35-year-old. He remained within the city and enjoyed coaching the 'Liverpool Way' across the world, as well as after-dinner speaking and a host of events, but always representing the Reds. His allegiance as a boy continued into his life after football.

The sad news of David Johnson's passing during the production of this book was certainly a sad day for Merseyside. After a year-long battle with throat cancer, the local great passed away in November 2022, aged 71. Both clubs came together to pay their respects, as did the many team-mates he had at Goodison Park and Anfield. Widespread love poured in for the Doc, who showed during his life that he would always fight for whichever shirt he was to wear. This honesty and integrity meant that he was only ever going to be remembered fondly. From the brief personal experience of talking with him so close to his death, it was obvious that he wasn't well, but he was also clear that he was happy with a brilliant life lived in Merseyside football.

Had Johnson never played for Liverpool or even supported them as a boy, it's fair to say his standing would be better among Everton supporters. Despite not having too much in the way of protest for his departure to Ipswich, you can understand a sour taste in the mouth when he succeeded so well at a club he admitted to supporting as a boy. There's no question the Scouser gave everything when he wore a blue shirt but he achieved so much more as a Red. In the '100 players who shook the Kop' fan vote, Johnson finished 77th, which shows that he's held in high regard by Anfield fans. He was never the darling of Goodison Park but, as part of Bob Paisley's silverware-collecting team, he proved to be a vital team member.

For Johnson to be the first player to have made more than 100 appearances for both clubs but still have a relatively negative relationship with the Everton supporters shows that rivalry and angst was growing in the stands, if not yet in the boardroom.

Kevin Sheedy

Name	Kevin Mark Sheedy
Born	21/10/1959, Builth Wells, Wales
Liverpool stats	5 matches/2 goals (1978–82)
Liverpool honours	League Cup 1982
Everton stats	369 matches/97 goals (1982–92)
Everton honours	First Division 1984/85, 1986/87, European Cup Winners' Cup 1985
Combined stats	374 matches/99 goals (1978–92)
Direct transfer?	Yes (signed for EFC from LFC for £100,000 on 26/05/1982)
Remembered (%)	LFC 92%/EFC 100%/Ave. 96%
Legend (out of 10)	LFC 4/EFC 9.3/Ave. 6.7
Traitor (out of 10)	LFC 6.1

IN JIMMY Payne and Tony McNamara we saw two players who attempted to move to the other side of the park to reignite their former potential and get their career going again. David Johnson had probably the most promising career but, like with Johnny Morrissey, he went and thrived with the other Merseyside team. Despite Kevin Sheedy being the man with the second-highest cumulative appearances for both Liverpool and Everton, seeing as just five came in red, it's easy to see where his legacy lies. Like Johnson enjoying the glory days of Liverpool's success in the 1970s and 1980s, Sheedy was part of a triumphant Everton team during his ten years at the club. His story will always be intertwined with Goodison Park but will also always begin at Anfield.

If Johnson's Everton career is unfairly judged by Everton supporters because of what he went on to achieve at Anfield, then the same can't be said for Sheedy because he didn't have a Liverpool career. Despite spending an initial five years at the club after arriving from Hereford in 1978, the Wales-born midfielder wasn't given a chance to showcase the talents possessed in his sweet left foot.

He impressed during reserve fixtures, alongside the likes of Howard Gayle and Sammy Lee, who would go on to challenge the first team much more than he was ever allowed to. Sheedy was playing well enough and had impressed enough with Hereford to have received youth international call-ups for Ireland (the nation he went on to represent at Euro 88 and the 1990 World Cup). Damage to his ankle ligaments in 1981 also hindered his progress with the Reds but Paisley was keen to play the midfielder, although often during friendly matches and when tinkering with a new system to try out with the first team.

Sheedy had enjoyed three years with Hereford but had seen a huge drop in playing opportunities now that he had made the move to a successful Liverpool. He proved to be little more than a stop-gap player who would fill the hole of injuries. After signing in 1978 as an 18-year-old, it wasn't until he was 21 that he was handed a start by Bob Paisley. Across just five matches for the club, two were appearances off the bench (one for the final minute of the match), two were starts in comfortable League Cup victories and the other his debut against Birmingham City in a 2-2 draw.

His finest moment in a red shirt came during a 4-1 Anfield victory over Middlesbrough in the League Cup in November 1981. *The Guardian* ran with the headline: 'Sheedy's sharpener for the match' and went on to report: 'Bob Paisley preferred Sheedy, the former Hereford player, who endorsed the manager's choice with the first goal, a low drive from 25 yards after half an hour of torpid football.' Sheedy had given Anfield a glimpse of the left foot that was set to score twice more inside the stadium but not for the team in red.

That was that, really. Had he not gone on to represent Everton, the insignificance of Sheedy's Anfield career would never again really need to be covered. He spent the vast majority of his four Liverpool seasons in the reserves, waiting patiently for opportunities that were very rarely handed to him. In a later interview with Everton, he went on to explain how the next chapter came about:

> I was in digs in Anfield, playing the last game of the season for Liverpool Reserves against Preston. I got a phone call from Colin Wood, who was a newspaper writer for the *Daily Mail* and he asked if I would be interested in signing for Everton. I said, 'Of course, I'd be delighted to.' He said, 'Well put the phone down and Howard Kendall will ring you up.' So, I put the phone down thinking it was a prank from one of the lads but, sure enough, the boss Howard rang and said he was going to come and watch me play for Liverpool against Preston and for me to do my best.
>
> Obviously I must have impressed him because a week later I got a phone call saying, 'Come and sign for Everton.' The minute I met Howard, the boss, he didn't need to sell the club for me – I knew about the tradition of Everton, I'd watched a number of games midweek while I was still a Liverpool player and so I'd seen the likes of Sharpey make his debut, Kevin Ratcliffe get into the team, Adrian Heath making his debut after signing for £750,000. I saw the team the boss was

putting together and so it was a great move for me, just moving across the city.

A bit of pressure obviously because, coming from Liverpool, the Everton supporters would have thought if I wasn't good enough for Liverpool why would I be good enough for Everton? I had to impress.

The 22-year-old certainly did, he was out of contract and a fee of £100,000 was decided by tribunal to be enough to force a direct transfer between the clubs. Although Paisley was uneasy to see Sheedy leave and to a local rival, he knew that opportunities were going to be few and far between, especially when competing with the likes of Graeme Souness, Terry McDermott and Ronnie Whelan for a place in the team. His ten years at Goodison showcased the midfielder's talents of vision and passing, a dream for his new team-mates Graeme Sharp and Andy Gray. His aforementioned left foot was also pivotal in some key successes that were to follow across the park. Even in games where it felt like the Irish international may have been missing from action, half a yard of space with his magic left boot was enough for something special to happen. One Everton supporter described it as: 'The best left foot in life!'

When free kicks were awarded to the Blues, rival fans would fall silent in the anticipated dread of what would invariably happen. A chorus of 'Sheedy, Sheedy' would ring out, before the ball flew into the back of the opposition's net. One of the most famous instances of this came in March 1985 during an FA Cup quarter-final against Ipswich Town, after Paul Cooper handled the ball outside the visitors' box. Trevor Steven and Peter Reid stood either side of the Welsh-born set-piece specialist but it was clear who was set to take it. With the opposing keeper standing by one post, rearranging his wall, Sheedy cheekily took a quick run-up and whipped it into the top-left corner of the mostly vacated goal. Referee Alan Robinson adjudged for it to have been taken too quickly though, so the goal was ruled out. However, the Blues had another opportunity to score. Now, with everyone settled, Sheedy ran up again and the No.11 audaciously placed it in the other corner this time, much to the adulation of his adoring supporters. It was a lesson in taking free kicks by the midfielder.

There were also two Merseyside derby free kicks that were set to be dispatched by Sheedy. Both were scored at Anfield, at the Kop end against Mike Hooper, but unfortunately for the Irish international they were in 3-1 victories for Liverpool. Both were also efforts that levelled the score at 1-1, so there was cause for celebration on each occasion, an opportunity that the Everton hero certainly made the most of. His first came in the first leg of the final of the short-lived Screen Sport Super Cup, a competition brought about following the ban on English teams in European competitions after the Heysel Stadium disaster of 1985. Thus comes the first opportunity to discuss a moment that many will trace the modern rivalry/tension/hatred between clubs back to. As no player discussed in this book took part in the match in question, there's little reason to delve into the detail, rather just the repercussions.

* * *

The bare bones and facts of the day read, via a BBC article:

> About an hour before kick-off at the 1985 European Cup Final, a group of Liverpool fans crossed a fence separating them from a neutral area containing mostly Juventus fans.
>
> As they fled the threat, the fans were crushed together in a section of terrace hemmed in by a

concrete retaining wall, which eventually collapsed. Thirty-nine people died. The game was played despite the disaster in order to prevent further disorder, with Juventus winning 1-0.

Among those killed were 32 Italians, four Belgians, two French fans and one from Northern Ireland. It resulted in all English football clubs being banned from playing in Europe for five years.

The blame for Heysel was initially laid entirely on Liverpool fans, and 14 were later found guilty of manslaughter and jailed.

However, an investigation did concede that some culpability lay with the authorities, and the crumbling state of the Heysel Stadium.

It's hard to write about this subject without giving an opinion. Seeing as the events have, to some extent, split a city, it's likely not to be the same opinion shared by all readers. On a simple and very generalised level, Liverpool supporters take responsibility for what happened at Heysel but there are other factors that they feel need to be considered. This event was a straw that broke the camel's back in an era of hooliganism, and English football fans were all tarred with the same brush, particularly when competing in European competition. There's no doubt that the actions of the Liverpool fans that day caused the unnecessary and tragic deaths of Juventus supporters but there's blame to be placed elsewhere too. European footballing authorities selected a substandard stadium. Heysel was falling apart and pieces of concrete could be easily lifted out of walls and barriers, such was the disrepair. There were also too many Juventus supporters placed in a supposed 'neutral zone' between fanbases. When they too started throwing missiles and aggravating a tense atmosphere, the stadium and policing wasn't fit to cope with it. No one should have to prepare for a match where they expect a charge to occur but this is what happened and 39 people were killed. Those deemed guilty were charged for their crimes and, following the European ban, some rival supporters believe that this event has been somewhat brushed under the carpet and forgotten about.

Not for some Everton fans though. On a pure footballing level, the two seasons that preceded the Heysel disaster saw the Blues win the FA Cup and finish as losing finalists, get to the final of the League Cup, win the Charity Shield and also the European Cup Winners' Cup, plus the 1984/85 First Division title. They followed that up with a second place, then won the league for the first two seasons of the European ban, even with star striker Gary Lineker leaving so that he could compete at the highest level. Everton have never won the European Cup but at this time they were very much competing with a team that had done so four times – Liverpool. There's some animosity built around losing an opportunity to win the major European prize because of an event involving their neighbours, one that was out of their control.

The Hillsborough Stadium disaster in 1989 was not a hooligan-related event but many uneducated and ill-informed supporters across the country believe it was. Then, 97 Liverpool supporters were unlawfully killed due to the actions of police and stadium officials, which led to a long fight for truth and justice, something that is still going on today. There's a feeling among some that Heysel has been forgotten but Hillsborough lives on. It's important to stress that this is certainly not an opinion shared by all, or indeed even most Everton fans, but some feel that their chances of European success was ruined because of the fatal actions of their neighbours, and this has grown into a toxic relationship between their fanbases over time.

Liverpool and Everton were supremely successful in the 1960s, 70s and 80s but the last league title won by the Blues was during this European ban. The Reds ended their long wait for a league championship in 2020 but the distribution of trophies has been a lot less evenly split since the turn of the millennium. The start of the growing gulf between teams, in terms of silverware, can be traced back to Everton not being able to compete in European football.

It wasn't a trigger point of immediate change in a relationship between two clubs, as Blues and Reds still mixed in crowds and families were still split. Everton's reaction to the Hillsborough disaster in 1989 was nothing short of amazing, the line of scarves that stretched through Stanley Park between the clubs demonstrating this, and the 'Friendly Derby' was still intact. The 1984 Milk Cup Final that preceded the Heysel disaster showed two teams unified in a squad picture after the match. The city was together more at that stage than it possibly ever had been.

However, the 1986 and 1989 FA Cup finals both saw the Reds claim victory over the Blues. The lack of a league title since 1987 and a trophy since 1995 has caused some Everton fans to point back to Heysel as the moment everything changed. Losing two finals in the years soon after Heysel and each year passing without a trophy led to anger. Possibly the real long-term aftermath of missing out on Europe and being able to keep their best players will continue to affect a certain group of Everton fans, and this will always, by some, be brought back to the actions of Liverpool supporters who were to blame for the deaths of Juventus fans at Heysel.

The events in Belgium could be very crassly pointed to as 'fair game' for abuse, as some Liverpool fans were to blame and Everton felt the repercussions of this. For some to then try to combine this with Hillsborough, though, just isn't right, and the modern-day use (certainly not just by some

Everton supporters) of chants such as 'murderers', '*The Sun* was right, you're murderers', 'always the victim, it's never your fault', and miming of walls being pushed and faces being crushed by walls and fences are performed with the intention of referencing the events at Heysel and Hillsborough.

It's impossible to write a book about these two clubs in the context of the 2020s rivalry between them without delving into the possible causes in a decline in the relationship between them. The first-ever all-Merseyside cup final was the Milk Cup in 1984, where chants of 'Merseyside' rang out at Wembley. This was the best and most unified footballing city standing side by side inside the ground. Blue and red flags waved in unison and it was a rivalry that existed nowhere else. Now, nearly 40 years later, it's just like everywhere else and it's sad to see. This was just an attempt to explain why that may have happened and there can only be sincere apologies provided to anyone who disagrees or is upset with the above.

* * *

As we return to Kevin Sheedy, standing over the ball about to take a free kick in the Screen Sport Super Cup Final first leg, he was met with the strange decision by Mike Hooper to put his wall in the centre of the goal and to stand directly behind it. This invited the former Red to have a shot at goal, which was never wise. The ball flew into the bottom corner of the net as Sheedy brilliantly hit across the ball and bent it goalward. The game and two-legged final was to end with the Reds lifting the small trophy at Goodison Park but was also a precursor for one of the Irish international's most famous goals in blue.

Seven months later Sheedy was standing in a very similar spot and, despite Everton supporters taking over nearly a quarter of the Kop that day, you could hear a pin drop as the free kick was given and memories were cast back to his last effort. Many Blues began to feel as if a Sheedy free kick was as good as a penalty, and it was clear that the Liverpool fans did too. His subsequent goal and celebration made him a hero.

Speaking about his derby goal in 1987, Sheedy said:

> It was probably one of my best strikes ever, it was about 25 yards out and as soon as it left my boot, I knew it was in. It nestled right in the top corner and for some reason I went to give a two-finger salute to the Kop, which I got away with. I got called before the FA and managed to talk my way out of it and it's a special memory. There was nothing meant in it, it wasn't planned or anything like that and I still get the Liverpool supporters laughing about it as well, they take it in good spirits as well.

This is probably a key reason why many Liverpool fans don't deem Sheedy to have ever been their player, as putting two fingers up to his former supporters certainly won't endear you to them. On a day where Steve McMahon scored for Liverpool and Gary Ablett assisted Ian Rush's goal that saw him level Dixie Dean's Merseyside derby record, it was quite a day for the men who feature in this esteemed list of players.

It seems unfair to boil Sheedy's Everton career down to three free kicks, as he was a crucial part of their successes in the 1980s, which included winning two league titles and the European Cup Winners' Cup across a decade where he made 369 appearances and scored a mightily impressive 97 goals. His decisive goal against Rapid Vienna provided the Blues with their first European trophy. Arguably more influential, or appreciated, in blue than David Johnson was in red, Sheedy was certainly a hero and a stalwart of the team, even if not always the greatest player in it. When Everton were great though, so was the Wales-born midfielder, exemplified by his European final goal and being in the First Division's team of the season in the two campaigns when he helped bring the league title to Goodison Park.

The silverware and success that came during his Everton days will always be fondly remembered, but when an Evertonian hears the name of Kevin Sheedy the first thing that comes to mind will always be his unerring left boot and an eye for goal from any set piece. His tally of free-kick finishes was more than anyone else in the 1980s and proved a decade-long deadly weapon for the Blues. He left Everton at the dawn of the Premier League era, aiding Newcastle United's promotion to the big time before again stepping down the divisions to Blackpool. Youth and caretaker coaching roles followed at Tranmere, Everton and Al-Shabab, before most recently a role at Dick Forshaw's old club – Waterford.

He's very active on social media today and it's not hard to see on which side of the park Sheedy's allegiances remain. Who can blame him either. His talents would have seen Liverpool utilise him much more in many other eras within the club's history. Competition was so high, though, that it forced him to move away from Anfield and there's no doubting he made the right decision for his career. Paisley's initial reaction of regretting allowing the Irish international to leave the club showed that his talents were appreciated but, like with Johnny Morrissey, the Reds only had themselves to blame for not playing him more. In this instance though, it seemed that everyone was the winner. Sheedy deserved a chance to shine at Goodison Park and it's fair to say he certainly did that. The £100,000 spent was certainly a bargain, especially as the midfielder is in the club's all-time top-ten goalscorers, alongside familiar names Dave Hickson and Edgar Chadwick.

Now a Blue through and through, Sheedy is adored by the Everton faithful and it's not hard to see why.

Steve McMahon

Name	Stephen Joseph McMahon
Born	20/08/1961, Halewood, Liverpool
Everton stats	120 matches/14 goals (1979–83)
Everton honours	None
Liverpool stats	277 matches/50 goals (1985–91)
Liverpool honours	First Division 1985/86, 1987/88, 1989/90, FA Cup 1986, 1989
Combined stats	397 matches/64 goals (1979–91)
Direct transfer?	No
Remembered (%)	LFC 100%/EFC 100%/Ave. 100%
Legend (out of 10)	LFC 7.8/EFC 3.9/Ave. 5.9
Traitor (out of 10)	EFC 7.4

STEVEN GERRARD made a bold prediction about Trent Alexander-Arnold in his autobiography, written in 2016: 'Trent Arnold has a terrific chance of making it as a top professional. He's quite leggy but he's got a lovely frame and seems to have all the attributes you need. He has the right attitude and comes from West Derby, home to Melwood. So Trent is another Scouser and, apparently, just as I tried to be John Barnes and Steve McMahon, he grew up pretending to be me while playing in the Merseyside parks.'

The above highlights the regard in which Steve McMahon is held by some Liverpool supporters. Of the 34 players to have crossed the park, no one has appeared more for both clubs than McMahon and, unlike second-place Kevin Sheedy, his appearances are much more evenly dispersed between clubs. In fact, of all the players, only Gary Ablett recorded more appearances for the team that he played fewer times for (if that makes sense). The reason for all these stats, though, are to illustrate that you would assume he was looked upon favourably by both clubs but that doesn't seem to be the case.

When some Everton supporters were interviewed for this book, a variety of responses included: 'Can we all start singing, "Fuck off McMahon"?', 'He was a good player but he's the biggest traitor', and one supporter pretended to spit on the floor and walked away from the rest of the questionnaire. McMahon was the second-highest-rated traitor of all the players involved in the questioning too, so it's clear that his four years at Goodison Park aren't necessarily remembered fondly.

Nevertheless, that's where the professional story of Steve McMahon begins. In an interview with Leadernomics, the Halewood-born midfielder described his early life:

> I started at grassroots level, playing in the park and playing school football. I got recognised by Tom Fairfoul who was the Everton scout at the time and he recognised something in me and thought I had talent and he asked me, at the age of 11 I think I was, would I like to join Everton as a schoolboy.
>
> I was brought up an Evertonian anyway, so when I got asked to join Everton I didn't hesitate – it was a joy, it was a dream come true. I couldn't sign the schoolboy forms until I was 14 and then you have two years before the club has to make a decision. I actually wasn't signed at the time, Everton said I was too small – talented but too small to be a footballer. History shows that I

proved them wrong. I kept going, I kept pestering them and, within six months or so, they decided to sign me as an apprentice, which meant I started getting paid. It wasn't much but it got me onto the path of being a professional footballer and every day I used to go to training until I was 18 and the club had to again decide if I was going to be a professional.

I was fortunate that at 18 they offered me a three-year professional contract, which I gladly signed. Within a short period of time, I made my full debut for Everton. It was a great honour for me to play for Everton and eventually captain Everton which was also a great honour.

The story of a boyhood Blue working his way up from an 11-year-old to eventually captain the club sounds like a fairy tale – what could possibly go wrong? McMahon broke into an Everton team that had just finished 19th in the First Division, so Gordon Lee was prepared to bed some fresh blood into his team. The 18-year-old was thrust straight into the first team and missed just nine matches in his maiden campaign. Finishing 15th, then 8th and finally 7th in his three years at the club, he played in 106 of a possible 132 league matches during his time at Goodison Park.

Gordon Lee was building a new, young squad, with the likes of Eamonn O'Keefe, Joe McBride, Imre Varadi, Paul Lodge and McMahon all being entrusted with playing time. The end of his first year as a professional Evertonian ended with McMahon witnessing Lee lose his job though, to be replaced by Howard Kendall. The former player at Goodison Park joined as player-manager but was to make just six appearances during the campaign before hanging up his boots. The boyhood Blue may have worried whether he would fit in with the new boss. However, the fact that no player in the squad made more appearances than McMahon that season shows that he was clearly a key part of the team that the new man in charge was forging.

Kendall's second season proved to be McMahon's last and also saw David Johnson and Kevin Sheedy sign for the club. McMahon played over 40 times in that campaign too, so it's again strange to think, at this point, how his legacy could be so poor among Evertonians. If it comes to Merseyside derby performances, then there wasn't much to be too overawed by in terms of big goals and victories, despite meeting Liverpool on seven occasions during his time at Goodison Park. Seeing as the final two seasons that McMahon spent with Everton ended in the Reds winning the league, the team in blue were often at the receiving end of the sound of 'we're the pride of Merseyside'. Not so much a nasty chant but rather a playful reminder of who was currently on top.

One such derby that McMahon took part in, in January 1981, may not have been magnificent for him in terms of personal performance but helping Mike Lyons win his first match against Liverpool in 20 attempts and move into the fifth round of the FA Cup made it a great day for all Blues. One segment of the match report in *The Guardian*, though, shows how the propaganda machine was in full flow when it came to diminishing the image of Scousers. John Roberts wrote:

> Everton's obsessive need for victory was expressed with frightening passion by their supporters, hundreds of who scaled the eight feet metal fences with ominous ease and mobbed their player at the conclusion of the match. Some managed to reach the field, and momentarily there was a possibility of violence. This was averted by speedy and undemonstrative police intervention.

In an area where unemployment has long been an accepted fact of life there is no doubt that many of the 53,804 spectators at the game will not have a job to occupy them this morning. Such circumstances are inclined to intensify and exaggerate an identification with, and a pathetic dependence upon, a team and its fortunes. Small wonder the atmosphere was that charged.

A later derby saw McMahon injure Ray Kennedy with a crude tackle that saw him leave the pitch. *The Guardian* went on to write: 'All it needed was a turning point, and this was inadvertently provided by young McMahon, paradoxically one of the few Everton players worthy of sharing a pitch with Souness, McDermott, and the rest of the European champions.' The turning point, though, was allowing Dalglish to operate in a more creative role after Kennedy's injury, the Scot scoring twice in a 3-1 victory. However, this description showed that the boyhood Blue was capable of keeping up with the 1981/82 league champions.

McMahon's final season in blue brought two further Merseyside derbies. For the Goodison match, McMahon was given a feature in the matchday programme and explained how his boyhood hero was Alan Ball and the fact that his brother John, who was part of the youth set-up at the time, although he never managed to make it as a first-team player for Everton, was driving him to training because he hadn't passed his test. Congratulations was also passed on to the player, who was set to record his 100th appearance, and there looked set to be many more to follow. His final match at Anfield as a Blue came in March 1983 and *The Guardian* reported: 'Everton were the better side in the first half, during which McMahon out-played Souness in midfield.' The midfielder was capable of competing with the best and in big matches too. Another insight into the rivalry between the clubs was also provided:

> The rest of the country has become a little wary of Merseyside whose people are often seen as trigger-happy both at work (when they can get it) and play. The rest of the country should have been at Anfield on Saturday.

> Of course, derbies all have their own special character, but few are as civilised as the Merseyside events. The rival supporters traditionally journey to the match together. You often see cars trailing a red scarf from one window and a blue scarf from another. When they get to the ground, the occupants tumble out to do battle but their weapons are words.

> Segregation, normally the first principle of crowd control, is hardly necessary. The uninitiated observer must have winced on Saturday when he saw several thousand blue-bedecked Evertonians being shovelled into the Kop of all places, but the locals knew they and the resident reds would simply get on with enjoying the match together, which they did.

> Bob Paisley's last derby as Liverpool manager was a pleasant occasion, then, even if the football tailed off into goalless anonymity after a bright start. He was glad to take the opportunity of praising the supporters of both clubs, saying: 'It's about time they got the credit they deserve. Nobody banters harder than Merseyside supporters, and they can even get a bit obscene at times, but they don't fight. They are a perfect example of the old saying about sticks and stones.'

For McMahon, taken at face value, when it came to the end of the 1982/83 season he was a young player full of promise. He had plenty of appearances under his belt and a possibility of breaking into the England squad after successful appearances for the Under-21s. Howard Kendall's team looked to be on the up, although there had been no real chance of securing silverware up to this point. As a boyhood Blue, it would be easy to buy into sticking around and continuing to help the team push on to match Liverpool's current success. However, this is the part where Evertonians first fell out with the midfielder. Back to McMahon's interview with Leadernomics:

> My contract was up, I did my three-year stint and I believed my value was worth more. I was playing for England Under-21s and I was established in the first-team, I'd played over 100 games now for Everton and I think I deserved a better contract. Howard Kendall was the manager at the time but I made the decision to leave because of the contractual situation and Aston Villa came in.
>
> It was heart-breaking and I actually could have gone straight to Liverpool but out of respect and the situation and the way that it happened, I decided to move to Aston Villa because it was the right decision at the time. I didn't want any of the hassle of moving straight from Everton to Liverpool.

Again, this may seem somewhat respectful from the player but any Blue standing on the terraces of Goodison Park would have killed to swap places with him. Most other situations of previous transfers had a degree of explanation about them. Sheedy wasn't playing, Johnson was a boyhood

Red, Morrissey wasn't getting a game, Hickson was at the end of his career, McNamara and Payne were being phased out of the team. McMahon, though, was, as he said, living his dream.

Finances have a big part to play in many decisions in life but for a fan in the stands to try to relate to this decision of leaving your club when you're such a vital cog within it is almost unfathomable. Villa had won the First Division and the European Cup over the previous three seasons, so McMahon was joining a team with pedigree but also one that finished just one place above Everton in his final Goodison Park campaign.

Perhaps if McMahon had gone to Anfield straightaway, it would have actually led to less hatred from his people. The midfielder was a strong performer in the Villa team but the Everton supporters already had distaste for him turning his back on their club in favour of more money elsewhere. The Villa Park team finishing three places below Everton in his first campaign was a welcome sight, then Kendall's team winning the league the next season meant that Everton fans could laugh at the player who had left to further his career. He was now set to move to Liverpool though, and this just added a new level of hatred against a boyhood Blue turned Red. Instead of getting all the anger out of the way in one fell swoop, he had a two-staged exit leading to his arrival across the park.

There seems little need to delve too far into McMahon's life at Villa Park, other than to mention the previous worries that he had of joining the Reds in May 1983 were removed by September 1985. Perhaps the outpouring of loathing from Everton fans had made the decision to join his childhood foes easier. Liverpool had already attempted to sign the midfielder when he was a Blue, and now Kenny Dalglish needed a tough-tackling and creative replacement for recently departed Graeme Souness. After proving his equal on many occasions, being a local lad and seemingly having cut his ties with the Goodison Park faithful, the move made sense for everyone.

McMahon was to join Dalglish's team in a midfield, with Jan Mølby, Kevin MacDonald and Ronnie Whelan. If the critical words of some Everton supporters could be used to describe the hatred of the Scouser, then perhaps the pretty consistently frank descriptive phrase of many Reds can be used now. That phrase is that he was 'hard as fuck', and his battles with Peter Reid perhaps best depicted the unity and growing tension between red and blue.

McMahon, a boyhood Blue, faced up against Reid, a childhood Red, on seven Merseyside derby occasions. Football is the language of Merseyside and the fans on the terraces could never contemplate changing their allegiance to the other club. That didn't stop the likes of McMahon and Reid, plus Carragher and Coady to come, being adored by the fans they used to personally oppose. Scousers like Scousers but, moreover, they like someone who is willing to fight for the badge. Dave Hickson was willing to break every bone for Liverpool and that was enough to win over the fans in the late 1950s. Perhaps the reason that David Johnson wasn't ultimately accepted on his second visit to Goodison Park is that changing too many times makes it seem somewhat disingenuous.

With McMahon and Reid though, their new adoring supporters were willing to forgive their misdemeanours in early life and that love and feeling of belonging that was awarded to them has seen both change their allegiances long after their playing careers ended. Interestingly, both men are friends to this day too, and this group of players could perhaps be covered in their own book, but will be covered briefly later.

This era of both clubs duelling for major honours is particularly depicted by the actions of the two men. McMahon has the silverware edge, despite not being part of either club's European successes. The Scouser in red was a winner and he was a crucial part of Dalglish's new team at Anfield. His dogged and determined play in midfield meant that he was an uncompromising foe with oodles of talent that could be used to split open a defence. The fact that the £350,000 spent by the player-manager on the Villa man was his first signing shows that he was confident success would follow. When he was first introduced to the Anfield crowd, McMahon was playfully met with the singing of 'Everton reject!'

McMahon's skill of unlocking defences was certainly one that improved with time but perhaps the best way that he could win over his new fans was by scoring his first goal, which of course came against Everton. September 1985 at Goodison Park saw the Reds go 2-0 up inside 15 minutes and appear to be cruising. Each time McMahon picked up the ball he was met with loud jeers but he was to soon silence the home fans with a low effort from distance that put his team three goals up at the break. The former Blue was caught in possession and allowed Graeme Sharp the opportunity to close the gap, with Gary Lineker adding a second with ten minutes remaining. It may not have felt as important as it proved to be when it hit the back of the net but McMahon's first goal was a derby-day winner. This helped further solidify the hatred from the Blues and establish him as a Red to his new fans.

Speaking about the match during a BT Sport documentary, *Two Tribes*, McMahon described the unsavoury events that followed this match:

> In my third game for Liverpool, I scored in the derby. It was my first game at Goodison in a

Liverpool shirt. We won 3-2 and, of course, I celebrated. I could not have dreamt of it going any better. You get brought in by Kenny and you've got to take on the mantle of Graeme Souness, so there was a lot of pressure.

My car got absolutely trashed outside the ground, but, as it happened, it was an Aston Villa one, which I had not yet given back. To start with, the hatred was beyond belief and I was a little bit bitter. But it was a wonderful time for me. It was an intense and fearsome rivalry – but it was great.

His first Anfield season ended in First Division success but, seeing as MacDonald started in front of McMahon for the 1986 FA Cup Final, it was clear that his position in the team was far from assured – despite playing 36 times. The next season saw a maturing 25-year-old play his highest tally of matches in a single campaign, although with Everton claiming the First Division title. Dalglish hit back by signing John Barnes and Peter Beardsley, as he built a squad fit to win it all.

Providing for a forward line that was as potent and exciting as he had in front of him meant that McMahon grew in confidence and seniority within the Liverpool team. Some Dalglish-esque moments of skill and vision illustrated a growth in ability too and he managed to score an array of brilliant goals in a red shirt. Boxing Day in 1987 saw a piledriver from distance away to Oxford United, while a similar effort, preceded by a cheeky nutmeg, against Manchester United in the April showed it wasn't a one-off. Then his chip in the 9-0 victory over Crystal Palace showed he had a wide array of scoring talents too.

McMahon was a favourite of Dalglish and signed a long-term contract to remain at the club. However, the events of Hillsborough in 1989 led to the ultimate departure of the legendary player and manager. When Liverpool lost the league to Arsenal in the most dramatic circumstances, images of McMahon informing all his team-mates that they were one minute from glory became much replayed. It was followed by Michael Thomas's late league-winning goal.

Few would expect the mental weight of overseeing this emotionally charged period to lead to Dalglish's 1991 resignation days after a dramatic 4-4 draw at Goodison Park, but one Scot left in place of another. Graeme Souness took the hot seat but his vision of doing things his own way resulted in McMahon and many others being displaced from the team. McMahon had been named captain of the team but felt disenfranchised with the direction of the club and the new boss. Less than a year after the man he had replaced in the Anfield midfield replaced Dalglish, the England international left the club for Manchester City and new manager – Peter Reid. He made an Anfield return with the Citizens and was booked for a tough tackle on Ian Rush, so clearly there was no love lost.

The 30-year-old then took the obligatory step down the footballing ladder. His three years at Maine Road were followed by his own time as a player-manager with Swindon Town, before managerial spells with Blackpool and, most recently, Perth Glory. TV work followed in Singapore with ESPN and Fox Sports and he moved into coaching camps in the local area.

McMahon perhaps felt the brunt of hatred more than any other player mentioned so far, perhaps best demonstrated by his car being attacked following his derby goal. It's hard not to understand the upset and anger of Everton supporters when one of their own left in the hunt for money and/or success. Aston Villa not succeeding made the Blues smug, as they had proven their former player wrong but his return to the city proved that there was still plenty of time for him to make amends. Supporters of the age of Steven Gerrard holding McMahon in such high esteem shows how valued the England international is by the red side of the city and this gulf in feeling towards the midfielder makes him an interesting character.

Only David Johnson experienced similar levels of animosity but there really had been none quite like McMahon at the time he made the surprising decision to abandon his home and (eventually) cross the park.

Peter Beardsley

Name	Peter Andrew Beardsley
Born	18/01/1961, Hexham, Northumberland
Liverpool stats	175 matches/59 goals (1987–91)
Liverpool honours	First Division 1987/88, 1989/90, FA Cup 1989
Everton stats	95 matches/32 goals (1991–93)
Everton honours	None
Combined stats	270 matches/91 goals (1987–93)
Direct transfer?	Yes (signed for EFC from LFC for £1m on 05/08/1991)
Remembered (%)	LFC 100%/EFC 100%/Ave. 100%
Legend (out of 10)	LFC 8.1/EFC 7.9/Ave. 8.0
Traitor (out of 10)	LFC 5.1

NO PLAYER, according to the people questioned to help with this book, had a higher average club-legend rating with both sets of supporters than Peter Beardsley. Plenty of the other players in the book have won more than the England international, as he never even won a trophy with Everton, but few are more respected. For a player who not only played for both clubs but also played for a united foe in Manchester United, the shared love and appreciation of the player is hard to ignore. This could be due to the age group of people asked, or a variety of other arbitrary reasons, but these figures can perhaps draw a conclusion that Beardsley is the best player to have represented both clubs. A non-Scouse factor may help too, as neither fanbase can feel let down that he abandoned them or that Beardsley was 'one of them'. Even with a direct transfer from Liverpool to Everton, many still appreciate everything he did for the Reds and then with the Blues. There are, no doubt, players who are better appreciated by an individual club but, during his six-year spell on Merseyside, the Hexham-born attacking midfielder somehow managed to unite a city in mutual appreciation of his talents.

The usual task of hopping from club to club on the journey before and after a player's arrival would take up half a book in this case. Starting his career with Newcastle United, a place where Beardsley's heart did appear to truly lie, he managed to hop teams rather intriguingly, with spells at Carlisle United, Vancouver Whitecaps, Manchester United, back to Newcastle and then finally over to Liverpool. The end of his career was even more nomadic but thankfully the bulk of this tale can be told from 1987 to 1993, although there's no place to fully cover his attempt at the rap in 'World in Motion' (you need to watch that).

As mentioned with Steve McMahon, Kenny Dalglish was building a new squad, and the signings of John Barnes and Beardsley, partnered with local scoring hero John Aldridge, provided one of the most exciting line-ups in English football. The magical Geordie certainly didn't appear to look like a superstar but as soon as he got a ball at his feet things started to happen. Like many who came before and will come after him, though, the initial stint in red showed the burden of being the club's record signing for £1.9m, and the presence of Barnes on the other wing was both a help and a hindrance.

With Barnes shining, Beardsley was initially compared to him but also the focus was purely on the Watford man, so some forgot about the Geordie's price tag. In his first 20 matches for the Reds, there were only four goals for the big-money transfer but, with the team sitting top of the league, it was clear that Dalglish had faith in the talents of his new man. As 1987 became 1988 though, something clicked and the 27-year-old began playing like the player everyone had been waiting to arrive.

In January alone, Beardsley scored six times, with one finish against Arsenal the pick of the bunch. Commentator for the day, John Motson, described the hype around the match with the Gunners:

> It's another sell-out at Anfield, in a season where gates have frequently been closed an hour before kick-off. Seats are so hard to get that even John Barnes was turned away from the Liverpool ticket office when he tried to buy some yesterday. His birthplace Jamaica is one of over 50 countries that will watch the BBC coverage of this match, 10 are taking the transmission live. Jan Mølby is working for the Danish TV and Michel Platini is here for the French and their projected worldwide audience is 200 million, the biggest ever it's said, for an English league game.

The Reds won 2-0 and Beardsley entertained the millions watching. He collected the ball in the middle of the pitch, pushed it past one defender, through the legs of Michael Thomas, before delightfully chipping it over an onrushing John Lukic. The Kop showed their appreciation with a chorus of 'There's only one Peter Beardsley' ringing out around the ground. He certainly impressed the watching Platini too, who said, 'It was a Continental performance. Liverpool played their football on the ground. Arsenal were more typically English, playing the ball through the air. Beardsley's goal might have been scored by a top French or Italian player.'

In all, Beardsley scored 18 goals in 48 appearances in his maiden season for the Reds, which saw Dalglish's team win the league. Beardsley was a mercurial talent and the only criticism could come in the form of him not scoring enough goals, especially due to the number of times he was ripping open defences and the powerful shot he had showcased on multiple occasions. He worked so hard on the pitch too, and his combination of talent and work ethic made him a dream player to manage and a darling of the crowd.

Speaking with the FA about this time, Beardsley said:

> Barnesy looked after me unbelievably. In my first season we went 29 league games unbeaten, and I was rubbish, I mean that honestly and I don't want any sympathy for that. Up until Christmas, I was really, really poor and scored about two goals before Christmas. I end up with 15 and with about six or seven games to go I scored the winning goal against Tottenham, which won us the league. It was amazing because I had genuinely been rubbish but in the papers the next day it was 'Beardsley wins the league for Liverpool', which obviously wasn't true but it was unbelievable to have something like that said about you.

The next season saw the return of Ian Rush, but the 1988/89 season will always be remembered for three events that have been touched on already. The Hillsborough disaster overshadowed all footballing events for that campaign. The Reds lost the title in the last match to Arsenal in a month in which Dalglish's team were forced to play eight times in May because of the postponed fixtures that followed the tragic events in Sheffield. Three matches in six days started with the FA Cup Final, which went to extra time, then ended in heartbreak in that final match of the campaign in the final minute against Arsenal.

With the events of Hillsborough and then the league lost, the only solace was the Merseyside FA Cup Final. Beardsley played the full match and, in a pre-match interview with *MATCH* magazine, Steve McMahon was as kind to his team-mate as he was soft in his tackling: 'Known to team-mates as "Quasi" (as in "Quasimodo"), Peter and I are in competition for the worst haircut at the club. He looks like he had his cut while wearing a helmet whereas I haven't had enough hair to cut in three years! "Quasi" is a quiet bloke off the pitch who rarely says too much.' The final ended 3-2 after extra time and Ian Rush was again the derby hero.

Although both clubs would have desperately wanted to win the cup, the day was about more than football. After the tragic events in the semi-final of the competition, the city was not only mourning the loss of 96 supporters but also the cover-up and adverse reaction that was already taking place within the police, stadium officials and the media. Scousers were being painted as hooligans and criminals, rather than giving everyone else in the country what they wanted to see – the city and the two football teams united in a spectacle of football, kinship and humanity. Blue and red again stood side by side and the city was together in the face of tragedy.

Beardsley was part of the team that bounced back from the football heartache of 1989 to win the league again in 1989/90. It started with some revenge against Arsenal at Wembley in the Charity Shield, with a Barry Venison cross finding Beardsley at the back post – he lifted the ball calmly over Lukic to score the only goal of the match. This helped restore confidence and prove that the previous season's league loss was purely down to the unfair fixture scheduling that offered little sympathy for the harrowing events at Hillsborough.

Despite winning the league in 1989/90 and a successful start to the campaign that followed, Dalglish resigned and in came Graeme Souness. During this period, Beardsley was still a crucial member of the team but some minor injuries did pave the way for some short spells on the bench. He still played more than 30 times in each of his Anfield campaigns though, playing against no team more than Everton (14 times) and scoring more goals against them (six) than any other team. His final Merseyside derby goals came in Dalglish's final match as manager, the third derby in 11 days and 21st in five years, but none had been as dramatic.

Beardsley returned for his first start in over two months and made a quick impact, as reported by *The Times*: '[Kevin] Ratcliffe, in turn, contributed to Everton's initial downfall when he failed to control a clearance directed by [Steve] Staunton along a touchline in the 34th minute. [Ian] Rush accelerated away from one of his Welsh colleagues before bemusing another, [Neville] Southall. Although [Andy] Hinchcliffe blocked his attempt on the line, the rebound fell for Beardsley, who scored.'

His name again rang out as the Liverpool supporters inside Goodison Park celebrated the opening goal. Graeme Sharp restored parity within two minutes of the second half, his header beating Bruce Grobbelaar in goal. However, Beardsley was again to make an impact. 'Beardsley relieved Liverpool's uncertainty in the 72nd minute with a goal of pure inspiration. Using the mobility he had shown throughout the evening, he deliberately threaded a pass along the edge of the area before unleashing a firm and measured drive beyond the reach of Southall.'

Beardsley had proved that the demands of the Liverpool supporters for him to return to the team were right and he looked like being the star of the match but there was plenty more to come. Steve Nicol gifted Sharp his second goal, before Ian Rush scored a customary derby goal – all three goals coming within six minutes. Tony Cottee saved the tie with a last-minute equaliser, as he got in behind Gary Ablett for a calm finish.

Extra time followed, and it was the turn of John Barnes to score, with the famous front three for the Reds having all found the back of Neville Southall's net. Despite the brilliance of Beardsley's earlier strike, it was Barnes who provided the pick of the bunch with a magnificent curling finish into the top corner with his weaker foot. Howard Kendall was to be rewarded for his team's efforts, with Cottee again proving to be a late-scoring hero. It was another mix-up at the back for Dalglish's team but another example of a determined and resolute Everton.

It was a spectacle of Merseyside football once again, with four equalising goals for Everton, who left the pitch the happier and then won the second replay of the tie a week later. Dalglish had gone, though, and Beardsley only played 14 more times for the Reds, following Ronnie Moran's stint as caretaker. Only four of these appearances were under Souness.

Much like had happened with McMahon, the new boss was quick to change the way things were done at Anfield. Although a place in the team hadn't been assured under Dalglish, it was the new manager's decision that saw Beardsley leave the club. He was now a 30-year-old and it seemed as if Souness was sure his talents were on a decline, so the Geordie was swiftly shown the door after the arrival of Dean Saunders.

Everton were also in the market for Saunders but, with the Reds sealing the deal for him, they were forced to take up their second option – Peter Beardsley. The £1m fee spent on the England international in August 1991 proved to be a bargain and, as is so often the case with these deals, the

Merseyside derby was to be played in the same month as his arrival, so the former Red returned to Anfield.

In contrast to the treatment of McMahon, the previous man to cross the park, Beardsley was welcomed back to his old club as a hero. The Kop sang 'There's only one Peter Beardsley!' in thanks of his four seasons as a Red and in another example of the positive relations between clubs, even up to the 1990s. David Burrows opened the scoring within a minute and Souness's team defeated Kendall's 3-1. Beardsley recorded an assist for Mike Newell's goal but it was his reception from the Liverpool fans that would be the lasting memory: 'Just before the game the Kop chanted my name and I don't suppose that's happened too many times, an Everton player getting his name chanted by the Kop. But during the game, with Liverpool winning, the crowd started to chant, "What a waste of talent!" The Kop were a bit special to me on that day and I won't ever forget it.'

The playful second chant was again nothing more than that, and it was a truly unique moment of appreciation for a former hero. Now though, Beardsley was a Blue and was again fighting to hold down a consistent role in Kendall's team. He was the fifth player in the past 30 years to have swapped clubs but few have been as loved by both sides. The Geordie became an idol of Evertonians, despite just two seasons and starring in a relatively mediocre team.

His famed individual bursts of talent saw him score 32 times in 95 appearances and show everyone that he was still more than able to produce performances of supreme quality. His tireless effort for the team again endeared him to another set of supporters and, performing alongside the likes of Dave Watson and Martin Keown, they helped keep the fans enthused in a difficult season where the Blues finished 12th. One thing the Evertonians could hold over their rivals, though, was that not only had they captured the signing of one of their favourites but he had arrived for a third of the price of Saunders and finished the campaign with more goals.

A personal highlight for Beardsley came against Coventry City at Goodison Park, where the Geordie scored a sublime hat-trick for his new club. His first was fortunate, after a poor clearance from ex-Blue Brian Borrows hit the Geordie and found the back of the net. His second, though, was the best finish of the day, a flash of Beardsley magic that could be added to his collection of brilliant goals. On the edge of the box he struck the ball on the turn and found the top corner of the net. His third was a penalty, converted expertly into the bottom corner of Steve Ogrizovic's net. The England international's new home echoed with the sound of 'There's only one Peter Beardsley!'

The next season was a drab affair, Kendall's team failing to excite the crowd too much in the maiden Premier League campaign. There was one highlight though, of course provided by Beardsley. Goodison Park hosted Liverpool in December 1992 and, with the teams in 17th (Everton) and tenth (Liverpool), the drop-off from the golden years of past meetings was abundantly clear for all to see.

Mark Wright headed home from a Mike Marsh corner to open the scoring on the day, to welcome chants of 'going down' from the travelling Reds. Mo Johnston silenced those shouts with a brilliant left-footed effort past Mike Hooper in goal. With just over five minutes to go, the match turned on its head when Beardsley and Gary Ablett played a one-two around the Liverpool defence and the 31-year-old thundered a right-footed effort home to win the derby in some style. Thus, Beardsley became the second man, after David Johnson, to score for both clubs in the derby. His celebrations that followed would have only endeared him further to Evertonians and, when the match ended, his legacy was secured. It was Everton's first league victory in the derby in nine attempts and only their second home win of the campaign.

Some supporters ran on to the field to celebrate with the midfielder, his feet were kissed and some bowed down to their knees to worship their new hero. Everton weren't in a great place but Beardsley had helped deliver a huge moment that ensured they didn't enter too severe a relegation scrap in the maiden season of a new era of football. He and Gary Ablett had also shown that Souness and Liverpool's decision to sell to the Blues certainly hadn't worked out.

In need of money, an offer of £1.5m for Beardsley would see Everton make a profit on a player who, although being a rare shining light in the season, was now 32 years old. His hometown club Newcastle United was also a big lure for the experienced midfielder. With the Everton board not being in a position to turn down the handsome fee, it was time for his Merseyside story to come to an end. Kevin Keegan secured the signing of his former team-mate and St James' Park was again to be blessed with his talents.

Four seasons with Newcastle were to follow, before a move to Bolton, a loan with Manchester City, a loan and then permanent deal with Fulham, two seasons with Hartlepool and finally a career that ended as a 38-year-old with Melbourne Knights. Coaching within the England and then Newcastle set-up followed too. Looking back on his whole career though, it seems that the decision of Manchester United to hand him just one League Cup appearance and sell him for £150,000 as a 22-year-old was the worst of the lot, although Newcastle twice paying for his services was also a poor financial decision on their part. For a man to represent both Merseyside and Manchester clubs is also not a move that has been repeated by anyone else.

Liverpool's decision to offload Beardsley for just £1m in 1991 seems even more baffling when he went on to play seven more seasons in the First Division and Premier League and played nearly 300 further matches. Souness certainly could have utilised the talents that were still clearly with the England international, who made 11 further appearances for his country during this time too. Everton were, of course, the first benefactors of Liverpool's poor transfer decision and, had the Goodison club been better when he was with them, there's no doubt he could have helped lead the team to silverware.

With the demise of Beardsley's Merseyside career being Liverpool selling him too early and Everton not being of his standard when they signed him, it helps to explain why he's loved by both clubs. Steve McMahon worked so hard on the pitch for both teams but abandoned his roots in search of silverware and increased wages, before then joining the club he was supposed to be opposed to after being raised as a Blue. Beardsley, though, was a man who also gave 100 per cent effort but, having no personal ties to either club, and his exits easily being explained by other mitigating circumstances, his transfers could be easily understood by supporters, so they appreciated everything he did for them.

Liverpool would certainly be the club more aggrieved, after seeing a player leave who was supposed to understand the club but, with it being so glaringly obvious that his departure can be blamed on Souness, this ill feeling certainly didn't transpire within the masses.

Beardsley probably holds the crown of being the most-respected and best-performing player to have represented both clubs with distinction. The interesting thing is that McMahon probably had a better, or at least similar, impact at Goodison Park but the way in which he moved between clubs means he's hated by Everton supporters, but Reds and Blues alike share a love and respect for Beardsley.

Gary Ablett

Name	Gareth Ian Ablett
Born	19/11/1965, Liverpool
Died	01/01/2012, Tarleton, Lancashire
Liverpool stats	147 matches/1 goal (1986–92)
Liverpool honours	First Division 1987/88, 1989/90, FA Cup 1989
Everton stats	156 matches/6 goals (1992–96)
Everton honours	FA Cup 1995
Combined stats	303 matches/7 goals (1986–96)
Direct transfer?	Yes (signed for EFC from LFC for £750,000 on 13/01/1992)
Remembered (%)	LFC 100%/EFC 100%/Ave. 100%
Legend (out of 10)	LFC 5.8/EFC 6.1/Ave. 6.0
Traitor (out of 10)	LFC 5.6

THE FINAL entry on this list to have won silverware with both Liverpool and Everton is another man who sees his legacy have a mutually accepted level of appreciation for his talents, services and loyalty on both sides of Stanley Park.

From the creative and attacking players that have preceded here, Gary Ablett adds a more defensive and perhaps less enthralling footballing twist to proceedings. Not since Neil McBain, who crossed the park in 1928, have we seen a defender covered, so this provides some variation on the above. Ablett's name lives on as rhyming slang in the city for a tablet but his legacy on the pitch is so much more than that. We may have zero Merseyside derby goals to ponder (although an assist was covered earlier), which seems unimaginable when the almost inevitable moments of irony came before too, but there are still so many interesting matches and stories to cover.

In Ablett, though, there's a defender who has the distinction of being the only player to have won the FA Cup in red and blue and a man who also went on to coach both clubs at youth level. Unfortunately though, it's also a story with a tragically abrupt ending.

Ablett joined Liverpool as a 15-year-old and worked his way up to the first team, much like Steve McMahon at Everton. However, unlike many that have come before, there never seemed to be a guaranteed place in Dalglish's team for the Scouser, so he found himself in and out of the team, covering for injuries and fatigue. Such was the success of the Reds at this time, though, that despite playing well whenever called upon, he found himself back out of the squad. Elegant on the ball, tough-tackling and with a tall and skinny build, he certainly looked set for a decent career.

Scoring and assisting on his home debut may have had Liverpool supporters thinking they had unearthed a goal threat too, but as this was his only goal in 147 appearances, that wasn't to be the case. His performance in that match against Nottingham Forest, attracted attention from *The Times*, which reported: 'For one so young, Ablett produced a quite memorable display. He carried out his defensive duties with elegant poise and underlined his rich potential by scoring Liverpool's third goal after 68 minutes with a quite delightful volley.' The joy on his face after the goal was a joy to behold.

Competition with Gary Gillespie and Barry Venison proved tough but Ablett never shirked the challenge of trying to impress the manager and get into the squad. He made his debut as a 21-year-old and spent six seasons battling to hold down a starting role at Anfield. It did always seem that the defender was never going to be the long-term option and always had to prove his worth. He never let anyone down though, and this was a quality that lasted throughout his life.

Versatility can often work against some players, and Ablett was viewed as a man who could come and fill a role, keeping it warm for someone else, his ability to play across the back four being invaluable. Being a boyhood Red perhaps allowed the defender to be more patient than his talents may have deserved. There were 49 appearances in the 1988/89 season, which has already been covered, but the defender was also given the start at Wembley.

The meeting with Everton in the FA Cup Final saw Liverpool dominate, but a fourth-minute finish by John Aldridge (assisted by Steve McMahon) wouldn't be followed by any more goals until Stuart McCall dragged the Blues back into the match with an 89th-minute finish that took the final into extra time. Ian Rush then proved to be the difference, scoring either side of another McCall goal that he volleyed in brilliantly. The season ended in defeat to Arsenal but also soon saw the arrival of Glenn Hysén. The Swedish defender swooped in and took Ablett's place in the team, which he had marshalled superbly for an entire campaign that should have ended in double success.

Now almost 24 years old, Ablett certainly had time but few would disagree if Ablett had started to wonder what more he could do. He was playing in a tremendous team that was successful but just wasn't quite *the* man for Dalglish to trust for an entire campaign. In the new Swedish centre-half, Steve Staunton, David Burrows, Barry Venison and the experienced Alan Hansen, competition was tough. However, a sign that the club still trusted the Scouser was the decision to reject an approach from Middlesbrough for his services.

Gary Gillespie's fitness struggles opened the door to more appearance in 1990/91 but the Anfield story changed for everyone when Souness took charge. It was initially a positive appointment for the Scouser, whose fortunes changed in terms of playing time, but the team was getting worse in terms of results. The defender was in the team for the first half of the season but when Everton came in with a bid of £750,000 it was agreed that it was time for Ablett to go where he would receive the first-team football his years of service at Anfield deserved.

The moral dilemma of those that came before in this list, particularly with Scousers, was still present for Ablett when he agreed to leave Anfield. It was certainly a move that made sense for his career progression but, seeing as he had waited so long to get a place in the team, even with a drop in quality since Souness took over, it does seem like a strange time to give up on your dream of representing your boyhood club as a mainstay of the team. Perhaps having seen the likes of McMahon and Beardsley depart Anfield also helped ensure that it was the right time to leave the Reds behind. It was an era of transition, mainly because the new manager had accelerated the need for this to happen, so it made sense. If not now, then when could the 26-year-old go and make a name for himself? It felt too that Ablett had left Anfield with the blessing of the Liverpool fans, something that no doubt would have made the decision easier.

Signing for Everton in January 1992, Ablett was immediately a key part of Kendall's team and played every match for the remainder of the campaign, missing just two in the following season. Beardsley, who arrived five months before Ablett, was the key man for the team and was trusted by Kendall to have a consistent role in proceedings with the Blues.

The season of 1993/94 saw the introduction of permanent shirt numbers, so the No.6 settled even further into the team, but the Blues were struggling. Fewer than 14,000 supporters attended a 1-0 victory over Southampton and Kendall's second spell as Everton boss came to an end when he resigned after the match. Everton were in 11th place, so by no means in a crisis, but there had been some serious stagnation. There hadn't been a trophy since the First Division title in 1987 and, other than losing the FA Cup Final in 1989, there hadn't looked to be much of a chance of one coming.

Again, it seemed, Ablett was a trusted man but in an unsuccessful team in transition. After being a mainstay over the past two seasons, new manager Mike Walker dropped him after his fifth match as manager and the Scouser didn't return to the squad until they were firmly in a relegation battle. He played four of the final five matches of the season, which culminated against Wimbledon at Goodison Park. Everton began the day in the relegation zone, behind Ipswich, Sheffield United and Southampton, all by a single point. A win was essential but not a guarantee of avoiding relegation for what would be just the third time in the club's history.

Anders Limpar's decision to handle the ball in the box after just four minutes to give Wimbledon the opportunity to score from the spot was ridiculous, the spot kick being converted. Ablett tried to restore the deadlock after a Kevin Sheedy free kick soon after but it didn't beat Hans Segers in goal. Calamity followed as Dave Unsworth and David Watson challenged each other for the ball, before Ablett then deflected Andy Clarke's effort past Neville Southall to double Wimbledon's lead. Anders Limpar's questionable clash with Peter Fear resulted in a penalty in the 25th minute, Graham Stuart scoring to add some belief into Goodison Park that the great escape was again possible.

The visitors had several chances in the first and second half to extend their lead and, with little over 20 minutes remaining, the Blues were going down. That was until a rocket from Barry Horne, who belted a volley into the top corner, so what seemed like such an unlikely victory was now again possible. The magic moment that followed was to be converted by Stuart, whose side-footed effort provided his second of the day. Now fingers had to be crossed for results to stay in Everton's favour. Full time still hadn't guaranteed survival but moments later it was rubber-stamped and the Blues were safe.

When Ablett put the ball into his own net, he must have felt that relegation was secured and he would be handed a huge portion of blame. Instead they could plan for another Premier League season, one that wasn't set to be too much more successful but did end in an FA Cup Final. Joe Royle was to take over as boss after a poor run of results for Walker. In the cup, Everton defeated Derby County, Bristol City, Norwich City, Newcastle United and Tottenham on the way to the big match.

Alex Ferguson's Manchester United were big favourites in the final, finishing 13 places above the Blues, but Royle's 'Dogs of War' were out for an upset. After half an hour, Paul Rideout converted after Graham Stuart's effort rebounded off the bar. That was to be all that was needed for glory and Ablett helped keep United out for the rest of the match. The Scouser was interviewed afterwards and was asked about the significance of winning the trophy for the whole city of Liverpool: 'Liverpool have ended up with the Coca Cola Cup and we've got the FA Cup. Red and blue, it'll be all families together and people will be celebrating all around Liverpool tonight.'

That was to be the final major achievement in Ablett's Merseyside playing career, as the following season saw him play second fiddle to Andy Hinchcliffe. A loan move to Sheffield United followed, before moves to Birmingham City, Wycombe, Blackpool and Long Island Rough Riders in the United States. Retiring as the only man to have won the FA Cup with both clubs, it then became a pick of the clubs for Ablett as a coach too. He started with Everton Under-17s for four years, before winning the league during a three-year stint as Liverpool Under-21 boss.

Ablett also took a step up to senior management with Stockport County. He was set to join the Ipswich coaching staff in 2010 but was taken ill during a training session. What followed was the devastating news of his diagnosis of suffering from Non-Hodgkin lymphoma. This blood cancer led to a 17-month battle with illness during which the former defender was nothing but a shining beacon of positivity and inspired many with the way in which he remained so resolute.

In January 2012 it was announced that Ablett had died. He was just 46 years old and his funeral within the city united both red and blue once more. It seemed as though no one in the city, no one in football, had a bad word to say about Gary, and his tragic death was a huge shock and crushing blow to so many people across Merseyside.

In terms of his playing legacy and place on this list, Ablett was a boyhood Red who was so well respected that even leaving for Everton didn't diminish the respect that the Anfield faithful had for him. He perhaps wasn't as talented as some of the names that have most recently been covered here but he was a committed, hard-working, loyal and respectful man and footballer. He was probably unfortunate to find himself playing for both clubs when he did, although the famous FA Cup medals he won will ensure that his legacy within the history of both clubs will never be forgotten.

David Burrows

Name	David Burrows
Born	25/10/1968, Dudley
Liverpool stats	193 matches/3 goals (1988–93)
Liverpool honours	First Division 1989/90, FA Cup 1992
Everton stats	23 matches/0 goals (1994–95)
Everton honours	None
Combined stats	216 matches/3 goals (1988–95)
Direct transfer?	No
Remembered (%)	LFC 83%/EFC 77%/Ave. 80%
Legend (out of 10)	LFC 5.5/EFC 4.6/Ave. 5.1
Traitor (out of 10)	LFC 5

THE INITIAL aim for this book was to speak to as many living members of this celebrated and unique set of players as possible. With exhaustive tactics and avenues pursued in order to get to speak to each and every person, eventually it was successful with David Burrows. Unfortunately, not with any other individual though. Because of this we have a slightly different look at the career of the former full-back, thanks to the generosity of the Midlands-born defender.

Because the questions about his career that work best around this book could be asked and answered directly, there seems little need to interrupt the story when it's been so well told by the man himself. Other than the unforgivable lack of questioning about deputising for Bruce Grobbelaar when the goalkeeper was sent off during a European match against

Spartak Moscow, here's David Burrows on his career with Liverpool and Everton.

Growing up outside the city, what was your perception of Liverpool and Everton as a youngster and did you have a favourite?

For me it was more so Liverpool because of the European nights in the 1970s, which we used to watch all the time because Liverpool were always my second team. I was a West Brom fan as a kid but watching Liverpool on the TV and seeing Anfield and the Kop, Kevin Keegan and John Toshack, they are the memories I have. Not too much notice was taken in our house of Everton at the time, so it was always the red side of Merseyside that caught my eye.

In 1988 you completed your move to Liverpool. Was there any interest from Everton at that time?

Yes, well funnily enough I went to Everton as a kid as a 14-year-old. I was sent by a local scout up to Bellfield for the day, I watched a game and then I was introduced to some of the staff at Everton. I later received two letters from the club wanting me to sign as a schoolboy, with the potential of an apprenticeship with them later on. I've still got those letters at home. Actually my mum kept them but that didn't work out. I was still a 'home boy', I had a close family and didn't really want to move too far from where I grew up.

As a Liverpool player you won the First Division and the FA Cup. What was your favourite memory from your time at Anfield?

Winning the championship as a footballer is a big, big thing, as I'm sure you know. To win a league championship is the absolute ultimate and, once you have got a league championship under your belt, you know you go into a different category as a player and as a club. But me being able to get my hands on the FA Cup was a close second.

As a kid I grew up watching every FA Cup Final from about 1974 until now really, so that was a big deal as well for me. But lifting that trophy at Anfield when we won the championship, it's what every player wants to achieve in their career, and I was lucky enough to achieve that.

Little did everyone know how long it would take for it to happen again at Liverpool!

What was your favourite derby moment against Everton?

It would obviously have to be my goal. I've never lost a Merseyside derby playing for both clubs actually, so I have got a good record from that point of view. My memory of my goal for Liverpool was that it was after a couple of minutes, and it was very early in the match. It was against Neville Southall at the Kop end and it's a moment in my life I will never forget. For someone to score in the Kop end in the Merseyside derby, it was very special – it really was.

What was your worst memory in the Merseyside derby?

My worst memory was my first derby. I had a bit of a torrid time. I hadn't been there very long, it was a televised match and Trevor Steven was playing against me as outside-right for Everton and I had a tough day. I gave a penalty away as well, which didn't help too.

When you came to leave Liverpool, was it hard to make that decision or was the decision made for you?

It was a change of regime more than anything. Kenny had gone, Ronnie Moran took over in the interim and, when you're used to someone for two or three years and all of a sudden all that has changed, it was a complete change.

With Kenny, you always felt it was okay to go and speak to him, there was a genuine warmth about him, but I never felt that with Graeme [Souness]. Graeme always seemed to keep himself away from the players but Kenny, you always felt more comfortable with Kenny, well I did personally, in Kenny's company. I didn't with Graeme, I'm not saying that was Graeme's fault, it's just how I felt and that's my fault as well. But I never felt Graeme appreciated myself personally and one or two others.

This was a championship-winning team from two years previous and within 12 months of Graeme's arrival at Anfield the team had been completely depleted. Players were going out left, right and centre and other players were coming in. Were they Liverpool players? Should Liverpool have been interested with players like that at that time?

I always felt on edge and I wasn't comfortable. The first thing was I got injured and I wasn't fit to play. Then he brought me into his office and said, 'Look, I'm bringing someone else in and I want you to go in exchange.' I had just signed a contract, this is crazy, I just signed a five-year contract, literally six months before, perhaps even less than that. Then, all of a sudden, he wants me to go on a part-exchange with someone. Obviously that's a manager who is not sure of what he wants.

If he wanted me to go or as an exchange, there is no way he would have offered me a new five-year contract, so not only did he now want me to go, he was going to have to pay me a lot of money as well, which is not good business at the end of the day, so his judgement was not very clear. That's how I saw it for me personally and I felt 'no, I'm not going to win this guy over, I think it is better for me that I have a change'.

As soon as I spoke to the West Ham contingency, when you have got Harry Redknapp in your living room and Billy Bonds pleading with you, 'Please, we want you to come, you will be a massive part of our club, we need people like you,' I thought right, let's give it a go.

So that's how it came about, I just felt I wasn't wanted by Graeme like I was with Kenny, so when it was like that, I thought the best thing to do was maybe move on.

How important to your career was Kenny Dalglish?
Well, he was one of the best and nicest and most genuine people I've ever met in my life.

When you left to join West Ham, was there any interest from Everton then?
No, not at all, not an inkling there was a possibility of Everton being interested at all. I think it happened so quickly that I don't think there was time for other clubs to get involved. At the time it was done so quickly my agent didn't have time to put the word around for a few weeks that I might be available, so it was done and dusted very quickly.

Had Everton made the move, would you have been tempted at that time?
Yes, I think so. I knew a couple of others that had done it. I knew Gary Ablett, who I was close to at the time and he had done it and made a success of it. Peter Beardsley, who I roomed with for a few years at Liverpool and I had kept in contact with, had done it as well.

Whether Peter was as happy as Gary, I don't know but he had made the move, so I wasn't worried about that because I knew other people had done it. Looking back now as I'm a lot older, there is a lot more added pressure and vice versa, from one club to the other.

Apart from my first-ever derby, which I have spoken about previously, I always seemed to play quite well, I always seemed to have a good game. I was instrumental in something in the derbies with my aggression against some of the other players on the Everton side, which the Liverpool fans seemed to enjoy, so I wasn't sure how popular I was at Everton but, with hindsight, it possibly was the best move for me to go to West Ham.

What was your opinion of Liverpool on the day you left?

I was heartbroken really. I didn't have time to take it all in, perhaps a good job in a way because I would have refused to go, I think, if I had had a few days to think about it. I wouldn't have gone, I would maybe have fought for my place, sat in the reserves and done it that way, but I was heartbroken. To play for Liverpool, to win a championship, to win the FA Cup, and with all my family. I had a son who had settled in really well on the Wirral and, you know, it's an upheaval and I was upset to leave, but at the time I knew it was right. The team was losing ground and the players that were coming into the club were not replacing the ones that were going out and it was a matter of time before there was a decline and that is exactly what happened.

What do you think your legacy is at Liverpool?

Good question; my legacy is, I just like to think, that I was an honest lad and gave everything for the shirt, that would be my legacy. As I have said before, I wasn't the most gifted of left-backs that Liverpool have had but what I did was I made sure that, when I went out on the pitch, I made sure there was nothing left when I finished and that was my goal. You maybe have to ask a few of the hardcore Scousers though.

When you left Liverpool, what were your thoughts of Everton as a club?

Everton was always a big club. I remember when I played at West Brom in the reserves, you used to play at Goodison Park and I always used to think, 'This is a lovely club, it really is.' With the history they had, don't forget they had a really good run in the mid-80s when they were a top team, and we all watched the Andy Grays and the Peter Reids and Derek Mountfield. They had a great tradition as well, so it definitely would have been a club I would have liked to play for at some point.

What was your opinion of Everton fans as you left Liverpool?

I didn't really have an opinion at that time. They were playing catch-up with Liverpool and perhaps had begun the struggle of playing second fiddle to Liverpool, after their success in the 80s. I had always had a bit of banter with the Everton fans when I was on the pitch, they obviously didn't really like me as an opposition player. Whether they would have liked me as one of their own I don't know, maybe you would have to ask some of those. When I played in the derbies I knew the Everton fans didn't like me because of the way I was. I was sort of a little bit aggressive, wanted to win and obviously that antagonises the opposite fans.

The decision to leave Liverpool, would you do that again?

Under the same circumstances, yes, under the same scenario today, yes, I would.

If Kenny had still been there or Ronnie or Roy, no not at all. I think when you leave Liverpool, I always thought, unless you were going to somewhere like Man United, it was sort of a step down, it was definitely a step down and that was evident all the way through the rest of my career after leaving Liverpool. There was nothing that touched the same sort of heights, if you like, not only on the pitch but the same heights as a club, nothing got near it afterwards but at least I had won the championship and been involved in two FA Cup finals, and that is something nobody can take away from you. I have my medals and my record is there. I am happy with all of it.

You spent one year at West Ham before your move to Everton. What attracted you to Goodison?

Well, we couldn't settle in London. We had done our best but the life difference between Liverpool and London is extreme. For five and a half years we had been used to a life and we had to change it completely and we found it difficult as a family. I found it difficult as a player and, again, going from Liverpool to West Ham, I had to adapt to the club. I don't want to say anything derogatory against West Ham, but it wasn't at the same level as Liverpool, of course it wasn't, but I knew that and I knew I was going to be a bigger fish in a smaller pond, where before I was a small fish in a big pond at Liverpool. We just couldn't settle and, at the end of the day, I spoke to my agent, and I said, 'Can you put the word around that I might be available?' and he spoke to several clubs. We spoke to Ron [Atkinson] at Aston Villa but they couldn't afford the money at that time. They had spent their budget. He told me to hang on for another season, but we couldn't do that.

Then I got a phone call from my agent that Mike Walker was interested and would I be interested in going to Everton? So, you've got two options: to go home to the Midlands, that was my priority, there was no two ways about that; I would have signed for Ron Atkinson the next day. I would have walked up the motorway to sign for him but that didn't come about. So, I thought, 'right then, okay, we will go back to

Merseyside and move back into our house', which we hadn't sold by the way.

So, we were straight back into our routine but I am playing on the Blue side rather than the Red side. I didn't hesitate at all after I had spoken to Mike Walker, who I had found very enthusiastic; I didn't know him at all until I had spoken to him at Everton. He needed a little bit of help as well. He was struggling to get results and hadn't found the balance that he wanted and I thought, 'Yes, let's have a go.' I quite liked the man personally and that always helps if you get on really well with your manager.

Did being a former Liverpool player affect your decision?

Yes, I suppose I thought about it, I knew there was going to be consequences and hostilities even, but my family life was as important as my career at that point, if not more important. Had to have my family settled, so I didn't really think too much about what it was going to cause. I knew West Ham were really, really disappointed for me to go, that's for sure, but once a player sets his mind on going, you might as well let them go because it is the start of the end.

Do you think moving to Everton has affected your legacy as a Liverpool player?

Good question! I think it all depends on who you speak to, I don't know, I couldn't answer that from my point of view. I would like to think it didn't but then what the general feeling is of players who have gone from Liverpool to Everton, what sort of legacy they have left, I don't know if it's affected their legacy.

Do you regret moving to Everton, looking back?

Football-wise, yes, I do regret it. Like we have just touched on before, maybe it did damage my five years at Liverpool, I don't know. Football-wise, I wasn't in good shape when I left West Ham. My 12 months had been reasonably successful on the football pitch, but I went to Everton probably in the worst condition I was as a footballer throughout my career. It was a battle to get fit straightaway. I had one or two little problems with my back, which we were trying to hide when I was playing with painkillers and what not, so it wasn't a good period really for me to go and play for Everton. If I had signed for them maybe two years later, then they would have seen a different player, that is without a shadow of a doubt, but if I had stayed in London, my football would have stagnated, that's for sure, and I wouldn't have got out of it if I had stayed there another 12 months or two years longer.

If a Liverpool fan had walked up to you in the street and called you a traitor, would you have agreed or thought that was too harsh?

I would have said, 'I get it completely, I get where you are coming from but am I traitor because I signed for Everton or am I traitor because I left Liverpool?' This is another question.

I would agree with them to a certain extent, from a football point of view. Yes, perhaps I was a traitor but I didn't want to leave Liverpool Football Club in the first place. I was pushed out so I don't feel as though I'm being a traitor, I feel as though I was pushed out of the club and just because I have gone and played for their local rivals that doesn't make me a traitor, but I get his point of view as well because, obviously, it's their club.

Did anything like that ever happen?

Once or twice but, again, as I have said to you before, I have never had a situation at Liverpool or on Merseyside where I didn't like what was coming out of someone's mouth that was aggressive or nasty or really derogatory. I've never had that situation, maybe I didn't go out enough, I don't know! But no, I've never had anyone insult me in the streets of Merseyside, no.

I did spend a lot of time in the city as well. I still have a lot of friends there; we go back now and again to see them. We still have banter. I still get 'remember that game when you were shite?!' I say, 'Yeah, I do agree with you, I remember the shit ones, but I remember the good ones as well!' I will always say something positive like, 'What about that cross I made for the winning goal when we won at Man City,' or something, 'Oh yeah, yeah, yeah.' So, we still have that banter.

That is the good thing about it, I always remember my time at both clubs, that the people there always had banter and they managed to make a joke out of everything and that is what you miss as well. When you go to other cities, you do, you miss that.

Did Liverpool show any interest before you moved to Everton?

Yes, we had spoken to Roy [Evans] and he was very keen for me to come back once Graeme [Souness] had left but they had Julian Dicks there, so I said, 'What is the point?' I know they were trying to get Steve Staunton back as well. For me and Steve [Staunton], Ronnie [Moran] and Roy [Evans], well we were their sort of prodigies if you like. Ronnie and Roy moulded me and then moulded Steve as well, so they knew that they were getting 100 per cent when they came back in for me and for Steve. But I wasn't in a position. There is no way West Ham would let me go back but Steve went back, and he had had a really successful time at Villa as well. As soon as Steve went from Villa, I got a phone call from Ron [Atkinson], so it's a bit of a merry-go-round, isn't it? I ended up playing for Ron in the end, he got me when I went to

Coventry from Everton, so I ended up playing for him again in the end.

When you signed for Everton, who did you think was the best team on Merseyside at that time?

At that time, Liverpool were the better side but they were declining, they couldn't maintain the standards. Graeme had, sort of, well from my point of view, he had taken the club backwards to a certain degree and he certainly didn't progress the club in his time there. But some managers win, some managers lose and that is the chance you take, but I felt Liverpool were a club in decline at that point.

You weren't at Goodison long but what was your favourite memory as a player?

I think it was playing with Big Dunc, I loved him. He was a big inspiration. I loved just being on the pitch with Duncan [Ferguson]. I was fortunate enough to cross a couple of balls to him for a couple of his goals and the biggest memory is playing alongside some really good lads and he was one of them.

I wasn't there that long or to have many other sorts of memories or legacies. We had a good cup run. I was fully involved with the cup but then when I got transferred to Coventry the team went on to win the FA Cup that year. I didn't get any bonus, by the way, which I have told the club! But hey-ho!

What was it like playing for Everton against Liverpool?

That was really difficult. I was really nervous before the match. The priority for me, playing at Anfield in a blue shirt, was whatever happens, we don't get beat.

You can look at it in two points of view. For the first you don't want to get beat but then from a personal point of view you don't want to make a fool of yourself. You have got to try as professionally as you can.

It was a good result for us at that time [0-0]. We were struggling so it was better for us than it was for Liverpool.

How were the Liverpool fans with you during the match?

They were okay, I believe. I didn't really take too much notice of the supporters' comments anyway. I think, if I remember the evening, I got a yellow card, which could have been a red card, so I was stirring up a little bit of aggression in the stands towards me from the Red side, but I remember clapping the Everton fans when I was walking off and they seemed really happy with the result and with our performance. Yes, it was good and when I came away from Goodison Park I thought, 'Well, I've never been beaten in a Merseyside derby and that's something to take with me.'

What were the Liverpool fans like with you while you were an Everton player?

I didn't put myself into situations like nightclubs or anything like that. I wasn't one of those kinds of people. I know one or two others may have had a bit of stick left and right, but I really can't recall any particular moment where I felt somebody was aggressive towards me. There was always banter, a bit of stick flying about, saying bluenose and all that, but I have no memories of anyone being untoward towards me.

What were the Everton fans like after you signed for them?

It's difficult, we were struggling at the time, it probably wasn't the best time to play for Everton. It always seemed to be a struggle and it probably wasn't my best period on the pitch. So, if you speak to any Evertonians and they said, 'It wasn't your best time on the pitch,' or they say, 'You didn't play as well for us as you did for Liverpool,' I would agree with them. But everyone has their own opinion and that is what football is all about.

Why did you leave Everton for Coventry in 1995?

Well, I spoke to Joe Royle, who was absolutely brilliant by the way – what a great man he was, and he said, 'Look, I have had Ron Atkinson on the phone for the last two weeks, he wants you to go to Coventry, he wants you to be one of his first signings at Coventry,' and he said, 'What do you think?'

I said, 'Well, what do you think?' He said, 'Well, I've got Andy Hinchcliffe, who is in the team at the moment. He has had a bad time, but he has come out of that, he looks like he is progressing, he is doing well, he's playing really well. I can't play you over Andy. If you had asked me a month ago, I wouldn't have said that to you but that is the situation. I don't really want you to go, I want you to stay. I really like you as a player but it's up to you.'

As I said before, I would have walked down the motorway to play for Ron Atkinson, and Joe Royle knew that. I spoke to Ron, and it meant I was going back to the Midlands, and I knew Ron really well. I knew he was really fond of me from when I was a kid and as soon as I spoke to him that was it, the clubs agreed a fee and it happened.

I think I knew at that time my Everton career wasn't going to take off. The team was struggling as well a little bit financially, so I thought I would have a fresh start. I spoke to the chairman at Coventry. They were putting a lot of money into it. They had given Ron the job because they wanted to progress. So, that's what happened, I was getting back home to the Midlands after all that merry-go-round, and I was happy to be there and happy to be with Ron.

There doesn't seem to have been any bad blood at Everton, but do you think being a Liverpool player affected you settling in there?

Yeah, I mean it was difficult settling in and trying to make an impact at the club and Everton fans knew what I was like as a player, playing for Liverpool. If they didn't see that same sort of player, they were going to be on my back, they would let me know. You always had that weight on your shoulders, so yes, I think it did affect me.

Did Liverpool come in again before you went to Coventry?

No.

Would you have gone there after Everton?

I don't think so, I think I had reached the point where I knew my Liverpool days were over. I had 12 months at West Ham and six months at Everton and I thought it was time to settle down again. I had two kids and I am dragging them around the country left, right and centre. It's time to settle down, I've got to get back in the Midlands and get my feet planted back down, get my head down and re-establish myself as one of the better left-backs in the country, and that is what I tried to do and Ron was all for that. He said, 'You need to get yourself back to where you were at Liverpool and that is what I want to see.' He told me straight. He knew me from a 14-year-old kid so he knew what he was getting. He was very blunt, very sharp with me: 'I want to see that player that was at Liverpool.'

So that was my goal and that was the confidence boost I needed to really get myself right physically and mentally, to get on with my career. So that's what happened at that time, and I couldn't have wanted to play for a better man.

What was your opinion of Everton as you left the club?

It was a case of I really liked Joe Royle and Willie Donachie but I never felt I settled in, I never felt I belonged there. My parting thought was, 'I don't think if I had been there two years, that I would have settled or really fitted in.'

Do you have a legacy at Everton?

I think it would be 'David Burrows played for us for six months after he played for Liverpool!' I don't think I left one. A lot of people don't even remember me playing for Everton because it was such a short period, so that is difficult for me to answer. I left in an FA Cup-winning season, which is a positive note I suppose.

What was your opinion of Everton fans when you left?

Similar to Liverpool fans in a way, especially the Merseyside ones. I mean, we all know they both have fans from north, south and east but it is the Merseyside fans that will tell you the truth. I always felt that they were genuine. If they didn't like something they would tell you, if they like something they would tell you. You knew where you stood with both Liverpool and Everton fans.

Though I do get a lot of stick from Everton fans now, more than I do with Liverpool!

On your last day as an Everton player, what was your opinion of Liverpool?

I felt they were on the decline; they hadn't restabilised. I thought how lucky I was to have had a great time with Kenny and a great team and having won things and, unfortunately, I was witnessing a decline in the club.

If you had your time again, would you still leave Everton?
Yes, I think so, yes, definitely. I would have made the same decision if it was tomorrow.

You're one of few people alive today that have played for both Liverpool and Everton. You're one of 34 people to have ever done it and one of 15 to have done it since the Second World War. Do those numbers surprise you at all?
That there's only 11 of us left [the interview was carried out before the death of David Johnson], that surprises me, yes. I didn't realise there was so few.

Who did you have a greater attachment to, Liverpool or Everton?
Liverpool. I spent more time there and was more successful.

Do you still look out for the scores for both teams today?
Yes, I always look out for the scores for all my old teams, all of them and every match.

In the 2021/22 season you were hoping Everton would avoid relegation and Liverpool would go on to win the Premier League?
Yeah, that would have been perfect, but we went through a period where it looked like Liverpool would win the league and Everton were going to be relegated and that would have been awkward. So, I was pleased in the end that Everton maintained their Premier League status.

Do you have any regrets about playing for either club?
No.

Do you think playing for both teams takes away from your legacy of playing for either club?
No, not at all. If I am only one of 11 left, that's a bit of an icon for me.

If you could have only played for one of the two teams, who would it have been?
Liverpool.

Having played in other local derbies, how do you view the rivalry between Liverpool and Everton?
Well, the teams that I played for, I was part of the local rivalries growing up in the area, so it was always intense and always a lot at stake. But I can't think where you are going to get a bigger rivalry than Liverpool and Everton, anywhere else in the world.

When you played for West Brom you would have had an idea about Merseyside derbies. Did that change when you actually played in them?
Not at all. I had watched many Merseyside derbies before and it lived up to every expectation I had and even more when you are actually there and you are walking on the pitch. You can feel the build-up too. It's two or three days before and then all the consequences two or three days afterwards. In fact, it goes on and on for a period of a few weeks, whereas other games you get it out of your system within a few days. This drags on.

If Liverpool play Everton in a derby today, who do you want to win?

Had it been the end of the 2021/22 season, I would have wanted Everton to win to help maintain their Premiership status. But had it meant Liverpool would win the league and Everton went down that would have been a million-dollar question! I can't answer that, I'm just glad it didn't happen!

The Kop or Gwladys Street?

The Kop.

Anfield or Goodison?

Anfield.

Best Liverpool manager you played under?

Kenny Dalglish.

Best Everton manager you played under?

Joe Royle.

Best out of the two?

Kenny Dalglish.

If you had your career again, would you do anything different at either club?

No, I have no regrets, I don't look back like that, no.

Did you achieve all you wanted to at both clubs?

Yes, I achieved what I wanted in winning the championship and the FA Cup and getting into the England squad. I always feel that I overachieved when I look back on my career.

Finally, what would your combined Merseyside XI be from the players you played with?

My Merseyside XI, unfortunately, is not too difficult. The period I played for both clubs was a tale of two ends of the table, as you know. So, I'm afraid the league-winning team of '90 has to get priority.

1. Bruce Grobbelaar
2. Steve Nicol
3. David Burrows (of course!)
4. Gary Gillespie
5. Alan Hansen
6. Steve McMahon
7. Steve McManaman
8. Ronnie Whelan
9. Ian Rush
10. John Barnes
11. Duncan Ferguson

Only Big Dunc would make it from the Blue side. May not be too popular, but there you go.

Again, sincere thanks to David Burrows for being so honest and giving his time to help this book and to be able to provide a different approach on one player in this long list. Burrows was again like McMahon, Beardsley and Sheedy in that Graeme Souness forced their hand on leaving the club. His life at Goodison Park was certainly not as successful as the defender's days at Anfield but had he stayed for a full season there would have been a winners' medal in the FA Cup for both teams too.

It's interesting that Liverpool were again interested in signing Burrows after the departure of Souness and it feels as though Roy Evans was trying his best to reunite the many successful members of Dalglish's squad and the young players he and Ronnie Moran had nurtured with the reserves.

Burrows is a hark back to players that came in the deals between/involving both clubs from decades before. His legacy is entirely Liverpool-related and, as he said himself, many don't even know he ever wore a blue shirt. He was a dependable and solid full-back who may have had a better legacy had he been given more time at both clubs. His experience with Liverpool led to an uncertain period in his life, where everything was unsettled by a perhaps ill-conceived move to London. This meant he couldn't resettle while playing for Everton and it was clear that a move back home to the Midlands was what he needed.

Listening to him talk about his home and family life, although perhaps not the first time we've ever heard this from a footballer, adds a new dimension for the reasoning for all moves before and to follow. Although Blues and Reds can't comprehend wanting to play for the other side, it's hard to ignore that both clubs are in the same city. To be offered a chance as a footballer, even if you're a local lad and have fervently supported the club all your life, to change clubs but not have to move house, uproot your family and see them change jobs and schools is such an attractive one. Until you're in the moment, it's hard to know whether you would cross the park.

For Burrows, Souness cut his Anfield career short, and this led to a chain of events that meant when he played for Everton he couldn't settle. The Scottish manager had such a huge impact on many players and events at Liverpool but also a remarkably large number of players on this special list.

Don Hutchison

Name	Donald Hutchison
Born	09/05/1971, Gateshead
Liverpool stats	60 matches/10 goals (1990–94)
Liverpool honours	None
Everton stats	89 matches/11 goals (1998–2000)
Everton honours	None
Combined stats	149 matches/21 goals (1990–2000)
Direct transfer?	No
Remembered (%)	LFC 100%/EFC 100%/Ave. 100%
Legend (out of 10)	LFC 5/EFC 5.8/Ave. 5.4
Traitor (out of 10)	LFC 4.5

AN IMMATURE Don Hutchison had several embarrassing moments at Anfield before he matured with Everton and went on to captain the club. When David Burrows questioned whether some players that Graeme Souness was attempting to bring to the club were the right fit, it's fair to assume that the teenager from Hartlepool United wasn't someone who fitted into life with Liverpool and his actions off the pitch curtailed his brief career.

It was, however, under Kenny Dalglish that a deal to sign Hutchison was agreed with the Fourth Division club but he was loaned back to them before he arrived in the summer of 1991.

He only made three substitute appearances in his first campaign at Anfield, accumulating less than an hour of football, but his performances in the reserves led to some ambitious compliments on his talents.

The 1992/93 campaign was his breakthrough one at Anfield, the 21-year-old being given an extended run in the team by Souness. A League Cup tie against lowly Chesterfield provided the future Scotland international just a second start for the club. It was a poor match in terms of a result but a young team fought back from three goals down to earn a 4-4 draw, Hutchison scoring Liverpool's second and assisting the third on the night. He had clearly done enough to impress though, and was rewarded with a run in the team.

Faith in the young midfielder was rewarded when he scored four times in four successive matches, culminating in a 2-2 draw at Old Trafford. The way in which Souness had forced change within Anfield saw Steve McManaman (20), Jamie Redknapp (19) and Hutchison (21) start the match against the old rivals. The former Hartlepool youngster scored with a speculative effort from distance, which included a deflection from Steve Bruce that helped beat Peter Schmeichel.

Faith in the youngsters was certainly admirable from Souness and there's no doubt that Hutchison was benefitting from the trust placed in him by his manager. Although there has been more than a fair amount of criticism placed in the way of the Scot, his young and much-changed team finished the season in fifth place and the board were in support of him staying at the club for another season. His absence from the final match of the season was odd, though, and the decision to promote Roy Evans as assistant showed that his successor was waiting in the wings. There's no doubt that coming off the back of a 42-match campaign, Hutchison was set to be part of the plans for the future too.

The 1993/94 season was to be a strange one for Hutchison, to say the least. He came into the campaign confident of holding down a starting role again but Souness was erratically changing his line-up. Three different keepers were tried and everyone seemed to have spells in and out of the team. The crushing FA Cup knockout to Bristol City spelled the end for the manager, who handed in his resignation. For Hutchison, who was handed just two starts by new boss Evans before the end of the campaign, it marked the end of his chances too. It didn't help either that the midfielder's goalscoring prowess completely dried up, with all ten of his Liverpool goals coming in the previous season.

This was just on the pitch though. Hutchison made a public balls-up, as written in *The Guardian*:

> While on holiday in Ayia Napa in 1994, an inebriated Hutchison hid his wedding tackle behind a Budweiser label. When a bystander's snaps appeared in the tabloids, his manager at Liverpool Roy Evans declared: 'If Hutchison is flashing his **** again that's out of order.' Hutchison had form. A year earlier he had spotted female students videoing their graduation celebrations in a wine bar, unzipped his flies and announced, 'Zoom in on this!' After the Ayia Napa incident he was fined £5,000, dropped, transfer-listed – and eventually shipped off to West Ham (where he was known to fans and team-mates as 'Budweiser').

Not quite Dick Forshaw levels of criminality but some glaring similarities between the pair. That was that. From a youngster who had so much potential, to transfer-listed and out of the door to West Ham. Two years in London were followed by another two in Sheffield, where the Scotland international flourished under Howard Kendall. As the former Everton boss returned to manage the club for a third time, he took the now 26-year-old with him after the player had pleaded with the manager to take him back to Merseyside. Speaking with Toffee TV, he explained his desire to move back to the city with the Blues: 'When I knew the move was going to happen, I just couldn't wait. I loved my time on Merseyside when I was at Liverpool. I lived in the Albert Dock, which was great for a single lad, good bars round there and great Italian restaurants as well and I loved Scousers – I still do.'

Hutchison had matured by the time he arrived at Goodison Park though. He had filled out into his frame and wasn't afraid to get stuck in for his team. He arrived in February 1998 and played every match up to the end of the season, helping the Blues retain their Premier League status. The penultimate match of that campaign saw Kendall's team head to a title-chasing Arsenal, who needed a win to claim the league title. The Gunners destroyed Everton 4-0 but some huge tackles from Hutchison showed his new fans that he was part of the fight to keep their top-flight status intact. Final-day drama included a missed Nick Barmby penalty, but a chaotic draw with Coventry was enough to stay up on goal difference.

The following season saw Walter Smith take the helm at Goodison Park and Hutchison make 36 appearances under the new boss. He was trusted by the Scot to be a key part of the team again, fighting off some initial competition from Olivier Dacourt and John Collins, to earn the role as stand-in captain whenever Dave Watson was absent. The new manager encouraged the players to be more tough tackling in training, never mind just the matches, and Hutchison rose to the challenge again.

It was to be another poor season though, and the decision to sell Duncan Ferguson rocked the dressing room, especially when the team was struggling so much for goals. The season ended with no player reaching double figures but Kevin

Campbell filled the void with nine in the final eight matches. He forged a great relationship on the pitch with Hutchison and Francis Jeffers, with four wins in the final six matches helping save the club once again.

The next season Hutchison was again heavily involved, his attacking abilities proving vital. When the Blues travelled to Anfield for the Merseyside derby, Everton fielded Hutchison, Barmby and Abel Xavier, with Liverpool starting Sander Westerveld in goal. Jeffers and Campbell carried on their brilliant end-of-season form to put the Blues ahead inside five minutes on a September evening on the dawn of the new millennium. There were no further goals but three red cards did follow. A clash between Westerveld and Jeffers ended in a scuffle and two dismissals, leading to Steve Staunton deputising in goal. Steven Gerrard was also later sent off and the deputy in goal had to be on hand to stop both Barmby and Xavier adding a second late in the match. Everton could and should have scored more but little did many travelling fans realise that was to be the last victory at Anfield for 21 years.

It was to be a less stressful end to the season and Hutchison was a key part of the team. He felt respected by Smith in terms of playing time and acting as stand-in captain but not in terms of his wages. This led to a mid-season standoff between club and player, the midfielder spending five weeks out of the squad as he was dropped. Hutchison claimed it was agreed by Smith that he could have a pay rise from £5,000 per week to just shy of £15,000, but when it came to negotiating with the club, they offered £8,000. Understandably, the Scotland international went to see the manager and question what was happening. He was met with anger, a hand around his throat and being pinned up against the wall after being accused of lying. Weeks of training alone ended with a chance back in the squad towards the end of the season but it seemed as though the damage was done. This is all Hutchison's take on proceedings, of course, but whatever the events that came before this dramatic breakdown in relationships, it ended with him leaving the club.

Before the departure was rubber-stamped though, Hutchison and Everton felt they were robbed by Graham Poll from securing a Merseyside derby double over Liverpool. The incident was reflected upon by the referee, writing for the *Daily Mail*:

> I fell foul of this basic error also at Goodison Park, during a Merseyside derby. With the game goalless, Liverpool goalkeeper Sander Westerveld collected the ball in the final seconds.
>
> I jogged back to the centre circle, checked my watch, which showed that time had elapsed and blew my whistle as I thought Westerveld had booted the ball up-field.
>
> Unfortunately, he had kicked it into Don Hutchison and the ball was on its way into the Liverpool goal. I stood firm and the 'goal' did not count.
>
> I was wrong back in April 2000 and have to apologise to any Everton fans that I meet even now – they never forget! I never repeated the act of blowing at an inappropriate time.

This apology will do little to appease any Everton supporters, much like one from Clive Thomas after his decision in 1977, or Herbie Arthur in 1893. A move back to his native north-east followed for Hutchison. The boyhood Newcastle fan moved to Sunderland, before then playing for West Ham and Millwall. The Scotland international born in England was never shy of upsetting people with his football club choices!

Hutchison retired at Luton Town as a 37-year-old in 2008 and has since gone into a career as a pundit. During this time he was asked on ESPN FC to pick his favourite Merseyside club: 'If you had to push me and I really had to lean towards one, it would be Everton because I captained Everton. I loved my time at Liverpool but I was a youngster, I was a teenager, I didn't know what I was doing. When I got older and I got a little bit more wiser and more responsible, I captained Everton. I was there for four years and captained them for about two years.'

It does feel as if Liverpool Hutchison and Everton Hutchison were two different people. The Scotland international arrived at Anfield at the perfect time for his progression, with a new manager who was eager to give youth a chance, so it should have created a perfect environment for him to thrive. The fun he had on the Albert Dock, though, suggests he lacked guidance and leadership from those within the club. His football dried up at Anfield but so did the team. When Souness departed, it could have welcomed a new era for Hutchison under Evans but off-field stupidity, partnered with a run of uninspiring performances, led to a move away that suited all parties.

By the time Kendall brought Hutchison to Everton, there was again no reason for any Reds to feel aggrieved at his decision to do so. Having the new Blue boss as his gaffer in Sheffield added more reason for him to make the move than his brief time across the park should have warned him off it. Aiding survival and then thriving under Smith, so much so that he wore the armband with distinction at Goodison Park, means that he deserves to be remembered fondly for his efforts. A breakdown in communication and relationships of epic proportions seems like a sad way for his career to end on Merseyside. The midfielder possessed enough passion, determination and talent to fit into a team that was fighting repeatedly to retain their Premier League status.

If more time had been afforded to Hutchison at either club, who's to say what could have happened for all involved. The old adage of no smoke without fire could be used to explain the relative cloud he left under at both clubs though. For Liverpool fans almost insignificant, but for Evertonians he could have been a captain and mainstay of a team for many years had the club decided to offer him a wage that seemed more than fair for his contributions.

Nick Barmby

Name	Nicholas Jon Barmby
Born	11/02/1974, Hull
Everton stats	133 matches/24 goals (1996–2000)
Everton honours	None
Liverpool stats	58 matches/8 goals (2000–02)
Liverpool honours	League Cup 2001, UEFA Cup 2001, FA Cup 2001
Combined stats	191 matches/32 goals (1996–02)
Direct transfer?	Yes (signed for LFC from EFC for £6m on 18/07/2000)
Remembered (%)	LFC 100%/EFC 100%/Ave. 100%
Legend (out of 10)	LFC 5.6/EFC 3.2/Ave. 4.4
Traitor (out of 10)	EFC 8.5

HERE HE is, public enemy No.1. That is, of course, if you're of an Everton persuasion, and as Nick Barmby is the man with the highest traitor rating of all the players to have dared to cross the park, this should help explain his standing on one side of the city.

Growing up in Hull, Barmby played at Sunday league level up to a teenager and his talents found him studying at the FA's School of Excellence. This set-up was hugely beneficial to helping launch a career in professional football with Tottenham. As a child, his favourite player choice may help to explain some future decisions. Speaking in an interview with Joe Walmsley, the midfielder said, 'There's only one King Kenny, he was my idol and a lot of people's idol. The first time I saw him play on TV, I was instantly drawn to the way he played. He was a clever footballer, great footballer, just a genius of a footballer and I just tried to emulate and play like him.'

With Spurs, his initial chance with the team came against his hometown club Hull City, and Barmby scored twice as an 18-year-old in a testimonial for Gareth Roberts. He spent three seasons at White Hart Lane and first thrived under manager Terry Venables and alongside team-mate Paul Gascoigne before moving on to Middlesbrough in 1995. He was a record signing at the Riverside, and Bryan Robson's team held their own in the Premier League, which attracted interest from Everton. The England international explained his decision to join the Blues:

> Merseyside, when it comes to football – wow. It's a religion, it's a brilliant place to play your football whether it's for Everton or for Liverpool. The fans get behind their team, they love the team, they're passionate – both red and blue.
>
> The Evertonians are very, very, very passionate people and I had four great years at Everton. To be fair, the first couple of years didn't go that well because we were fighting relegation which, for a club like Everton, we shouldn't have been doing that really. There was a few scares and we stayed up on the last day which again, we shouldn't have been in that position.
>
> Walter Smith came in from Rangers and he steadied the ship and started to build but unfortunately Andrei Kanchelskis and Gary Speed left – two of the best players really. To play at Goodison under the lights and in derby games was special. One of my first games was the derby game

at Anfield and we drew 1-1 but I always remember
Gary Speed scored in the last 10 minutes and I
just saw pockets of Evertonians in the Kop. I just
thought, 'Wow, that's unreal!' and I don't think it
could happen now. The same was with the Kopites,
some of them were in the Gwladys Street and you
just thought, 'Wow, this is a special derby.'

For me, I've been lucky enough to play London
derbies and North-East derbies but nothing
will ever touch the Merseyside derby. For me, a
Merseyside derby is incredible.

Barmby's time at Goodison Park was relatively successful.
He was a club-record transfer in 1996. His aforementioned
missed penalty against Coventry City in May 1998 could
have cost Everton their Premier League status and some
might say it would have seriously damaged his reputation in
a blue shirt but that was still to come. He was joint third-top
goalscorer and made the third most appearances for Kendall's
team, certainly helping to provide a positive spin on a poor
campaign.

Walter Smith's first Goodison Park season was met
with injury issues and just four league goals for Barmby. It
was a frustration for him to not be more involved as Kevin
Campbell inspired another relegation escape. Then 1999/00
was the midfielder's best season in blue, in which he played
more than anyone else that season. His ten goals in 42
appearances included the two impressive derby performances
for the Blues in that campaign.

What followed certainly means that his efforts that
season have and will be largely forgotten but the 26-year-
old was a crucial cog in Smith's Everton team that finally
delivered a season in which the Goodison faithful could relax
and not fear relegation. Barmby's performances were set to

be rewarded by the club and he was expected to sign a new deal. In the light of Don Hutchison and John Collins also leaving, some may have understood a departure but when Liverpool made an offer it was a shock for everyone to see a deal completed. Performances for England at Euro 2000 stalled negotiations between Barmby and Everton and the offer to double his wages at Anfield was clearly too much to turn down.

It was the first transfer directly from Goodison to Anfield since Dave Hickson 41 years earlier and it was set to receive similar levels of backlash. A statement from Everton read: 'Everton and Liverpool have today agreed the transfer of Nick Barmby to Liverpool in a package worth up to £6million. The clubs wish to emphasise that negotiations have continued over the past week in a spirit of goodwill and integrity and they both wish each other success in the forthcoming season.' The message conveyed that there was still a good-natured relationship between the top echelons of both clubs but the fans weren't quite so forthcoming in their spirit of goodwill.

Everton thought he would sign a new deal but Barmby was informed of the Liverpool offer and told the club that he wanted to cross Stanley Park, a decision that rocked Merseyside. As the midfielder was a key asset but still with one year left on his deal, the Blues could try to convince or force him to stay. However, the 26-year-old was determined to go and the Goodison Park hierarchy knew that this would be the best way for them to handle the situation with at least some money for the player. There were hopes that another club could come in to match the offer and save some indignity of losing a key man to a local rival, something that Manchester United and Chelsea tried to do, but it never materialised.

As soon as it was publicly announced that Barmby wanted to leave Everton for Liverpool there was never to be any going back and the player would have known that. As

reported in the *Liverpool Echo*, former Everton Shareholders'
Association spokesman Tony Tighe said:

> The fans will never forgive him for this. His career
> was in the doldrums for three years after he came
> here but we stood by him and kick-started his
> career. Now he has kicked us in the teeth by saying
> he wants to move across the park.
>
> That will hurt the supporters deeply and he'll
> never be welcome at Everton again. I had ordered
> a Barmby number eight shirt in our new kit for
> my young son to be collected on July 1st but I will
> now cancel it.

If the Evertonians interviewed for this book are anything to
go by, then this statement by Tighe is correct – they haven't
forgiven Barmby for crossing the park and in the manner
he did. Again speaking with Joe Walmsley, the Hull-born
midfielder discussed the controversial move:

> Liverpool to Everton, the Evertonians act as if
> 'oh yeah, we've got one up on Liverpool there,
> we've got one of their players'. I knew the stir it
> would cause, especially with me being at Everton
> for four years. I had a year left on my contract,
> a few clubs were in for me and Liverpool came
> in for me and I thought, 'I've always wanted to
> play for Liverpool and King Kenny was my hero.'
> I knew it would cause a stir, which it obviously
> did at the time.
>
> It was stressful for me and the family and I was
> obviously more concerned about my family but, to
> be fair, the amount of people I've talked to over the
> years now – I know they're never going to forgive

me, or at least the majority won't. At the time it wasn't the done thing.

Gérard Houllier unveiled his new signing in front of the understandably interested media and Barmby was immediately involved in the Liverpool squad. He played every match of the season up to 29 October when red met blue at Anfield.

The script was written for the new signing to score his first goal against his old club and he duly delivered. The No.20 was hoping to help Liverpool end a run of just one victory in the last 12 meetings between the clubs. It was clear from some early challenges by Michael Ball and Mark Pembridge that they wanted to ensure their old team-mate wasn't given an easy time though.

A foul by Pembridge on Barmby led to a free kick taken by Steven Gerrard. His long ball was headed clear by Abel Xavier, before a Christian Ziege cross/shot hit the Portuguese defender and deflected to find the head of Barmby. You might say it couldn't be written but it was the most obvious story that ever could have been told. His header found the back of the net and his name rang around Anfield, ensuring that his polarising reputation on Merseyside became even more severe. The game ended 3-1 to the Reds and Barmby reflected on the goal and the day:

> My wife and family had a police escort from
> Queen's Drive into Anfield and the manager told
> me that everything was fine and my family was
> fine, then I went out and played. The first 20
> minutes was normal, as frantic as all derbies are
> with the tackles flying in. I remember Christian
> Ziege the left-back had a shot and it deflected and
> as it deflected it bounced up and it was coming

towards me and I just sort of guided it, and as I guided it you know it's in.

The goalie was funny, Paul Gerrard, I used to room with him and as it looped over his head he said, 'You little ...' I sped off celebrating and we won the game 3-1 but the atmosphere was incredible. Normally the manager didn't allow us days off but after the game he said, 'Have a day off, go home and let the dust settle.' But yeah, it was some day, I must say!

That was to be the start of what was a magical season for Houllier's team. Three trophies were set to follow as the Reds played in every possible match available. Barmby played in 46 of them and scored a penalty in the successful Worthington Cup Final shoot-out after coming off the bench against Birmingham City at the Millennium Stadium in Cardiff. Injuries during the second half of the season led to Barmby not being brought on in the UEFA Cup triumph against Alavés or to even make the squad for the FA Cup Final against Arsenal. Fitness issues meant that the midfielder struggled to displace Gary McAllister, Didi Hamann, Danny Murphy, Igor Bišćan, Patrik Berger and a young Steven Gerrard towards the end of the season. Barmby did start in the 4-0 victory over Charlton on the final day of the Premier League season though, and that was by no means a dead rubber, with the win ensuring Champions League football at Anfield next year. The open-top bus tour that followed the amazing season was to be a special memory for all involved.

Barmby more than played his part in one of the great seasons though, and helped secure the first trophies at Anfield since the 1994 Coca Cola-Cup. His reward was a starting role in the Charity Shield victory over Manchester United and an opportunity to play in the Champions League.

Injuries hampered his progress again, however, and with so many talented young midfielders coming through, Houllier had little space to allow a 28-year-old Barmby back into the team that came close to winning the league in 2002.

With no bad blood, the club and player parted ways in August 2002. Barmby moved back home to Hull City via spells with Leeds and Nottingham Forest. Eight years as a player with his hometown club came before a year of managing in 2012. From there the England international stepped away from football and remains a very private person, choosing to remember his football memories personally. He still lives in Hull and helps run a family construction business with his wife.

Barmby made a point of saying that these transfers between clubs only end with a sour taste when players move from blue to red. Using the case studies of Dave Hickson, David Johnson, Steve McMahon and Nick Barmby – there certainly can be some weight added to that claim. However, there's also no way that had the same transfer happened the other way around, the same hatred wouldn't have transpired in exactly the same way.

Barmby was a club-record signing for Everton who, without setting the world alight at Goodison Park, did help to ensure they avoided relegation and were able to stabilise under Walter Smith. He certainly wasn't the only player to jump ship or be pushed overboard, but the way in which he left and the club he went to made it irreparably unforgivable. There's almost no need to try to praise his career at Everton because very few would care to entertain it.

In a red shirt, the 2000/01 season will live long in the memory and it's fair to assume Barmby would have played a greater role if not for the fitness issues that affected him. No one expected McAllister to be so crucial, and with young players like Gerrard and Murphy, Houllier reluctantly had no place for the Hull-born midfielder. Being a Red as a child though, seeing what he went through to get to Anfield, scoring in the derby and collecting five winners' medals, all means that there's certainly no regrets from the player.

It's hard to imagine that a transfer between the clubs will ever be met with this amount of controversy and outrage again and none have ever been so bold as Barmby was in pushing for a move across the park. The hatred from Everton fans certainly isn't met with equal measures of love from the Reds but there's no doubting that the player will always be thankful he forced a move and achieved his childhood dreams.

(Liverpool squad picture 1961/62, Morrissey front row far right). Johnny Morrissey, sold behind Shankly's back. A much-loved stalwart of an Everton side he won two First Division titles with.

Johnny Morrissey (Pictured for Everton vs. Nottingham Forest in 1971).

(Pictured for Liverpool vs. Real Madrid in 1981) David Johnson, 'the Doc' was the first man to make over 100 appearances for both Merseyside clubs.

*David Johnson
(Pictured for
Everton vs. Leicester
City in 1972).*

*(Pictured for Everton vs. Rapid Vienna in 1985) Kevin Sheedy – after next to no
Liverpool career of note, the Irish international with a wand of a left foot and a
wicked free kick thrived at Goodison Park.*

(Pictured for Everton vs. Leeds United in 1979) Steve McMahon, no player has more combined games for both Merseyside teams.

Steve McMahon (Pictured for Liverpool vs. Everton in 1989).

(Pictured for Liverpool vs. England XI in 1988) Peter Beardsley, arguably the most loved man on both sides of the park.

Peter Beardsley (Pictured for Everton vs. Norwich City in 1992).

(Pictured for Liverpool vs. Everton in 1989, Ablett far right). Gary Ablett, the only man to have won the FA Cup with both Liverpool and Everton.

Gary Ablett (Pictured for Everton vs. Manchester United in 1995, Ablett far left).

(Pictured for Liverpool vs. Derby County in 1990) David Burrows, a promising left-back forced out of Liverpool by Graeme Souness and returned for a brief spell with Everton.

David Burrows (Pictured for Everton vs. Queens Park Rangers in 1994).

(Pictured for Everton vs. Arsenal in 1999) Don Hutchison, filled in as captain for Everton and aided their Premier League survival before leaving over contract disagreements with Walter Smith.

(Pictured for Everton vs. West Ham United in 1999) Nick Barmby, enemy No.1, voted the biggest traitor after completing the first transfer from blue to red in 41 years.

(Pictured for Liverpool vs. Everton in 2000).

(Pictured for Everton vs. Middlesbrough in 2000) Abel Xavier, a relatively brief spell with both clubs but remains the last player to directly transfer between both clubs, back in 2002.

Abel Xavier (Pictured for Liverpool vs. Bayer Leverkusen in 2002).

(Pictured for Liverpool vs. Arsenal in 2001) Sander Westerveld, the treble-winning goalkeeper left Anfield under a cloud after a brief but successful stay.

Sander Westerveld (Pictured for Everton vs. Newcastle United in 2006).

(Pictured for Liverpool vs. Anzhi Makhachkala in 2012) Conor Coady, the most recent player to have played for both Merseyside clubs and with Everton's looming move to Bramley-Moore Dock, possibly the last to cross Stanley Park.

Conor Coady (Pictured for Everton vs. Liverpool in 2022).

(Pictured for Liverpool vs. AC Milan in 2005) Rafa Benitez, a club legend at Anfield and sacked by Everton, with two vastly different spells at both clubs.

Rafa Benitez (Pictured for Everton vs. Liverpool in 2021).

Abel Xavier

Name	Abel Luís da Silva Costa Xavier
Born	30/11/1972, Nampula, Mozambique
Everton stats	49 matches/0 goals (1999–2002)
Everton honours	None
Liverpool stats	21 matches/2 goals (2002–04)
Liverpool honours	None
Combined stats	70 matches/2 goals (1999–2004)
Direct transfer?	Yes (signed for LFC from EFC for £750,000 on 30/01/02)
Remembered (%)	LFC 83%/EFC 92%/Ave. 88%
Legend (out of 10)	LFC 4/EFC 3.2/Ave. 3.6
Traitor (out of 10)	EFC 5.8

FROM NO transfer from blue to red in 41 years, to a second in just 18 months. Abel Xavier caused a lot less of a storm when he arrived at Anfield compared to Nick Barmby but he does remain the last player to directly move between the clubs. He was also the first man from outside of the British Isles to be part of this illustrious list. Despite all of this though, perhaps the one everlasting memory from both sides of Xavier is his hair.

Born in Mozambique, Xavier moved to Portugal after his home country became a colony of the European nation and that's where his football career took off. Spells with Estrela da Amadora and Benfica were followed by the start of the right-back's journey around the world. Italy with Bari,

Spain with Real Oviedo, the Netherlands with PSV and then England with Everton.

Walter Smith solidified his defensive options with the Portuguese international full-back. The 26-year-old was given a run of matches in the team and Everton were unbeaten in his first five appearances. This new-look defence looked set to ease worries of another relegation scrap but Xavier started picking up some injury problems. It wasn't until March that season that he was able to put a run of four starts together.

Xavier impressed enough to earn a call-up to the Portugal squad for Euro 2000 and Everton were pleased with his progress during a first season in English football. Now donning his famed eccentric hairstyle, the defender played for his nation against France in the semi-final of the competition. During the match, the right-back was adjudged to have used his hand to block a goalward effort from David Trezeguet during a golden goal period of extra time, Zinedine Zidane scoring the resulting penalty. Portugal were out and Xavier was handed an initial nine-month ban for the way in which he protested the referee's decision.

He returned to Goodison Park as a defender with widespread notoriety thanks to his impressive displays in the competition, his new hairstyle and the lengthy ban that he had received. Walter Smith was spending the Nick Barmby money on the likes of Alessandro Pistone, Steve Watson, Thomas Gravesen, Niclas Alexandersson, Alex Nyarko, Paul Gascoigne and Duncan Ferguson. The signings had little positive impact, however, and it was another dispiriting campaign that ended in 16th place.

The concerning decision for Xavier to appeal his UEFA ban seemed to make little sense to a team not playing in Europe. He was, though, eyeing a way to make himself a more attractive transfer option for a move away from

Goodison Park. The right-back only featured 11 times that season as Smith didn't want to reward his public plea for European football. Injuries within the squad handed him the opportunities he was given but personal fitness issues again hampered his progress and relations had fractured with the boss. So 2001/02 was to be the final season for the Portuguese international at Goodison Park, and the reduction of his ban to six months meant that he was now free to play in UEFA competitions.

Xavier had proved that he could play across the defence and help in midfield if needed. Despite upsetting some with his desire to play in Europe, the defender was happy to remain at Everton but awaited a new contract to be offered. With the club cash-strapped and his deal ticking down, the 28-year-old held the power in negotiations. The Blues couldn't offer him an extension at that time, so when Liverpool made an offer he listened. Speaking with *The VAR Show*, the Portugal international said:

> I played two-and-a-half years with Everton and both clubs had more than 100 years of existence and I am one of the few players to play for both of them. It was a difficult move because the relative passion we need to understand, the emotion of the people and when I made that change, I was very respectful towards Everton. Everton was experiencing a difficult time, we were fighting relegation and there were economic problems in the club and Liverpool approached me in a very respectful way. They said, 'Abel Xavier, we would like to have you. In six months' time you can run down your contract but we would like to offer you in 15 days to be able to play Champions League football.'

As a player, it was a very difficult decision because socially, you're going to make a lot of impact. I need to move my house, I need to live in a different area of the city, I need to have bodyguards to protect me because of the emotions. People don't believe it's possible that I could go and play for a rival from across the park. When you do things with the right respect for both sides, when you do things and tell people your vision – it's very pleasing that when I come back to Liverpool now, I'm very welcome by both sides. It was a very, very difficult move.

Markus Babbel was ruled out for the rest of the season when he contracted Guillain–Barré syndrome, so Liverpool needed a right-back. It was a bargain deal for Liverpool, a last chance to grab any much-needed money for Everton and the offer of Champions League football for Xavier. Despite following in the footsteps of Nick Barmby, the response was a world of difference. Although the Blues had been left short-changed, there was little to complain about regarding the player – when the finances were simply not available to offer him the chance to stay. Had Xavier wanted to hurt the club, he could have played out the last six months and then had a pick of clubs and wages, but now he was able to somewhat help Everton with his departure.

Xavier was thrust straight into action and, after failing to score in his 49 matches with Everton, he found the back of the net on his Liverpool debut. It was more salt being rubbed in the wounds of the Goodison faithful when his deflected effort found the back of the net inside 15 minutes of his debut on a day when the Reds won 6-0. Next came his Champions League dream, being handed the start against Galatasaray at Anfield. His third match was the Merseyside derby at the same ground.

You could forgive any Evertonian for putting their mortgage on the Portuguese defender scoring in the match, especially after the Barmby goal in the previous season. Xavier was playing his sixth derby and only once had he been on the winning team, when Kevin Campbell scored the only goal at Anfield in 1999. This derby ended 1-1 though, and damaged Liverpool's title hopes.

Houllier's team finished the season in second place, seven points behind Arsenal, and were knocked out of the Champions League at the quarter-final stage when a Xavier goal wasn't enough to help defeat Bayer Leverkusen. The next season was to be his last though, as a fall-out with the manager meant that his four starts in the Premier League at the beginning of the campaign were to be his last. The 30-year-old was loaned out to Galatasaray in January 2003 and never played for either Merseyside club again.

A nomadic career followed with Hannover 96, Roma, Middlesbrough and LA Galaxy over the next five years. He then moved into coaching with Olhanense, Farense, Aves and Mozambique. A step back from coaching as a 46-year-old opened the door to punditry in Portugal, where the unique style of Xavier is often showcased for all to see. The man with 20 appearances for his country also returned to represent a Liverpool Legends squad at Old Trafford in 2022.

Another interesting character and a unique one. No one other than Abel Xavier had moved from outside the British Isles to experience life as a Blue and a Red before he did so in 2002. At the time of writing, the fact that he's the last player to have moved directly between the clubs, and that it occurred over 20 years ago, shows how infrequent these deals have become.

His Everton legacy is one shrouded in some controversy around his desire to reduce a UEFA ban and bolster his chances of finding a new club. However, it's clear that he wanted to leave Goodison Park respectfully and, in his own haphazard way, he did this. Xavier could have fleeced the club and lined his own pockets more and, in a time of financial need, even leaving for Liverpool benefitted the club more than it hurt their pride.

Had Xavier had a better career, then the reaction may have been more Barmby/McMahon/Hickson-like, but he was a decent player who never really held down a consistent starting role, so his departure was easy to take. Liverpool fans would have revelled in taking a good player from their local rivals but he was always a stop-gap filler for the stricken Babbel, who they hoped would soon return. It was a deal that worked for everyone and, given the fall-out with Houllier, Everton may have actually been the winners as they recouped money when they could have lost out.

Liverpool didn't recoup any money for Xavier's services and, although it wasn't a deal that didn't work out for them, little was gained by signing the Portuguese defender. Xavier's legacy on Merseyside will only grow the longer it takes for another direct transfer between the clubs to take place. As a footballer though, his legacy is much less than any of the more recent deals, perhaps going back to days of Tony McNamara and Jimmy Payne for a similar impact.

Sander Westerveld

Name	Sander Westerveld
Born	23/10/1974, Enschede, Netherlands
Liverpool stats	103 matches/42 clean sheets (1999–2001)
Liverpool honours	FA Cup 2001, League Cup 2001, UEFA Cup 2001, European Super Cup 2001
Everton stats	2 matches/0 clean sheets (2006)
Everton honours	None
Combined stats	105 matches/42 clean sheets (1999–2006)
Direct transfer?	No
Remembered (%)	LFC 100%/EFC 100%/Ave. 100%
Legend (out of 10)	LFC 5.9/EFC 3/Ave. 4.5
Traitor (out of 10)	LFC 5.3

WE NEAR the end of the story with Sander Westerveld and, in many ways, he almost doesn't deserve to be on this list. The Dutchman's time at Goodison Park is almost irrelevantly short but, if David Murray and John Whitehead have been covered, then why stop now!

Westerveld spent a little over two seasons with Liverpool but managed to cram a lot of memories and trophies into this time. The Dutchman made his name in the Netherlands after being promoted through the youth team at Twente. He made his debut as a 20-year-old and was then transferred to Vitesse in 1996. His three-year spell there helped his new team qualify for Europe and earn a national call-up in the week before his move to England.

June 1999 was to see Westerveld come into a Liverpool team that had struggled to cope with the inconsistent performances of both David James and Brad Friedel. Signing on a British transfer record for a goalkeeper showed the size of his potential. The 24-year-old looked set to provide a possible long-term option in goal that would ensure some stability for Gérard Houllier's new-look defence. Arriving in the same summer as Sami Hyypia and Stephane Henchoz meant that it was a slight gamble by the French manager but they were three ultimately successful signings.

The 1999 Merseyside derby wasn't the best introduction to Westerveld's new supporters, losing to Everton and being sent off in just his ninth match. This incident with Francis Jeffers was to somewhat mar his career at Anfield, as the fans always feared that the opposition could get into his head again. By that match too, the Dutchman had kept just one clean sheet and there were some real fears that he was never going to be able to control and command his own penalty area. What helped, though, was that his solitary shutout had come against the previous season's runners-up – Arsenal. Westerveld also saved a Davor Šuker penalty in that match.

Ending the 1999/00 season with 15 clean sheets in 39 matches, however, shows that Houllier's defensive overhaul was paying off. The Reds finished fourth but with plenty of room for the team to mature in the new millennium. European football was set to return to Anfield and, with the fewest goals conceded of any team in the league that season, the manager's signings had worked.

The 2000/01 treble feats have already been covered but Westerveld's 61-match contribution shows that he more than played his part. However, that wasn't to say that some of his performances left a little to be desired. Many supporters pointed to the UEFA Cup Final against Alavés as proof that, although the Dutchman was good, Liverpool could do better. If this team could achieve so much in cup competitions, then Premier League successes seemed to be looming large.

It was no secret that Chris Kirkland and Jerzy Dudek were at the very least being monitored by Liverpool. It's then understandable that this could cause some worries for Westerveld and would have knocked his confidence but all that was after the treble had been won. After starring in all three finals and the Charlton league victory that secured Champions League football, the 26-year-old was given the chance to play in the victorious Community Shield and Super Cup matches too, completing a unique set of medals.

Despite some seemingly public doubts in Westerveld's ability, he was handed a start in the August Premier League match away to Bolton. It was to be a day to forget for the man between the sticks, as the *Liverpool Echo* reported:

> This was a dreadful night for Liverpool and it may prove to be a worse one for Sander Westerveld.
>
> Despite reassurances he's Liverpool's number one, the Reds' pursuit of a new goalkeeper has been no secret for months. The timing of the match-costing error couldn't have been worse for Westerveld, especially with a Champions League transfer deadline looming.
>
> The last minute fumble from Dean Holdsworth's hopeful shot was a cruel way for Liverpool to lose this game. They shouldn't have lost, and didn't deserve to lose.
>
> When Holdsworth seemed content to do no more than hold the ball and see out time in the 89th minute, the nightmare unfolded.

It was an awful mistake and so late in the game there was no way back.

Westerveld had been a spectator for most of the match and virtually all the second half.

He's no doubt woken up this morning wishing last night didn't happen.

It proved to be as costly as some expected and Westerveld was unceremoniously dropped from first- to third choice keeper. He never played for the club again. It was a cutthroat move from Houllier and understandably left the Dutchman with a sour taste in his mouth. It seemed as though the French manager was waiting for a mistake so he could drop the stopper, and when it came about, there was no time wasted.

Treble-winning hero to third-choice in a matter of weeks. When the transfer window opened, Westerveld seemed set to close the door on Merseyside. Real Sociedad took the 26-year-old in December 2001 and he spent four years in Spain before an English comeback was realised with Portsmouth. He again struggled to earn an expected starting role, and when Everton needed an emergency loan following injuries to Nigel Martyn, Richard Wright and Iain Turner in 2006, they turned to the former Red. Speaking with This Is Anfield, the Dutchman explained how the move came about:

> I was playing for Portsmouth but was on the bench. On my way to watch Chelsea play Barcelona, David Moyes phoned me in the car and said he needed a goalkeeper who could play for a month. Straight away I said yes.
>
> I put the phone down and was like, 'Oh crap, it's Everton.' I always had a great connection with Everton because nine out of ten of my friends in

Liverpool were Bluenoses. I phoned them and they said, 'We'd love to have you there, everyone will understand, you're not going straight from Liverpool to Everton, you got kicked out of Liverpool.'

From the second I arrived, the atmosphere and the warmth of the fans at Everton made such an impression on me. It was one of the best experiences of my whole career.

I ran on to the pitch and they accepted me and were clapping their hands. I was really surprised, everything was positive.

It was almost like they were saying thank you, because they had three goalkeepers out, I was there to help and I tried to help them. It was a good opportunity to show myself to the world again and get some minutes under my belt. From the very first minute to the very end I was loving it.

I was even allowed to stay another month but my wife was pregnant and I told Moyes I had to go back. I'm still friends with a couple of players, [Mikel] Arteta and [Tim] Cahill, and even the kit manager. It's got a place in my heart.

There were some mixed thoughts at Goodison Park around the brief arrival of Westerveld but most could see it was purely to cover an emergency and, once Arsenal's Mart Poom failed to reach an agreement with the club, they had to act quickly. Evertonian memories were all running back to his treble-winning campaign with the Reds but also the red card that followed his clash with Jeffers. The Dutchman was now 31 years old though, and his Anfield days were five years ago. Due to the injury crisis, Moyes was left with the possibility of starting a 19-year-old John Ruddy or signing up 46-year-old goalkeeping coach Chris Woods, so it made sense to get someone else in, whoever he had played for in the past.

Westerveld was handed an immediate debut on his 28-day loan spell with the Blues and it understandably attracted a lot of media attention (fortunately people seem fascinated with players who have represented both Merseyside clubs!). However, it wasn't to be a dream debut for Westerveld, who watched his team lose 2-0 at St James' Park, thanks to a Nolberto Solano double, one of which was a superb, curled effort by the Peruvian. It certainly wasn't the fault of the Dutchman though. The *Daily Post* wrote: 'While the Newcastle result was obviously disappointing, at least Sander Westerveld's contribution represented a small plus. Once the fans got over the somewhat odd sight of an ex-Red in an Everton shirt, they couldn't help but be impressed with a decent performance from the big Dutchman. Many more of those and there's every chance he will have to have his wits about him tomorrow – and there might even be pleas for the manager to sign him up.'

His second and final Everton match came at Upton Park against West Ham and it was set to be another disappointing result. The first goal came from a brilliant passing move by the Hammers, Marlon Harewood's low drive giving the former Red no chance. A Leon Osman equaliser was hammered home but the Londoners' lead was quickly restored after a brilliant finish from Dean Ashton. James Beattie again levelled proceedings in the second half with a looping chipped finish but neither team were able to go on to win the match. Again though, it was no fault of the keeper that either goal had been conceded, with the *Liverpool Echo* summing up his game: 'Poor Westerveld. In two appearances, he has barely had a save to make, done whatever has been required of him with aplomb yet ended up conceding four goals.'

There followed two home matches as a substitute for Westerveld as Richard Wright had regained his spot. It was clear that Westerveld's services were no longer needed but it did provide the Dutch stopper an opportunity to be greeted positively by the Goodison Park faithful, and that's clearly something that he appreciated at the time.

He was also released by Portsmouth at the end of the campaign and spent the final seven years of his career in Spain, the Netherlands, Italy and South Africa, before moving into goalkeeping coaching. The Westerveld name lives on through Sem Westerveld, who, at the time of writing, is a young goalkeeper for AZ Alkmaar.

Westerveld's post-playing legacy is also heavily Liverpool-orientated, as would be expected. Playing alongside the likes of Abel Xavier in a host of Liverpool Legends fixtures, the Dutchman's achievements for the Reds and particularly the treble-winning campaign have also been remembered on a mural in the AXA Training Centre in Kirkby. The trophies of all keepers to have ever won a major honour with the club have been recreated on the wall in order to inspire the current crop and future generations that are looking to emulate those that have come before.

From the huge names and controversial deals of the past, there's no question that Westerveld certainly doesn't have quite the same amount of intrigue as some that have come before. The way in which his Liverpool career came to an end was undoubtedly not achieved in a way that befitted the efforts that had led to the club winning five trophies while the Dutchman was in goal. That no doubt aided his decision to accept an approach from Everton in 2006.

Five years had passed and both teams were quite far from where they had been when Westerveld first left Merseyside and he had little reason to show too much remorse to the Reds after his exit. However, as this was just a 28-day deal, it was clear to all involved that there wasn't any need for bad blood between any involved parties. All the Dutchman could have done was publicly reject a move to Goodison in order to improve his reputation at Anfield but then he wouldn't be part of this illustrious list of players.

Westerveld came and did a good job for both clubs, perhaps leaving both while still wanting more. His legacy will always remain at Liverpool though, and his 2000/01 efforts will never be forgotten by him, the supporters or in the history of the club.

Conor Coady

Name	Conor David Coady
Born	25/02/1993, St Helens
Liverpool stats	2 matches/0 goals (2012–14)
Liverpool honours	None
Everton stats	12* matches/1* goal (2022–present)
Everton honours	None
Combined stats	14* matches/1* goal (2012–present)
Direct transfer?	No
Remembered (%)	LFC 100%/EFC 100%/Ave. 100%
Legend (out of 10)	LFC 3.8/EFC 5.5/Ave. 4.7
Traitor (out of 10)	LFC 5.1

*Figures correct at the time of writing

TIME TO be truthful. When the idea for this book was first conceived, the idea of Conor Coady wearing a blue shirt would have been laughed at by most. Instead, the St Helens-born midfielder-turned-defender decided to ruin the USP of this book and join Everton on loan from Wolves. At the time of writing, the loan hasn't yet been made permanent but it's safe to say that the England international nearly had the dream start to his Goodison career, especially in relation to Merseyside derbies.

Before we delve into that though, the boyhood Red's first days in Merseyside as a footballer began in 2001. An eight-year-old Coady had an early dream realised when he signed his first junior contracts for Liverpool, and so began the early comparisons with Steven Gerrard, with the tough-tackling young midfielder gathering positive attention within the Kirkby youth set-up. A move to a defensive-midfield and then central-defensive position started comparisons with Jamie Carragher and it looked as if the local lad was set to have a long career with his boyhood team.

Kenny Dalglish recognised the talents of the youngster when he took over from Roy Hodgson as Liverpool manager for his second stint in charge of the club. Despite not managing to get a match for the first team, Coady received two substitute call-ups around his 18th birthday during 2010/11. During this time though, Coady was excelling in the reserves, where the following season saw him play every match in the league and in Europe for the young team. There were no senior appearances or call-ups to the bench in the first full season under Dalglish and there were some fears that Coady had failed to improve to a level that many within the club thought he could. However, he still shared reserve captaincy duties with Andre Wisdom and was regularly training with the senior squad.

The arrival of Brendan Rodgers saw a change in the style of play for Liverpool but also an improved number of opportunities for Coady within the team. The Northern Irishman involved the midfielder in six matchday squads and his first minutes on the pitch came against Anzhi Makhachkala in the Europa League. The group-stage match saw the 19-year-old start in Russia alongside the likes of Jamie Carragher and Jordan Henderson.

Rodgers was clearly using the competition to give opportunities to some younger players in his squad, and that bitterly cold evening also had fellow academy graduates Jon Flanagan, Andre Wisdom and Adam Morgan starting. *The Times* reported, 'Conor Coady, a 19-year-old making his full debut, was impressive as he recovered from a shaky start to produce a mature midfield display,' and the *Liverpool Echo* corroborated: 'Coady was tasked with offering protection in a deep midfield role and he rose to the challenge as he used the ball intelligently.' The match may have ended 1-0 to Anzhi, managed by Guus Hiddink and coached by Roberto Carlos, and including the likes of Samuel Eto'o, Lacina Traoré and Chris Samba in their starting line-up, but the youngster had proven that he was able to compete on a European level.

Coady shared his thoughts on his own performance, his first match in senior football, in an interview with Jamie Carragher on Sky Sports: 'I was nervous, really nervous and a bit panicky if I'm being honest with you. Every time I lost the ball, I felt like the world was ending. I'll always remember it because it was a big game for myself but I don't think it was one for the spectators.'

His only opportunity with the first team was to come in May of that season though, when the 20-year-old was handed a Premier League debut as an 89th-minute substitute for Philippe Coutinho. It was certainly a proud moment for the youngster, with a Daniel Sturridge hat-trick leading to a 3-0 victory for the Reds. There wasn't going to be much opportunity for him to shine in four minutes but it did show that there was a chance that Rodgers could utilise him further. However, it was never going to be easy to compete with Gerrard, Henderson, Coutinho, Lucas Leiva, Jonjo Shelvey and Joe Allen.

Rodgers decided that Coady should spend the next season on loan with Sheffield United in League One, where he impressed so much that an initial six-month deal was extended to a full season. In his 50 matches the boyhood Red had impressed during the 2013/14 season. However, the Reds had just come second in the Premier League and it was going to be hard for the 21-year-old to get a run in the team. There was a decision to make of whether he should wait and see if a chance at Anfield arose or leave to chase first-team football elsewhere. He explained his decision – again speaking with Sky Sports:

> Brendan Rodgers was good to me when I was young. I had a season training with the first team at Melwood, and learning off them, that was big for me, but I always knew it was tough. I was always realistic, I was learning a lot off the first team, how to play and do things.
>
> I knew at some point I'd have to come away from Liverpool to really experience being a first-team player. It was the best decision I ever made, and Brendan Rodgers was great for that; he pushed that to send me on loan and try to improve my game.
>
> Even being on loan at Sheffield United (in 2013/14), I loved the season and it was a great club for me to go to. Coming back I still knew it was going to be tough. Liverpool were always getting better, they were always improving, and the players in my position were ridiculous. But I just wanted to play football. I knew where I was at, the type of level I was at, but I just wanted to be part of a first team, playing in games which meant something, playing against men.

Huddersfield Town were the club that managed to capture the then midfielder but his three-year deal was cut short when Wolves signed him for £2m in July 2015. This was to be the start of a long and happy stay in the Midlands. Two years into his move he was put at the heart of defence in a three-man defensive set-up. This tactical change brought a new lease of life to both the club and the player. From 2017, Coady was named captain of the club and he helped guide them to Premier League promotion. The top tier was soon followed by European football and the former Red looked set for a long and happy career with the team in old gold. Club success brought international acclaim when he was selected as part of the Euro 2020 England squad.

There was to be a big shock at the beginning of 2022/23 when Coady was unceremoniously removed from the starting line-up by Bruno Lage at Wolves. Coady had played over 300 times for the Molineux club but, having been dropped, despite consistent performances and availability, he again looked for more first-team football. The main news around this, though, was where the boyhood Red ended up.

It's important to note now, that this book is being written at the end of 2022, ahead of the start of the Qatar World Cup, so there's still no confirmation of what has or will be further agreed with regard to Coady.

At the start of the season Everton became the surprise favourites to capture the local lad on an initial loan but with a reported option to buy of around £4.5m. It's certainly a brilliant deal for a 29-year-old with so much experience and a nearly perfect injury record, as well as a great understanding of the local area. Frank Lampard's team had just avoided relegation in the previous season and needed some defensive reinforcements, so the signing of Coady not only made sense but seemed like a great coup for the Blues.

There was always going to be a lot of media attention around the move though. He was a boyhood Red and he was about to cross the park. Coady was aided by a lack of any real hatred from either side because his football career was so brief at Anfield, so neither could be too upset with the move. There does seem to have been a deliberate lack of comment on his career with Liverpool and the defender is trying to show to all Everton supporters that he is Blue through and through. That would never be in doubt, though, because the former Wolves skipper has always been a true professional and, having played against Jürgen Klopp's team for so many years, his boyhood loyalties have often been removed for personal and professional gain. Talking about playing against the Reds during his days in Wolverhampton, the defender spoke with the *Express & Star*: 'Every week I look at Liverpool and hope they win. I supported them growing up but I'm playing for Wolves now.'

This line was quickly going to have to change when the 29-year-old became a Blue. Speaking with Everton's club website when the move was agreed, Coady explained the feeling of signing for the club: 'It was mad. When I got the opportunity to come here I didn't want to turn it down. I didn't want to miss it. As soon as I spoke to him [Lampard] I just thought to myself: He sounds incredible. It sounds absolutely incredible, the way he wanted to play, how he wanted to do things, what he wanted to do with the club and where he wants to take it. I wanted to be a part of it.'

Lampard put Coady straight into his team and the deal proved to be as successful as most thought it would be. Starting in the heart of the defence as part of a back four or five, the local lad was an immediate hit with Evertonians. His Liverpool allegiances were soon forgotten after a string of impressive performances. His brilliant fitness was vital, with the likes of Yerry Mina struggling to retain a place alongside him at the back, and the leadership qualities on show from the 29-year-old were abundantly clear.

September 2022 was to provide Coady his first Merseyside derby and nearly a dream introduction to a fixture he knew so much about. With 20 minutes remaining of a tense yet entertaining Goodison Park derby, Neal Maupay fired a ball across the box and found the defender in space to tap the ball home. What followed was the clearest indication of a change of allegiance for the player as he went crazy in celebration with his team-mates and new supporters. However, VAR was to spoil the party and the goal was disallowed. It was to prove a day for goalkeepers Jordan Pickford and Alisson Becker though, the match ultimately ending 0-0. Despite the goal being chalked off and the match ending in a draw, the new Blue discussed how it had provided him with one of the greatest moments of his career, in an interview with *Sportsmail*:

> A lot of people ask me about scoring against Liverpool and to be honest, I think it is a daft question.
>
> I have played football for a long time now and the one thing I give to any club I am playing for is everything every single day of my life. I'll push that club and try to make the people around me better.
>
> I know how big Merseyside derbies are, I grew up with them, I know what they are about, I know how big they are for Everton Football Club and we spoke about it before that game. It is a massive game for Evertonians, a massive game for the manager and the players.
>
> So, to have that feeling at the time [when the ball hit the back of the net], bearing in mind it got taken away, it was one of the best feelings I ever had in football, I'll be honest. I am giving my all for that club every single day.

A move to Everton, especially in the modern era, is always likely to cut ties with an elongated relationship with any Liverpool fans. Even though the former Red only played twice for the first team, there was always a sense of pride in seeing one of your own doing well. Liverpool fans had an affinity with Coady, and vice versa, but it's clear that would change as soon as he wore a blue shirt. The derby in September 2022 was marred by acts of idiocy by some supporters, with murals to Ian St John, Roger Hunt and Trent Alexander-Arnold being defaced with blue paint, including the message that read 'For fans supporting foodbanks'. This change from friendly relationships to a sour one was perhaps best depicted in this moment. It's by no means one way and there are idiots on both sides of Stanley Park. However, to see that change from a unified city to a divided one is so sad to witness.

There may have been a time when Coady could speak about Liverpool as an Everton player, like he did as a Wolves one. However, to be a star in the modern day it seems that all ties need to be cut and a decision will have to be made of where his heart lies. The defender will give 100 per cent for his new club and there will never be a doubt about that. What will be interesting, as his career at Goodison Park continues and possibly even into Bramley-Moore Dock, is to see whether a retired Coady will pick a club or remain a fan of both.

There always seems to be a favourite club for each player, and Coady's career in blue has already had many more minutes than his red one did, so it's likely to be Everton. No Liverpool supporter would have stood in his way to leave Anfield, but some would have been upset to see him join the Blues at Goodison Park. For that reason he's likely to double down on being a Blue and go on to have a long career there. With the aforementioned move to a new stadium, the injury record of the defender and his love for Merseyside, not only could Conor Coady be the last man to ever cross the park but he could go on to be one of the best to have ever done so.

The Managers

THE BOOK, or at least the main focus of it, has been completed. There are a couple of loose ends to be drawn up though, and that starts with the managers. Only two men have ever had the duty of managing both Everton and Liverpool but it's likely the first man wouldn't have even had a mention if it hadn't been for the controversy that surrounded the second ...

William Edward Barclay

Name	William Edward Barclay
Born	14/06/1857, Dublin
Died	30/01/1917, Liverpool
Everton stats	22 matches (9 W/2 D/11 L) (1888–89)
Everton honours	None
Liverpool stats	91 matches (52 W/17 D/22 L) (1892–95)
Liverpool honours	Lancashire League 1892/93, Second Division 1893/94
Combined stats	113 matches (61 W/19 D/33 L) (1888–95)
Direct transfer?	Yes (signed for LFC from EFC after clubs split)

KNOWN BEST as W.E. Barclay, this was an era when the board of directors was responsible for selecting the team for each match. The dawn of the first Football League campaign in 1888 saw the Dubliner elected as secretary, so he selected the team. John Houlding was president of Everton and the entire board still had a say in selections too but Barclay was to be the man tasked with choosing the team for each match at their new home – Anfield.

In modern-day standards, Barclay is classed as the first manager of both clubs but he was far from the tracksuit-wearing coach we're used to today. His youth was prosperous and saw him receive a good education and the opportunity to travel around the nation before settling in Liverpool as the governor of an industrial school, Everton Crescent. He aided young people within the city, while also being a wealthy man and thus moving in the same circles as Houlding. His interest in sport and kinship with the brewer provided an opportunity to get involved with St Domingo FC and then Everton.

Barclay was in charge for the 1888/89 campaign, the season that Preston North End completed their Invincibles season, but it was to be his only one in charge of the Blues. In August 1889 he handed in his resignation as secretary and this was 'accepted with regret' by the club. Dick Molyneux took over with immediate effect.

Barclay remained with the club up to the split in 1892 and, despite his loyalties clearly lying with Houlding, he was very much a voice of reason during the fractious relations within the club. Because his introduction to the committee had been through his business relations with Houlding and not the religious background of St Domingo, it was perhaps not a surprise that he was to remain at Anfield. However, during the final meetings of the board before the split, Barclay pushed for the departing members of the board to keep the name 'Everton' and he wanted a new team to be called 'Liverpool'.

Houlding wanted his new club to bear the name Everton in some capacity, partly as reference to the hard work he had put into building the club and partly to spite those who had left Anfield and abandoned him. Despite some protests from Liverpool Rugby Club, the name of Liverpool Football Club was finally accepted. Barclay agreed to remain by the side of the new club's president and took up the role he had held for Everton, thus becoming the first Liverpool manager.

He was again the head of a committee that helped select a Liverpool team that included the likes of Andrew Hannah, Tom Wyllie and Duncan McLean. An initial omission from the Football League has been attributed by some to Barclay, because the forms were incorrectly submitted to the Football Association at the time, which led to a season away from the formal football set-up that was to follow.

Barclay's scouting missions to Scotland helped build the initial 'Team of Macs' for Liverpool and showed his keen eye for a player. Although the Dubliner is attributed as being the first manager of the club, he did have a lot of help in the role, with John McKenna a key associate in running the football operations. Seeing as his fellow Irishman was to become the club's second-ever manager in 1895, he was soon to be favoured for his footballing and administrative skills.

However, Barclay did show during the club's maiden Lancashire League season and an invincible Second Division season that he had plenty of skills as a football manager and selector of a team. The Dubliner left his role in August 1895 and went on to work for the FA, such was his standing within the game. Life in Liverpool was certainly a defining moment within the life of Barclay and he never really had to cope with a rivalry as such, but he did have to deal with the drama that surrounded the forming of two separate clubs.

It's quite a feat to have not just managed both clubs but to also be the first man to have ever done so for each. Barclay will always be remembered for his work for both clubs but in a very different era of football and of relationships between them.

Rafa Benítez

Name	Rafael Benítez Maudes
Born	16/04/1960, Madrid
Liverpool stats	350 matches (197 W/74 D/79 L) (2004–10)
Liverpool honours	Champions League 2005, European Super Cup 2005, FA Cup 2006
Everton stats	22 matches (7 W/4 D/11 L) (2021–22)
Everton honours	None
Combined stats	377 matches (204 W/78 D/90 L) (2004–22)
Direct transfer?	No
Remembered (%)	LFC 100%/EFC 100%/Ave. 100%
Legend (out of 10)	LFC 9/EFC 1/Ave. 5
Traitor (out of 10)	LFC 4.4

WHERE TO start with Rafa Benítez? Probably 2004. There has been a conscious effort to not delve too far into the careers of the final few men in this book because this is about the players who have played for both. There could and probably will be a book written about the Spaniard's controversial decision to join Everton in 2021, especially after six memorable years with Liverpool, but this will be a brief examination of his time at both.

Liverpool replaced Gérard Houllier with a fresh-faced Benítez, the 44-year-old having won La Liga twice and a UEFA Cup with Valencia and looking set to be a successful manager. He immediately hit the floor running and key signings such as compatriots Xabi Alonso and Luis Garcia were crucial to a very famous night in May. Despite the Reds finishing one place below Everton in the league and failing to achieve a top-four finish, Istanbul was to provide some solace. Benítez's team famously fought back from three goals down and secured the most unlikely Champions League Final victory and thus managed to secure football at Europe's top table for another season. However, it also illustrated the managerial prowess of the young coach.

The FA Cup was to follow in 2006 and Benítez continued to improve his squad for a Premier League challenge. In 2007 AC Milan got revenge in the Champions League Final in Athens but that prompted the arrival of Fernando Torres, who was set to make a big impact at Anfield. He and Steven Gerrard formed a formidable partnership and, by the time the 2008/09 campaign came about, the Reds were desperately unlucky to lose out on the title to Manchester United.

An incident during the season led to much ridicule for the Spaniard though, as he used a press conference to list several 'facts' about Manchester United boss Alex Ferguson. Whether the comments were true or not, it heaped pressure on the players and, despite a 4-1 Old Trafford victory, Liverpool's lead at the top of the table ebbed away and they finished second.

Chants of 'Rafa's cracking up' and 'you're just a fat Spanish waiter' followed, as the manager was mercilessly ridiculed by opposition supporters. Those at Anfield still adored Benítez though, and he was famed for bringing the good times back to the club. He had provided silverware and European football back at Anfield and looked to be consistently challenging for the illustrious league title that had evaded the Reds since 1990.

However, 2009/10 was to be the curtain call for Benítez. A combination of losing key players, an inability to fund new ones and clashes with the club's now much-maligned American owners, Tom Hicks and George Gillett, was always going to end on a sour note. Liverpool finished seventh and it seemed as though a new era was dawning but not a positive one. Results had taken a turn for the worse but many pointed to the faults of the club's owners and not a man that the Kop had adored.

Benítez's donation of £96,000 to the Hillsborough Family Support Group followed the announcement that he had left the club. It reaffirmed that he understood Liverpool and the supporters, many of whom were willing to allow him a chance to rebuild. However, a combination of the manager and owners meant that would never happen. In 2011 the Spaniard returned to Anfield for the Hillsborough Memorial Service and was given a public thank you from the Family Support Group for his donation. The Kop rose to its feet and Benítez was captured in tears, the long applause leading to a rendition of his name being sung once again by his supporters.

Through the club's website, Benítez released the following statement:

> It is very sad for me to announce that I will no longer be manager of Liverpool FC. I would like to thank all of the staff and players for their efforts.
>
> I'll always keep in my heart the good times I've had here, the strong and loyal support of the fans in the tough times and the love from Liverpool. I have no words to thank you enough for all these years and I am very proud to say that I was your manager.
>
> Thank you so much once more and always remember: You'll never walk alone.

Take this moment and then fast-forward ten years to the day he became Everton boss. The Liverpool supporters had continued to show their love for the Spaniard whenever he returned to Anfield as an opponent, even during a testing spell of their loyalty when he took the Chelsea job on an interim period in 2012.

However, the news that he was now set to take the Goodison Park hot seat was a shock for Reds and met with displeasure from some Blues.

Despite spells at clubs such as Real Madrid and Napoli, Benítez's career had taken a downturn since he left Merseyside. He was adored by the Newcastle United supporters too but a fall-out with the board there and then a move to China made his appointment at Everton even more unlikely. Despite an impressive CV and an obvious understanding of both the Premier League and Merseyside, there were several members of the Everton fanbase that were staunch in their opinion that Benítez should never be given the top job there.

There was also a huge number of Everton supporters who reacted in a way that perhaps is best comparable to Liverpool supporters after signing Dave Hickson in 1959. They wanted to back the new man and were willing to give him a chance. However, the sight of banners outside Goodison Park before his arrival as manager was confirmed, reading 'Fuck off Benitez you fat Kopite c**t' and 'Benitez not welcome', showed that there were always going to be some fans that wouldn't be willing to give him as much time as others.

Historic comments of Benítez calling Everton a 'small club' in 2007 were also cited but the Spaniard was quick to try to make amends when he was announced as manager in June 2021. He moved straight back to the family home that had been kept on the Wirral and said in his first press conference:

To be fair, the Evertonians around my place they are quite happy and they were very supportive. Even the Liverpool fans, they were accepting that this is an opportunity for me to come back to the Premier League to compete for something. So it was quite good. Talking about the banners, we can talk about one or two people, you never know.

I think it's better to think about the positives. How a lot of people were encouraging me to do well and I'm happy with that.

Liverpool is my city, we have very good connections in the red side, in the blue side and now obviously a lot of people in the blue side. Now the blue side will be pleased if I am successful so I don't see a big issue. I think that the fans appreciate that we will be here working really hard for the team for the club and then if we can do well then nobody will be talking about that what happened in the past so I'm thinking about the future. I know that they will want us to be successful and I am sure that there we can do it.

It was a successful start. A nomination as Premier League manager of the month for August was followed by the Blues sitting in fourth place in October, after just one loss in nine matches as boss. Early form of bargain signings Demarai Gray and Andros Townsend showed that the Spaniard could work under a tight budget and there were whispers of a charge for European football.

Then came the injuries and drop in results, Benítez repeatedly bemoaned the absence of Richarlison, Dominic Calvert-Lewin, Yerry Mina, Allan, Tom Davies, Townsend, Seamus Coleman and others at certain points. In his next, and ultimately final, 14 matches at the club, Everton won just two and lost nine. They had fallen from fourth to 15th and looked set to continue heading in one direction. The decision of the board to allow the Spaniard to sell Lucas Digne at the start of the January transfer window but then to sack the boss less than a week later was bizarre. It pointed to a lack of football knowledge and leadership at the top of the club but there were still plenty of happy Evertonians once the news broke that Benítez was to leave Goodison. Banners had started appearing in the crowd calling for his head, and there were planned protests of supporters leaving early because of his leadership. Chants of 'Get out of our club' grew louder, and anger towards the manager and board grew stronger.

When Liverpool travelled to Goodison Park and comfortably beat the Blues 4-1, chants of their former manager's name could be heard in the away end and it was done to mock their local foes. Talk of 'Agent Rafa' spiralled around social media as Liverpool supporters revelled in the failures of those across the park and of their old manager. Seen as fair game now that he was on the other side, there was no time for pleasantries from the Reds.

January saw the end of Benítez's three-year contract after just 200 days. It wasn't a shock, especially seeing as they were now just six points above the relegation zone and had lost to lowly Norwich City.

Speaking with Sky Sports after his sacking, Benítez said:

> At the time Everton came in with the offer, I knew I would give my best and do everything to try to improve things. I knew it could be difficult because I was at Liverpool, so maybe I couldn't make some decisions. It was very clear for us at the beginning.
>
> I had a meeting with a head of one of the departments and I asked him, 'Do you think everything is fine?' He said, 'Yeah, everything is

perfect.' I thought £600million had been spent, it cannot be perfect when the owners aren't happy and the fans are not happy.

So I realised we had to change things inside, but I couldn't do it straight away because I was a former Red and it could be seen as 'oh, he's come in to change our club'.

In another club, I would have made those decisions. I did it in the past, because you know very clearly that is the way to improve, but there at Everton I couldn't do it.

There's no hiding the fact that the biggest gulf in club legend status between any man mentioned during the questionnaires and the lowest score of anyone both came with Rafa. He's still adored by many Liverpool fans but taking the Everton job certainly had the possibility to tarnish this for him. The main reason that the Spaniard will still have fans at Anfield is because he did such a bad job at Goodison Park.

For some rival supporters, Benítez was mocked for being a 'fat Spanish waiter' during his latter days at Anfield. The Liverpool fans backed him then but once he became a subject of mockery for Everton they took their own chance. Blues can be understood for having an initial distaste for the manager, although some certainly took it too far and, once the job became untenable, he had to go. Rafa was always going to be on a tightrope at Goodison Park and as soon as results and injuries went against him, so did some of the fanbase. His reputation at Everton is worse now than before he took the role.

For Liverpool fans it's an interesting one. Some, again as a sad insight into the current state of the rivalry, won't forgive him for taking a job across the park. Others will say that it made sense for him to come back home and take a

. job in the city again and they're willing to remove that from their memory because it didn't work out. A final set will love the fact that Benítez took the Everton job because it went so badly and they'll even love him more for it.

Over the next ten, 20 or 30 years Benítez will be welcomed back at Anfield like the legend that many perceive him to be following a successful six years in charge. He certainly won't be afforded the same greeting with Evertonians though.

The Don't Really Counters

I EXPECT there will be some readers at this point screaming at the book because several names haven't yet been mentioned. Apologies for any frustration caused and also for the crudely named heading of this chapter but we now enter another strange list of men who are going to be known as 'the don't really counters'.

These are players who are classed by some as having played for both clubs but they never actually made a senior appearance for both. Places on the bench, games for the reserves and in friendlies will all be on show here but, because they failed to perform in a senior match for both clubs, they don't really count. So, there's little need to reference their whole careers but a brief mention is certainly deserved here.

Alex Latta
1889–96 – EFC (148 matches, 62 goals – 1889/90 First Division title)
1896–97 – LFC (Eligible for official selection but never given a first-team appearance)

Harry Bradshaw
1891–92 – EFC (Part of the Everton reserve squad in the Lancashire Combination league)
1893–98 – LFC (138 matches, 51 goals)

Benjamin Howard-Baker

1919–20 – LFC (Signed amateur forms but never played a
first-team match)
1921 & 1926 – EFC (13 matches, 3 clean sheets)

Alf Hanson

1930–31 – EFC (Part of Everton's A-team and reserve squad
before being released)
1931–38 – LFC (177 matches, 52 goals)

Charlie Leyfield

1932 – LFC (Handed one A-team match on trial)
1932–37 – EFC (38 matches, 13 goals)

Jack Balmer

1934–35 – EFC (Nephew of Everton greats Bill and Bob
Balmer, spent two seasons as an amateur but refused offer
of £1 a week to become professional in 1935)
1935–52 – LFC (309 matches, 110 goals – 1946/47 First
Division title)

Roy Felton (Robert Francis Foster Felton)

1936–37 – LFC (Full-back who left Liverpool as a 19-year-old)
1937–38 – EFC (Played for the reserves before being sold
to Port Vale)

John Heydon

1946–49 – EFC (Three years in Everton's reserves)
1949–53 – LFC (67 matches, 0 goals)

John Gidman

1970–71 – LFC (Member of Liverpool's youth team but no
senior appearances)
1979–81 – EFC (78 matches, 3 goals)

Alan Harper

1978–83 – LFC (Boyhood Red spent his entire youth career with Liverpool but never made the first team)

1983–88 & 1991–93 – EFC (241 matches, 4 goals – 1984 FA Cup, 1985 UEFA Cup Winners' Cup, 1984/85 & 1986/87 First Division title)

Dave Watson

1978–80 – LFC (Part of Liverpool reserves set-up, sold to Norwich for £50,000 in 1980)

1986–2000 – EFC (528 matches, 37 goals – 1995 FA Cup, 1986/87 First Division title)

Alec Chamberlain

1987–88 – EFC (Unused understudy to Neville Southall)

1994–95 – LFC (Unused understudy to David James after injury to Michael Stensgaard – received a 1995 Coca Cola Cup winners' medal as an unused substitute)

Darren Potter

1995–99 – EFC (Boyhood Everton fan but released as a 15-year-old)

2001–07 – LFC (17 matches, 0 goals – part of 2005 Champions League-winning squad)

Andy Lonergan

2019–20 – LFC (Received winners' medals as part of UEFA Super Cup and FIFA Club World Cup victories in 2019)

2021–present – EFC (At the time of writing, yet to appear for Everton and is an understudy to Jordan Pickford and Asmir Begović)

Sammy Lee

There's also no natural place to briefly mention Sammy

Lee, who joined Liverpool in 1972 and played 295 matches, scored 19 goals and won four First Division titles, four League Cups and two European Cups at Anfield, before leaving in 1986. In 1993 he was part of Graeme Souness's coaching staff and remained with the club until 2004 when Rafa Benítez took charge. Lee returned to join Rafa in 2008 and stayed until 2011 under Roy Hodgson. In 2017 Lee was part of Sam Allardyce's coaching staff when he took the job at Everton and was at the club during his five-month tenure at Goodison Park.

The Carraghers

EXCUSE THE crude title again but here we'll briefly mention those who dared to cross the park but did so on a purely moral basis (some of them on a professional level too). All these players are said to have supported the 'other' side before going on to play for their new club. There are many examples of this but it feels as though none are more famous in the modern era than Jamie Carragher.

Some of these men never had the opportunity to play for their boyhood team but were handed the chance to play on the other side of the park instead. There are a lot of examples here and this may not be a full list because it's not always common knowledge who footballers supported as a child, and certainly not when we go back to the very early days of both clubs. Instead, here's a brief look at some of those who have played for the rivals of a team they used to love:

Everton supporters to have played for Liverpool:
Jimmy Payne – 1948–56
Ian Rush – 1980–87 & 1988–96
Steve McMahon – 1985–91
Steve McManaman – 1989–99
Robbie Fowler – 1992–2001 & 2006–07
David Thompson – 1996–2000
Jamie Carragher – 1996–2013
Stephen Wright – 1997–2002
Adam Lallana – 2014–20

Liverpool supporters to have played for Everton:
Johnny Morrissey – 1962–72
David Johnson – 1969–72 & 1982–84
Peter Reid – 1982–89
Alan Harper – 1983–88 & 1991–93
Dave Watson – 1986–2001
Mike Newell – 1989–91
Gary Ablett – 1992–96
Phil Jevons – 1996–2001
Nick Barmby – 1996–2000
Matthew Pennington – 2013–21
Ashley Williams – 2016–19
Theo Walcott – 2018–21
Dele Alli – 2022–present
Conor Coady – 2022–present

Conclusion

HOPEFULLY THIS isn't the page that you reach and think, 'What was the point of all that?' and hopefully there's now more appreciation for this special list of men.

As much as there has been somewhat of a conclusion to each player and their legacy at the end of each section, this is perhaps an opportunity for the key themes of the book to be summed up. A conclusion or possibly just a long ramble, this is an attempt to end a unique and interesting list of men and their impact on Merseyside and the rivalry between Everton and Liverpool.

There are so many different ways of grouping them together and there's no doubt that some are mutually appreciated, some have a bigger place in the heart of one team than the other, some barely even count because they hardly represented one club and had a bigger role for the other, while some did next to nothing for either.

The main questions will be from all of this:

- Why is the number of players so relatively low?
- Why has it been over 20 years since a direct transfer?
- Why had it been so long without any double agents until Benítez, Coady and Lonergan?
- Who is the most hated man on Merseyside of these men?
- Who is the most loved?
- What will the future of this rivalry hold?

Reading the above list of questions seems like one of the toughest homework assignments but here we go ...

For just 34 players in over 130 years to have made this short trip across the city is quite remarkable. Considering the personal upheaval that moving around the world and the country entails, you would expect that some players would push for a move across the park whenever possible. There's no answer to this, or any question really, as each person has their own thoughts and reasons for making a move. Loyalty will keep some players from moving but certainly not all, as we've seen. That will be the main reason though. Football is so passionate on Merseyside that even those outside the city feel the love for the game. Once you've played in front of either set of supporters or experienced a Merseyside derby, it will affect your future career decisions. This clearly wasn't true for Nick Barmby or Abel Xavier but many who came before and since will hold their relationship with the home crowd as a reason to remain loyal. Legacy is important to a lot of people and this seems to be the overarching reason for remaining at one club and not pushing to move to the other.

Abel Xavier's transfer in 2002 was the last time a player moved directly and that can point to a worsening relationship between the clubs during the ensuing period. After being twice stung by Liverpool taking some of their better players, you can understand Everton's stance of ensuring that it didn't happen again. Bill Kenwright is still present at Goodison Park, and perhaps once he leaves there may be an easing of this seeming halt on transfer dealings. There has also been a gulf in on-field performances during this time too and a larger gap between the quality of squads may relate to a reduced number of players moving between them.

For this to then all flip with Rafa Benítez, Andy Lonergan and Conor Coady is odd to say the least. All three men have very different reasons for these moves though.

Benítez was looking to return to his family home and the Premier League. It was the most controversial and probably least successful of the moves but, regardless of all other contributing factors, he wanted to come home. Lonergan wasn't really a Liverpool player and isn't yet an Everton one. He's clearly happy being a third-choice keeper and has no real reason to become too involved in this debate because he hasn't played a match. Coady had learned at Wolves that football is a game that will take you away from your home and teach you to fight for whichever club shows faith in you. The England international stopped getting game time at both Liverpool and the Midlands club and he made a decision that benefitted his career, nothing else. On top of this, though, and like with Benítez, he too was able to move back home to his family. A lack of a Liverpool career, despite a life supporting them, meant there was little chance that a professional bond would be broken and now he has the opportunity to be an Everton hero.

The most hated men in this long list are most probably Rafa Benítez, Nick Barmby, Steve McMahon and David Johnson, in that order. It's interesting that these men go in order of date, which again shows a worsening relationship between the clubs. The hatred towards these men is also more Everton-based and that's not trying to insinuate any reasons behind this. Most of the reasons for the Blue side having distaste is understandable and probably would be the same on the Red side, had it happened the other way round. This is an interesting turn of events though, but the less-negative deals in between these cases shows that every transfer is viewed in its own unique way by all involved.

The most loved is Peter Beardsley, while Gary Ablett had a certain level of mutual respect from both sets of supporters. With Beardsley though, his departure from Anfield is easy for Liverpool fans to take because of the role of Graeme

Souness. By not attributing blame or upset to the player for his departure, the fans can then forgive him for whatever his next move may be. The fact that it was Everton may have hurt at the time but the Kop singing his name during a Merseyside derby was a unique showing of his impact at the club. True too with the Blues, who, instead of resenting his days as a Red, welcomed a talented individual to their squad. The fact the Geordie was gifted and in a team that was certainly not the best made his class even more obvious.

The future looks bleak (what a way to finish!) and Merseyside has come a long way from parading the 1966 World Cup together during the Charity Shield match that season, singing 'Merseyside' during the 1984 Milk Cup Final and the show of solidarity in 1989 after the Hillsborough disaster. Now we see death threats to ex-managers, vandalising murals, constant social media abuse and the abhorrent chants of 'murderers'. Both fanbases have their fair share of idiots and it's slowly sullying the bond that used to be in place. Rival captains would wish the other team luck for the season and supporters would sit next to each other. The relationship has soured since the Milk Cup Final of 1984, and the events during the Heysel disaster can certainly be said to be a long-term cause of this. The disparity of silverware and the increase in ticket prices can also be cited. Fans can no longer afford to watch both teams, so have to pick one. Once Goodison Park is knocked down and the distance between the club grows bigger in every sense, it's hard to know how many more will ever cross the park again.

Everton and Liverpool used to be a derby and a bond that was like nowhere else in Britain, nowhere else in the world. Surely it's better to stand out to the rest of the world by being the friendly derby it used to be? The city is built on standing by each other and when times get tough there's nobody like a Scouser to go through it with. There's been enough media, governmental and social dirt thrown at everyone for that to be abundantly clear, and by targeting each other with hurtful messages, chants and vandalism, both sides lose. When blue faces red it should be an intense match with tackles flying, fans singing and an undying show of love for your team, but when it comes to anyone else we should stand together.

These 34 men dared to cross the park and play for the other club, and the reaction of upset and anger in some cases is good too. Football is so important and gets so many people through a mundane week at work that we need to resonate with those on the pitch in our colours and want them to fight for every ball like we do in the stands. If someone betrays that trust they should expect to hear and receive the backlash, but then perhaps the safest place would be a short trip across the park, because they'll be protected and loved there just as strongly. The two clubs are so similar and that used to be the grounds that brought us all together but, if we're not careful, it could pull us apart.

If Conor Coady is the last man to ever cross the park, he looks set to be a good one. Times have changed since Andrew Hannah, Patrick Gordon, Harold Uren and Dick Forshaw, but anyone who dares to make this transfer will always be remembered in a special group of players that have a truly unique insight into the love and passion shown by both Liverpool and Everton supporters. This was their story and thanks for taking the time to read it.

Statistics

Complete statistics in order of date of crossing the park:

Player	Everton Apps	Everton Goals	Liverpool Apps	Liverpool Goals	Combined Apps	Combined Goals	Remembered	Legend	Traitor
Andrew Hannah	44	0	69	1	113	1	-	-	-
Tom Wyllie	21	7	25	15	46	22	-	-	-
Duncan McLean	26	0	82	4	108	4	-	-	-
Patrick Gordon	22	5	30	8	52	13	-	-	-
John Whitehead	2	1 (Clean Sheets)	3	0 (Clean Sheets)	5	1 (Clean Sheets)	-	-	-
Fred Geary	100	85	45	14	145	99	-	-	-
Abe Hartley	60	28	12	1	72	29	-	-	-
Edgar Chadwick	300	104	45	7	345	111	-	-	-
David Murray	2	0	15	0	17	0	-	-	-
Don Sloan	6	0 (Clean Sheets)	6	0 (Clean Sheets)	12	0 (Clean Sheets)	-	-	-
Arthur Berry	29	8	4	0	33	8	-	-	-

Harold Uren	24	3	45	2	69	5	-	-	-
Tom Gracie	13	1	34	5	47	6	-	-	-
Bill Lacey	40	11	260	29	300	40	-	-	-
Frank Mitchell	24	8 (Clean Sheets)	18	8 (Clean Sheets)	42	16 (Clean Sheets)	-	-	-
Dick Forshaw	42	8	288	123	330	131	-	-	-
Neil McBain	103	1	12	0	115	1	-	-	-
Tommy Johnson	161	65	38	8	199	73	-	-	-
Billy Hartill	5	1	4	0	9	1	-	-	-
Jimmy Payne	6	2	243	43	249	45	24%	6.8	5
Tony McNamara	113	22	10	3	123	25	40%	3.9	3.5
Dave Hickson	243	109	67	38	310	147	85%	7.7	2.7
Johnny Morrissey	315	50	37	6	352	56	64%	6.8	3.8
David Johnson	105	20	213	78	318	98	93%	6.6	6.5
Kevin Sheedy	369	97	5	2	374	99	96%	6.7	6.1
Steve McMahon	120	14	277	50	397	64	100%	5.9	7.4
Peter Beardsley	95	32	175	59	270	91	100%	8	5.1
Gary Ablett	156	6	147	1	303	7	100%	6	5.6

David Burrows	23	0	193	3	216	3	80%	5.1	5
Don Hutchison	89	11	60	10	149	21	100%	5.4	4.5
Nick Barmby	133	24	58	8	191	32	100%	4.4	8.5
Abel Xavier	49	0	21	2	70	2	88%	3.6	5.8
Sander Westerveld	2	0 (Clean Sheets)	103	42 (Clean Sheets)	105	42 (Clean Sheets)	100%	4.5	5.3
Conor Coady	12*	1*	2	0	14*	1*	100%	4.7	5.1

Most Combined Appearances

Player	Combined Apps
Steve McMahon	397
Kevin Sheedy	374
Johnny Morrissey	352
Edgar Chadwick	345
Dick Forshaw	330
David Johnson	318
Dave Hickson	310
Gary Ablett	303
Bill Lacey	300
Peter Beardsley	270
Jimmy Payne	249
David Burrows	216
Tommy Johnson	199
Nick Barmby	191
Don Hutchison	149
Fred Geary	145
Tony McNamara	123
Neil McBain	115
Andrew Hannah	113
Duncan McLean	108
Sander Westerveld	105
Abe Hartley	72
Abel Xavier	70
Harold Uren	69
Patrick Gordon	52
Tom Gracie	47
Tom Wyllie	46
Frank Mitchell	42
Arthur Berry	33

David Murray	17
Conor Coady	14*
Don Sloan	12
Billy Hartill	9
John Whitehead	5

Most combined goals

Player	Combined Goals
Dave Hickson	147
Dick Forshaw	131
Edgar Chadwick	111
Kevin Sheedy	99
Fred Geary	99
David Johnson	98
Peter Beardsley	91
Tommy Johnson	73
Steve McMahon	64
Johnny Morrissey	56
Jimmy Payne	45
Bill Lacey	40
Nick Barmby	32
Abe Hartley	29
Tony McNamara	25
Tom Wyllie	22
Don Hutchison	21
Patrick Gordon	13
Arthur Berry	8
Gary Ablett	7
Tom Gracie	6
Harold Uren	5
Duncan McLean	4

David Burrows	3
Abel Xavier	2
Neil McBain	1
Andrew Hannah	1
Conor Coady	1*
Billy Hartill	1
David Murray	0

Most combined clean sheets

Player	Combined Clean Sheets
Sander Westerveld	42
Frank Mitchell	16
John Whitehead	1
Don Sloan	0

Combined club-legend rating (out of 10)

Player	Legend
Peter Beardsley	8
Dave Hickson	7.7
Jimmy Payne	6.8
Johnny Morrissey	6.8
Kevin Sheedy	6.7
David Johnson	6.6
Gary Ablett	6
Steve McMahon	5.9
Don Hutchison	5.4
David Burrows	5.1
Conor Coady	4.7
Sander Westerveld	4.5
Nick Barmby	4.4

Tony McNamara	3.9
Abel Xavier	3.6

Traitor rating (out of 10)

Player	Traitor
Nick Barmby	8.5
Steve McMahon	7.4
David Johnson	6.5
Kevin Sheedy	6.1
Abel Xavier	5.8
Gary Ablett	5.6
Sander Westerveld	5.3
Peter Beardsley	5.1
Conor Coady	5.1
Jimmy Payne	5
David Burrows	5
Don Hutchison	4.5
Johnny Morrissey	3.8
Tony McNamara	3.5
Dave Hickson	2.7

Most Everton appearances

Player	Everton Apps
Kevin Sheedy	369
Johnny Morrissey	315
Edgar Chadwick	300
Dave Hickson	243
Tommy Johnson	161
Gary Ablett	156
Nick Barmby	133

Steve McMahon	120
Tony McNamara	113
David Johnson	105
Neil McBain	103
Fred Geary	100
Peter Beardsley	95
Don Hutchison	89
Abe Hartley	60
Abel Xavier	49
Andrew Hannah	44
Dick Forshaw	42
Bill Lacey	40
Arthur Berry	29
Duncan McLean	26
Harold Uren	24
Frank Mitchell	24
David Burrows	23
Patrick Gordon	22
Tom Wyllie	21
Tom Gracie	13
Conor Coady	12*
Don Sloan	6
Jimmy Payne	6
Billy Hartill	5
John Whitehead	2
David Murray	2
Sander Westerveld	2

Most Everton goals

Player	Everton Goals
Dave Hickson	109
Edgar Chadwick	104

Kevin Sheedy	97
Fred Geary	85
Tommy Johnson	65
Johnny Morrissey	50
Peter Beardsley	32
Abe Hartley	28
Nick Barmby	24
Tony McNamara	22
David Johnson	20
Steve McMahon	14
Don Hutchison	11
Bill Lacey	11
Dick Forshaw	8
Arthur Berry	8
Tom Wyllie	7
Gary Ablett	6
Patrick Gordon	5
Harold Uren	3
Jimmy Payne	2
Neil McBain	1
Tom Gracie	1
Conor Coady	1*
Billy Hartill	1
Abel Xavier	0
Andrew Hannah	0
Duncan McLean	0
David Burrows	0
David Murray	0

Most Everton clean sheets

Player	Everton Clean Sheets
Frank Mitchell	8

John Whitehead	1
Don Sloan	0
Sander Westerveld	0

Most Liverpool appearances

Player	Liverpool Apps
Dick Forshaw	288
Steve McMahon	277
Bill Lacey	260
Jimmy Payne	243
David Johnson	213
David Burrows	193
Peter Beardsley	175
Gary Ablett	147
Sander Westerveld	103
Duncan McLean	82
Andrew Hannah	69
Dave Hickson	67
Don Hutchison	60
Nick Barmby	58
Edgar Chadwick	45
Fred Geary	45
Harold Uren	45
Tommy Johnson	38
Johnny Morrissey	37
Tom Gracie	34
Patrick Gordon	30
Tom Wyllie	25
Abel Xavier	21
Frank Mitchell	18
David Murray	15

Neil McBain	12
Abe Hartley	12
Tony McNamara	10
Don Sloan	6
Kevin Sheedy	5
Arthur Berry	4
Billy Hartill	4
John Whitehead	3
Conor Coady	2

Most Liverpool goals

Player	Liverpool Goals
Dick Forshaw	123
David Johnson	78
Peter Beardsley	59
Steve McMahon	50
Jimmy Payne	43
Dave Hickson	38
Bill Lacey	29
Tom Wyllie	15
Fred Geary	14
Don Hutchison	10
Nick Barmby	8
Tommy Johnson	8
Patrick Gordon	8
Edgar Chadwick	7
Johnny Morrissey	6
Tom Gracie	5
Duncan McLean	4
David Burrows	3
Tony McNamara	3
Harold Uren	2

Abel Xavier	2
Kevin Sheedy	2
Gary Ablett	1
Andrew Hannah	1
Abe Hartley	1
David Murray	0
Neil McBain	0
Arthur Berry	0
Billy Hartill	0
Conor Coady	0

Most Liverpool clean sheets

Player	Liverpool Clean Sheets
Sander Westerveld	42
Frank Mitchell	8
Don Sloan	0
John Whitehead	0

*Figures correct at the time of writing

Average league position per decade/how many players crossed the park in that decade:

Decade	LFC	EFC	Players
1890	10.9	3.7	7
1900	10.3	6.4	4
1910	12.2	7.2	3
1920	6.2	12.2	3
1930	12.9	12.7	2
1940	8	14	-
1950	20.2	20.4	3
1960	10	5.8	1
1970	2.3	10.4	1
1980	1.7	7.2	2
1990	4.4	12.4	4
2000	3.5	9.9	3
2010	5.4	7.8	-
2020	2	12.7	1

1980	LFC best decade
1890	EFC best decade
1980	Merseyside best decade

1890	Most players crossing the park
1940/2010	Least players crossing the park

Bibliography

Interviews:
David Burrows, Johnny Morrissey, Tommy Jones,
Steve Dunning, Paul Dunning, Tony Gore, Phil
Bickerstaff, Allan Woodward, David Addicott, Joe
Atkinson, David Lewis, Joe Flannaghan, Mark
Stanistreet, Paul Moore, Don Storr, Chris Whitehead,
Jeffrey Hughes, Adi Jeffery, David Scotland, Mikey
Lewis, Bill Benbow, Frank Taylor, Peter Richards,
Elliot Conway, Mike Parry

Books:
Baldursson, A. & Magnusson, G., *Liverpool: The
Complete Record.*
Baldursson, A. & Magnusson, G., *The Liverpool
Encyclopaedia.*
Barwick, B. & Sinstadt, G., *Everton v Liverpool: A
Celebration of the Merseyside Derby.*
Chilvers, G. & Platt, M., *Old Liverpool FC in Colour.*
Goulding, J. & Smith, K., *The Untouchables: Anfield's
Band of Brothers.*
Historic Newspapers Ltd., *Liverpool Headlines from
1906: A Newspaper History.*
Johnson, S., *Everton: The Official Complete Record.*
Jones, P.K., *Liddell at One Hundred: A Family Portrait
of a Liverpool Icon.*
Kelly, S.F., *Forever Everton.*

Kelly, S.F., *Liverpool: The Official Illustrated History 1892–1995.*

Liversedge, S., *Liverpool: The Official Centenary History.*

Marsden, A., *Liverpool Football Programmes.*

O'Brien, M., *The Everton Miscellany.*

Platt, M., *120 Men Who Made LFC.*

Platt, M., *The Essential History of Everton.*

Ponting, I., *Liverpool: Player by Player.*

Roberts, J., *Everton: The Official Centenary History.*

Rogers, K., *Goodison Glory: The Official History.*

Rowlands, G.A., *The Red Men of Liverpool Football Club.*

Rowlands, J.K., *Everton Football Club: 1878–1946.*

Walmsley, D. & Done, S., *The History of Liverpool FC.*

Williams, J., *Red Men: Liverpool Football Club: The Biography.*

Websites:

BritishNewspaperArchive.co.uk

LFChistory.net Arnie Baldursson and Gudmundur Magnusson

PlayUpLiverpool.com Kjell Hanssen

EvertonCollection.org.uk The Everton Collection

BlueCorrespondent.co.uk James Smith from Everton Chronicles

Index